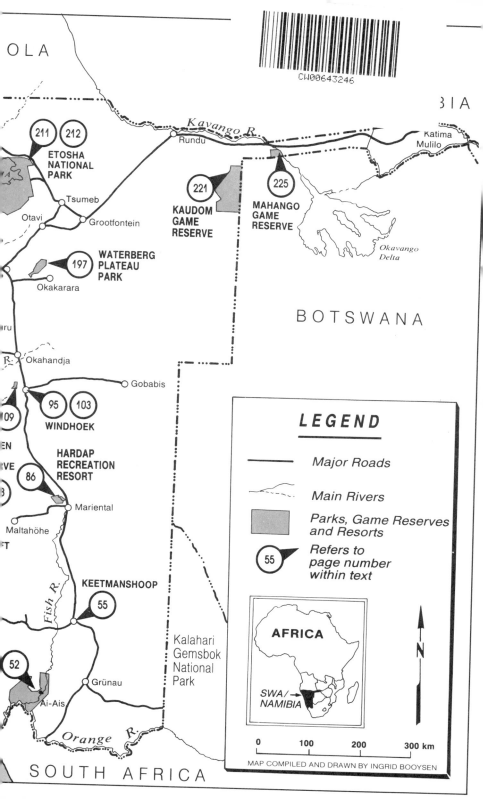

LEGEND

Maps

🏛	Rest Camp	◀	Border Post
▲	Campsite	✈	Airfield/Landing Strip
✳	Viewpoint	⊙	Waterhole
✚	Hospital	♙	Museum
i	Information Bureau	1	Hotel
✉	Post Office	▲^{2}	Places of Interest
℗	Police Station	🚌	Bus Terminus
♏	Hot Spring	=⌂=	Day Camping Facility
🏊	Swimming	▦	Sanddunes
⚑18	Golf Course	⬚	Built-up Area

⌒⟨	Perennial River	▬▬	Main Road
⌁⟨	Non-perennial River	━━	Secondary Road
++++	Railway Line	──	District/Farm Road
.—.	International Boundary	.....	Other Road
		▒▒▒	Park Boundary

VISITORS' GUIDE
TO NAMIBIA

VISITORS' GUIDE TO NAMIBIA

HOW TO GET THERE · WHAT TO SEE · WHERE TO STAY

Willie and Sandra Olivier

SOUTHERN
BOOK PUBLISHERS

Copyright © 1989 by Willie and Sandra Olivier

ISBN 1 86812 155 0

First edition, first impression 1989

Published by
Southern Book Publishers (Pty) Ltd
PO Box 548, Bergvlei 2012
Johannesburg

Maps by Ingrid Booysen
Set in Palatino
by Kohler Carton & Print (Natal)
Printed and bound by
Interpak, Natal

PREFACE

SWA/Namibia has variously been called "The Untamed Land", "The Land God Made in Anger", "Africa's Harsh Paradise" and "A Thirstland Wilderness". Despite these names, which conjure up visions of a harsh, inhospitable land, SWA/Namibia has been a popular tourist destination for many years, and more recently the country has experienced an unparalleled growth in tourism.

The experience of most tourists is of a brief visit and pleasant memories of SWA/Namibia. We are fortunate enough to live here and over the past three years we have been able to explore the country extensively. During our many journeys we realised what a need there is for a comprehensive tourist guide, as very often little or no information is available at many of the country's well-known tourist attractions. With this guide to help you, we hope that it will be easier for you to discover and appreciate the wide-open spaces, abundance of wildlife and contrasting scenery which presents an ever-changing kaleidoscope.

SWA/Namibia is said to be a Third World country, yet it has a First World infrastructure and facilities available to the tourist are amongst the best in Africa. Unlike many African countries, tourist attractions are, with a few exceptions, accessible by sedan cars. In some towns the German influence is still strongly felt and tourists are attracted to their *Gemütlichkeit* and attractive street scenes.

Do remember, though, that this ancient land is fragile. We ask you to help those who have their roots here and love this country to conserve its natural and historic heritage for future generations.

ACKNOWLEDGEMENTS

Visitors' Guide to Namibia has been made possible by the enthusiastic co-operation, assistance and advice of many people whom we would like to thank sincerely. We appreciate the assistance of all and, should anyone have been omitted inadvertently, we apologise. Our gratitude is due especially to the following: the Director of the Directorate of Nature Conservation in SWA/Namibia, Mr Polla Swart, and his staff, in particular Dr Eugéne Joubert, Dr Tony Williams, Dr Hu Berry, Mr Achim Lensin, Mr Rudi Loutit, Mr Steve Brain, Mr Hentie Schrader and Mr Treigue Cooper. The Head of the Desert Ecological Research Unit at Gobabeb, Dr Mary Seely, verified the section on the Namib Desert, while the Curator of the State Herbarium in Windhoek, Mr Mike Muller, checked the sections on flora. Our gratitude also to Mr Neels Coetzee for permission to examine the records of the National Monuments Council and Mr Johan Bruwer, Miss Anida Smit and Miss Vera Geleijnse of the Council for their friendly assistance. A word of thanks also to the Director of Geological Survey, Dr Roy Miller, and his staff for making our sections on geology intelligible, and to Mr John Kinahan of the State Museum for verification of our sections on archaeology. Our research was made considerably easier by the efficient help of the staff of the Estdorff Reference Library. Brian Jones assisted us with information on East Caprivi and Kaudom, while Mr Willem de Vries of Bethanie, Mrs Marlene Berger of Haruchas and Mr Anton Botha of Mariental, as well as Günther and Marion Schelke of Lüderitzbucht Safaris earned our grateful thanks for their hospitality and willingness to share their knowledge. Thanks also to Ingrid Booysen for the excellent maps.

Finally our appreciation to Southern Book Publishers' Managing Director, Mr Basil van Rooyen; the General Books Editor, Sally Antrobus; the copy editor, Frances Perryer, and all Southern staff involved in the production of this guide.

CONTENTS

HOW TO USE THIS GUIDE

Chapters 1 to 5 deal with the basics of travelling to and in SWA/ Namibia. As a detailed description of parks, game reserves, national monuments, towns and places of interest in each region is given in chapters 6–11, only a general résumé of sightseeing is given in Chapter 1, **What to do and see.** Once you know what there is to do, the best times for visiting the country, where to stay and how you can get around if you do not have your own transport, you are ready to tackle the **Regional notes on places of interest,** Chapters 6–11.

For practical purposes the country has been divided into six regions – South, Central, Namib Desert, Kaokoveld, North, and Kavango, Caprivi and Bushmanland.

Tourist attractions in each region are described more or less along popular tourist routes. However, as there are numerous routes to the same destination, the sequence of descriptions does not imply a suggested itinerary. Although all accessible tourist attractions are described, this does not necessarily mean that they should be visited – your final choice will be dictated by your particular interests and your time schedule. SWA/Namibia has known human conflict for many centuries and references to battlefields, military graveyards and fortifications are made from a purely historical point of view and not to serve as reminders of past conflicts.

Distances measured during our travels frequently differed from those on road maps which, to add to our confusion, often differed not only from one map to the other, but also from those on distance markers along the road. Discrepancies are generally small, but distances should be treated as approximate only.

References to trees in the text are numbered according to the *National List of Indigenous Trees,* while bird numbers are those used in *Roberts' Birds of Southern Africa.*

All possible care has been taken to ensure that information is up to date and reference is made to all planned facilities and developments. Visitors should, however, bear in mind that information does change from time to time. This is particularly true of telephone numbers.

AUTHORS' NOTE

Since the completion of the manuscript, agreement has been reached on the implementation of the United Nations' peace plan for South West Africa/Namibia. Information in respect of the various authorities could, therefore, become outdated or change.

CARTOGRAPHER'S NOTE

Information from official maps is reproduced under authority of the Office of the Surveyor-General dated 12 February 1988. I also wish to express my gratitude to the Directorate of Nature Conservation and Recreation Resorts for permission to reproduce maps of conservation areas.

1 WHAT TO DO AND SEE

SIGHTSEEING

SWA/Namibia is renowned for its game parks, game reserves and resorts, and the name Etosha has almost become synonymous with a visit to the country. In addition to the abundance of wildlife and the uniquely adapted flora, visitors are also attracted by the characteristic, starkly beautiful landforms. Rock engravings and paintings testify to the habitation of the country thousands of years ago, while numerous places of more recent historic significance can be visited by those interested. Detailed descriptions of places of interest are given in the **Regional notes on places of interest**, Chapters 6–11.

ANGLING

The coast of SWA/Namibia has long been regarded as a paradise for anglers and every year thousands of fishermen flock to the Namib coast. The Directorate of Nature Conservation and Recreation Resorts (DNC) has provided camping facilities at popular angling spots along the coast such as Mile 14, Jakkalsputz, Mile 72, and Mile 108, as well as camping and hotel accommodation, at Torra Bay and Terrace Bay respectively, in the Skeleton Coast Park.

At present licences are not required to angle in the sea, but the Directorate of Sea Fisheries intends to introduce several new regulations to protect the country's surf and rock angling fish from over-exploitation.

In terms of the *proposed regulations* anglers require a valid fishing licence. The total number of fish in the possession of a licence holder may not exceed 30, while the number of galjoen that may be caught is 8.

In respect of the collection of bait the proposed limits are as follows: armadillo 6, black mussels 50, clams 15, cockles 10, crabs 2, limpets

10, octopi 50, olly-crock 10, pencil bait 20, periwinkles (*Littorina*) 50, prawns 50, sea-crabs 15, sea-cucumbers 20 and Venus ears 10.

The proposed regulations will prohibit the collection of bristle worms (*Polychaetae*) and limit the number of white mussels to 25 per person with a valid angling permit. It is also proposed to limit the collection of red bait to bona fide anglers and only red bait washed up on beaches may be collected. One will also be limited to no more than 1,8 kg of red bait (excluding the shell) per person per day.

Oysters, bloodworms, limpets, black mussels, white mussels and prawns may only be collected by hand and not with a spade, fork or any other implement.

The proposed regulations prescribe that a permit is required to catch rock lobster. Eight rock lobsters may be caught daily per person during the rock lobster season, which stretches between 1 November and 30 April. (The limit in the Walvis Bay enclave is four.)

The regulation in SWA/Namibia in respect of minimum size differs from that in South Africa – the minimum size measured in a straight line down the middle of the back being 65 mm, compared with 85 mm in South Africa. It is forbidden to be in possession of female rock lobsters carrying eggs or showing signs of the eggs having been stripped off, or any rock lobster (male or female) which has a very soft shell.

Rock lobsters may be caught between sunset and sunrise only and no fish baskets or bow-nets may be used. The only permissible artificial breathing apparatus is a snorkel. They may not be caught in the lobster reserve at Lüderitz, which extends from Dias Point to Agate Beach.

Should you be unfamiliar with local angling regulations, details can be obtained from the inspectors of the Directorate of Sea Fisheries in Lüderitz (Magistrate's Court Building, Tel [06331] 2415) or in Walvis Bay (204, 2nd Street, Tel [0642] 5968).

Freshwater fishing

A number of dams and rivers offer opportunities for freshwater fishing. Popular species include large- and smallmouth bass, carp, yellowfish, kurper (bream) and barbel.

Favourite venues include Daan Viljoen Game Reserve near Windhoek, the Von Bach Dam (Okahandja), Hardap Dam (Mariental) and the Fish River at Ai-Ais. Licences can be obtained from the reception offices at these venues. To fish in the Goreangab Dam on the outskirts of Windhoek a permit must be obtained from the Windhoek Municipality, in addition to the angling licence required by the Directorate of Nature Conservation.

In the north of the country the Kavango and Zambezi rivers offer excellent opportunities for tiger fish and bream.

Ensure that you are well acquainted with the regulations regarding the number and size of fish which may be caught. Details can be obtained from the reception offices in the relevant resorts/game parks or from the DNC's head office in Windhoek, Tel (061) 63131.

MOUNTAINEERING, BACKPACKING AND TRAILING

Despite the few perennial rivers and excessive summer temperatures, several areas in SWA/Namibia lend themselves to mountaineering, backpacking and trailing.

The Fish River Canyon in the south of the country is one of the most popular trails in southern Africa and is hiked by some 2 700 backpackers every year. Covering some 86 km, the trail, which ends at Ai-Ais, is usually hiked in four to five days.

A popular area of long standing with mountaineers and backpackers is the Brandberg, where Königstein is the highest point in the country. The mountain can be ascended along several routes, but because of the extremely rugged terrain and the limited water, excursions should only be undertaken by experienced and fit backpackers after careful planning.

One of the greatest challenges to mountaineers is the Spitzkoppe, known as the Matterhorn of South West. Rising some 700 m above the surrounding plains, the mountain, rated as an E grade climb in some sections, was first ascended in 1946.

Two guided wilderness trails are conducted by field officers of the DNC – a three-day trail in the Ugab River and a four-day trail in the Waterberg Plateau Park. The Ugab River Trail was opened in 1985 and, unlike most other guided wilderness trails, no facilities are provided. Trailists must carry their own backpacks and sleeping is under the stars. On the Waterberg Wilderness Trail trailists are accommodated in wooden huts in a base camp from which walks are conducted daily. Carrying of a pack with the day's lunch and a first-aid kit is shared by the trailists.

The DNC also plans to open a hiking trail in the Naukluft Mountains which can be hiked in either four or eight days and a two-day (34 km) trail in the Daan Viljoen Game Reserve.

Those unable to undertake a backpacking, hiking or guided wilderness trail can take to the hills on any of a number of short walks. In Naukluft there is a choice of two day walks – the 17 km-long Waterkloof trail, which requires about 5–6 hours and the shorter Olive Trail (4–5 hours).

Two day walks have been laid out in the Daan Viljoen Game Reserve – a 7 km trail which is ideal for families and school groups and a longer, more strenuous trail of 13 km, while a circular route of either 9 km or 15 km can be hiked in the Hardap Game Reserve.

Visitors to the Etosha National Park are generally restricted to their vehicles. However, the Tsumasa Trail, on a hill near Halali rest camp, affords one the opportunity to stretch one's legs. A brochure describing trees and shrubs (which have been numbered), geology and birds of the area is available at the rest camp.

Information on the Fish River Canyon, Ugab River, Waterberg and Naukluft Trails can be obtained from the DNC. Visitors interested in backpacking and mountaineering can contact the SWA section of the Mountain Club of South Africa, P O Box 2488, Windhoek 9000. In addition to their monthly meetings, which usually take the form of an illustrated lecture, the club also undertakes regular backpacking and mountaineering excursions.

BIRD-WATCHING

To date over 630 bird species, including vagrants, have been recorded in SWA/Namibia. About 130 of these species generally occur nowhere else in SWA/Namibia but in the Caprivi and eastern Kavango.

Among the South West specials are rosyfaced lovebird (367), Bradfield's swift (413), Monteiro's hornbill (462), shorttoed rock thrush (583), Herero chat (618), rockrunner (662) and whitetailed shrike (752).

November through to April are generally the best months for bird-watching, as – in addition to residents – a large number of Palaearctic and Intra-African migrants also occur during these months.

The single best area for birding in the country is the Mahango Game Reserve in Kavango, where more than 300 species have been recorded.

Situated at the north-western edge of Botswana's Okavango Delta, the reserve attracts species which do not occur elsewhere in the country, such as western banded snake eagle (145), sharpbilled honeyguide (478), African skimmer (343) and Pel's fishing owl (403).

Well over 250 species have been recorded in the Windhoek area. It is likely that you will spot more birds here in a day than anywhere else in the country and, just before the onset of the summer rains, the experienced "twitcher" should be able to tick 100–120 species a day. The best spots are Avis and Goreangab dams, situated on the city's perimeter.

During dry cycles you are unlikely to see more than 100 species in the Etosha National Park, but during wet cycles the park is the habitat for up to 320 species. Fischer's Pan is the best wetland area in the park, while the Andoni Pan is best for such species as crowned crane (209) and pinkbilled lark (508). The Namutoni area is one of the best places to tick blackfaced babbler (561) while at Halali you have the best chance of spotting barecheeked babbler (564) and violet woodhoopoe (453). Scop's (396) and whitefaced (397) owls roost in the camp's trees.

The Walvis Bay/Swakopmund coastal area offers excellent birding opportunities. By visiting Walvis Bay Lagoon, the Bird Paradise, the rocky shores, Swakop River Mouth and the saltworks you could identify up to 90 species in a day during the summer months. Radford's Bay at Lüderitz is the best place in SWA/Namibia to get really good photographs of greater flamingo (96), while Halifax Island is the only place in the country where jackass penguin (3) can easily be seen from the mainland.

Some 260 species occur in the Hardap Dam reserve, among them Goliath heron (64) and Caspian tern (322) – both of which occur unusually far out of their normal range. Be on the lookout for osprey (170) between October and April. The best birding places are below the dam wall and along the irrigation canals.

The Waterberg Plateau specials include Cape vulture (122) (the northernmost breeding colony in southern Africa), Hartlaub's francolin (197), Rüppell's parrot (365) and Bradfield's hornbill (461).

Some 50 bird species occur in the desert and semi-desert areas. Your best chances of sighting Herero chat (618) are either at Spitzkoppe or on the road between Khorixas and Twyfelfontein. Elim Dune at Sesriem is a good spot for dune lark (503), while Gray's lark (514) favours the gravel plains of the coastal strip between Lüderitz and south-west Angola.

HUNTING AND HUNTING SAFARIS

SWA/Namibia is well known for its wildlife and the opportunities it affords hunters. In recent years game farming has become an important source of revenue to farmers and at present there are 314 officially recognised hunting farms, 25 guest farms and 20 safari undertakings in the country. To ensure the orderly utilisation of the country's wildlife resources, all aspects of hunting are strictly controlled by law.

Game is classified into three categories: specially protected, protected and huntable game. Springbok, kudu, gemsbok, buffalo, warthog and bushpig have been classified as huntable game and may be hunted during the season, which is usually between May and July.

A permit is required for huntable game and prospective hunters must obtain written permission from the farm owner, who decides what game may be hunted and the cost to the prospective hunter. The letter of permission must then be submitted to a nature conservation office or police station, which will issue the necessary hunting permit, which costs R25,00.

The numbers that may be hunted are three head of big game, or two head of big and four head of small game, or one head of big game and eight head of small game or 12 head of small game per hunter per year. The permit must be carried on the hunter's person during the hunt (unless accompanied on the hunt by the owner) and between the hunt and his return home and for as long as any of the meat is in his possession.

To ensure high standards and professionalism all hunt leaders are subjected to a rigorous test before they are registered. Trophy hunting permits are issued only to prospective hunters who can produce proof that they will be hunting under the guidance of a registered professional hunter or hunting guide, otherwise such permits are only issued to hunt leaders.

Trophy hunters may also hunt protected and specially protected game throughout the year, except for December and January, provided the necessary permit has been obtained from the Directorate of Nature Conservation. Registered professional hunters may hunt on any farm, provided the owner's consent has been obtained, while hunting guides may take clients hunting on registered farms only. A list of registered professional hunters and hunting guides can be obtained from the Directorate of Nature Conservation. Further information can be obtained by contacting the SWA Professional Hunters and Guides Association, P O Box 11291, Klein Windhoek 9000.

Hunting in the communal areas* is controlled by the Directorate of Nature Conservation who, in conjunction with the second-tier authorities, decide on the species and numbers of animals that may be hunted in the areas concerned. The necessary permit must be obtained from the nature conservation office in the communal area concerned. All revenue collected from hunting on communal land goes to the revenue fund of the respective second-tier authority.

The hunting season for game birds is usually during August and September, but this may vary. Visitors to SWA/Namibia (including South Africans) hunting on a trophy permit may shoot only two individuals of a particular species if such birds are listed on the permit. A permit is not required to hunt huntable birds during the hunting season, but hunters must be in possession of the written permission of the landowner. At the time of writing 20 bird species are classified as huntable. It must, however, be borne in mind that the list of species may be changed and hunters are advised to consult the Directorate of Nature Conservation on the current regulations.

In order to assist hunters in identifying huntable birds a small booklet with colour illustrations of the huntable species as well as similar, but protected, species has been published by the Directorate and is available free of charge on application.

PHOTOGRAPHY

Unspoilt scenery and wildlife make SWA/Namibia a popular destination with photographers and, in recent years, many award-winning photographs have been taken in this country.

On account of the harsh sunlight films with an ASA rating of between

---

* Areas inhabited by members of a particular population group where ownership of the land is vested in the second-tier authority, eg Owambo, Damaraland, Kavango, Hereroland, Namaland, etc.

50 and 160 are recommended for landscape photography. Early mornings and late afternoons are the most rewarding times for photography, but should you take photographs in bright sunlight a polarising filter is useful for reducing glare. Dust and fine sand are frequently a problem, especially in the Namib Desert, and you should store your camera and lenses in a chamois leather bag. Remember to bring a blow brush and special lens-cleaning tissues and take care not to scratch the surfaces of your lenses when cleaning these.

A cool box for your films is recommended if you are unable to have your film processed within a reasonable time.

2 WHAT YOU NEED TO KNOW

CLIMATE

With a mean average rainfall of 270 mm, SWA/Namibia is generally considered an arid country. More than 70 per cent of the country's rain is recorded between December and March and in general the rainfall, as well as the length of the rainy season, increases from the coast inland and from south to north. This trend is reflected by the average annual rainfall figures listed below.

Swakopmund	8 mm
Keetmanshoop	146 mm
Windhoek	365 mm
Grootfontein	611 mm
Katima Mulilo	700 mm

Rain usually falls in the afternoons as thunderstorms which soon pass over.

The months between May and September are usually considered the best time to visit the interior. Daytime temperatures are pleasant, but evenings are generally cold. The following table will give a good idea of temperatures throughout the country. Do not forget that they are *average* figures and summer temperatures of over 35°C often occur.

	Jan	April	July	Oct
Swakopmund	20/16	19/13	17/9	16/11
Keetmanshoop	35/18	29/14	21/5	31/13
Windhoek	30/17	26/13	20/6	29/15
Grootfontein	30/18	27/13	24/4	32/16
Rundu	31/19	30/15	26/6	35/18

Temperatures along the coast are usually cooler than those of the interior and in summer the coast offers welcome relief from the warm temperatures further inland. Fog occurs on average for 117 days a year at Lüderitz, the months between February and May receiving the most. Swakopmund has an average of 113 foggy days – fog being most prevalent between May and August. Berg winds and occasional sandstorms also occur during this period.

WHAT TO PACK

The aforementioned temperatures clearly dictate the type of clothing required. During summer (day and night) light clothing – cotton shirts, shorts or skirts – is necessary. Long-sleeved shirts and long cotton trousers are a good idea if your skin is sensitive to the sun, and also keep mosquitoes at bay after sunset. This clothing is also adequate for winter daywear but for early mornings, evenings and nights warm trousers, jerseys, track suits, balaclava, gloves and warm socks should be included.

Miscellaneous items not to be forgotten include a sunhat, sunscreen cream, insect repellant, anti-malaria tablets, sunglasses, binoculars, sturdy walking shoes and a bathing costume.

LANGUAGE

English and Afrikaans are the official languages of SWA/Namibia, although German is widely spoken. Afrikaans is the lingua franca throughout the country except in Caprivi, where only English is spoken.

EMBASSIES AND CONSULATES

At present, SWA/Namibia has no official overseas representation and all enquiries should be directed to South African embassies and consulates.

Except for the Portuguese Consulate in Windhoek there are no diplomatic representatives resident in SWA/Namibia.

ENTRY AND CUSTOMS REGULATIONS

At present (1988) there are no border posts between South Africa and SWA/Namibia and South African citizens and holders of South African permanent residence permits do not require a passport. Other visitors must, however, be in possession of a valid passport, while tourists who are required to obtain a visa for South Africa must also have a visa for SWA/Namibia, obtainable from South African embassies and consulates abroad. Proof of being able to leave the country, such as a return ticket, is also required.

Border posts between SWA/Namibia and Botswana are manned (on the SWA/Namibia side) between 08h00 and 17h00 at Buitepos (east of Gobabis) and between 07h00 and 18h00 at Ngoma (in East Caprivi), while a further border control post giving access to Shakawe is planned for Mohembo. As there are no border posts in Botswana at these points, you must report to the police station at Mamuno, Kasane and Shakawe respectively when travelling from Botswana to SWA/Namibia or vice versa.

There are no customs restrictions on travellers between South Africa and SWA/Namibia. Visitors arriving from any other country than South Africa are allowed 1 litre of spirits, 2 litres of wine, 300 ml perfume and 400 cigarettes/50 cigars/250 g tobacco duty free.

POLICE PERMITS

Since the end of 1987 it has not been necessary to obtain a police permit to travel through Kaokoland, Owambo, Kavango, Bushmanland, Hereroland East and Caprivi. However, you still require a military permit to travel through West Caprivi (refer to page 226). At the time of writing a dusk-to-dawn curfew was in force in Owambo and tourists arriving at the Oshivelo check-point 100 km north-west of Tsumeb in the late afternoon were not permitted to proceed into Owambo. However, this restriction might be lifted in the near future. Ensure that your identity document or passport is easily accessible as it is usually required.

HEALTH

No vaccinations are required at present and medical facilities of a high standard are available in the major centres.

Tap water in towns is purified and you need have no hesitation in drinking it. Care should, however, be exercised in rural areas.

Although SWA/Namibia is virtually free of tropical diseases, visitors to the north of the country should be especially aware of malaria, bilharzia and sleeping sickness.

Malaria

A bite by an affected *Anopheles* mosquito can transmit microscopic blood parasites, resulting in malaria. In SWA/Namibia you always run the risk of contracting this disease when travelling through the malaria endemic areas north-east of Grootfontein to Katima Mulilo. Etosha, Gobabis and the extreme south-east of the country are malaria epidemic areas where there is usually only a risk during summer. However, it is advisable to take anti-malaria precautions in both the malaria endemic and epidemic areas throughout the year, even if only passing through the area.

Consult your doctor or chemist at least a week before entering the area as to which brand of preventive tablet should be taken. Medication changes from time to time as the mosquitoes become immune to certain medication. Read the instructions carefully with regard to how long in advance, the frequency, and how long after leaving the area the course should be continued.

Symptoms of malaria are vomiting, general body ache and severe fever.

Bilharzia

This disease is caused by a parasite which lives in water and attacks the intestines, bladder and other organs of its mammalian hosts, which are humans, stock and game. Fortunately, it is only travellers to the Caprivi and Kavango who need fear bilharzia. Human habitation is usually associated with it, so avoid drinking, swimming or washing in water downstream from any human settlement.

The symptoms of bilharzia take at least six weeks to appear, although after three to four weeks there could be general lethargy and weakness. However, any sign of blood in urine or faeces should be reported to a doctor as soon as possible.

Sleeping sickness

Sleeping sickness is caused by a parasite transmitted to man by the bite of an infected tsetse fly. The fly is a little larger than the common house fly, grey with scissor-like wings and difficult to swat because of its hard body. Once again, it is only visitors to the Caprivi who run a risk, although the incidence is low because of selective spraying against tsetse fly.

Bites can be prevented by wearing long-sleeved shirts and trousers in dull colours and applying insect repellant to exposed skin. A sharp pain will indicate a bite, but this does not necessarily result in the disease being transmitted. If the bite becomes sore or inflamed, consult a doctor as soon as possible. Other symptoms include swelling of the lymph glands and a severe headache.

CURRENCY AND BANKS

The South African Rand is the valid currency and South African exchange control regulations are enforced in SWA/Namibia. International visitors may only enter or leave the country with R200 cash but there is no limit on the amount of travellers' cheques.

The major South African commercial banks – Standard, First National (formerly Barclays), Trust, Nedbank, Boland – are represented in Windhoek. Standard, First National and Bank Windhoek (agents for Volkskas) have branches in the major centres and agencies in smaller towns.

Automatic telling machines have been installed in Windhoek and Swakopmund by First National Bank, and by Boland Bank and Swabank in Windhoek.

Visa and Master cards are widely accepted, although many of the German pensions, restaurants and shops do not offer this facility.

PUBLIC HOLIDAYS

SWA/Namibia does not have the same public holidays as South Africa and the following is a list of those applicable in the country:

New Year's Day – 1 January

Good Friday – March/April

Easter Monday – the Monday following Good Friday

Workers' Day – 1 May

Ascension Day – May (40 days after Easter)

Day of Goodwill – 1st Monday in October

Human Rights Day – 10 December

Christmas Day – 25 December

Family Day – 26 December

ELECTRICITY

Electricity of 220 volts is supplied and sockets are for three-pin plugs, 15 amp types.

3 HOW TO GET THERE

ROAD

The main approaches to SWA/Namibia are either via Vioolsdrif, when travelling from Cape Town, or via Upington and Karasburg, when travelling from Johannesburg. Both these routes are tarred. Visitors can also travel through the Kalahari Gemsbok National Park, in which case about 270 km on the SWA/Namibia side between Mata Mata and Stamprietfontein is travelled on a good surface gravel road before joining the tarred road.

Distances between Windhoek and South African cities are as follows:

Bloemfontein	1 665 km
Cape Town	1 493 km
Durban	2 330 km
East London	1 955 km
Johannesburg	1 763 km
Kimberley	1 482 km
Port Elizabeth	1 916 km
Pretoria	1 819 km

From Botswana, SWA/Namibia can be approached by sedan car via Ngoma in East Caprivi and by four-wheel-drive via Mamuno/Buitepos east of Gobabis and Shakawe/Mohembo.

AIR

South African Airways operates daily flights between Windhoek and Johannesburg and Cape Town (except on Saturdays between Cape Town and Windhoek), while Namib Air, the country's national airline, operates scheduled flights between Johannesburg and Windhoek via Katima Mulilo, Rundu and Tsumeb. The airline also has regular flights from Windhoek to Keetmanshoop and Upington, where travellers can connect scheduled SAA flights to Bloemfontein, Cape Town, Johannesburg and Kimberley.

South African Airways runs a twice-weekly direct flight between Frankfurt and Windhoek.

RAIL

Passenger trains run three times a week to and from Windhoek and Cape Town/Johannesburg. Two of these carry goods as well as passengers and the journey takes four days. The once-weekly *Suidwester* is a passenger train only and completes the journey in two days.

BUS

F P du Toit Transport operates a twice-weekly return *Mainliner* service between Windhoek and Cape Town/Johannesburg. The journey between Windhoek and Cape Town takes 18 hours and between Windhoek and Johannesburg 20 hours. Hot meals, refreshments, videos, two-channel music and cushions and rugs are provided. Reservations in South Africa can be made with Computicket in Johannesburg and Cape Town, as well as Thomas Cook American Express travel agents.

The *Ekonoliner* service operates a weekly service between Walvis Bay and Cape Town – departing on Fridays from Walvis Bay and from Cape Town on Mondays. Reservations can be made with Woker Travel in Swakopmund, Tel (0641) 4950, and with Ritz Reise in Windhoek, Tel (061) 36670.

4 GETTING AROUND

BY ROAD

The road system in SWA/Namibia is one of the best in Africa and nearly all of the country's major centres are connected by tarred roads, which cover about 4 378 km (11 per cent) of the total network of approximately 41 715 km.

Motoring and traffic regulations

Driving in SWA/Namibia is, as in neighbouring countries, on the left-hand side of the road. As a rule the speed limit on main roads is 120 km/h, while a limit of 60 km/h is generally in force in built-up areas. It is compulsory for the driver and front-seat passenger to wear seat-belts.

Visitors, excluding residents of neighbouring states, must be in possession of a valid international driving licence if they intend driving in SWA/Namibia.

International road signs are used. Main routes (known as national routes in South Africa) are either tarred or a well-maintained gravel surface and are indicated by a "B" followed by the route number in a five-sided roadsign.

At present, secondary routes are numbered in a diamond-shaped sign, but this will gradually be replaced by a rectangular sign, with a "C" followed by the route number. Consequently, both the old and the new route numbers have been included in this book's route descriptions. This could also cause confusion when using old maps, but the routes are generally well signposted. Secondary routes (referred to as provincial routes in South Africa) have gravel surfaces which vary from fair to good.

District roads are indicated with a "D" followed by the route number in a small rectangular roadsign. The condition of these roads varies from good to poor and the surface can become sandy or corrugated. A "P" followed by the route number indicates farm roads, which are best avoided.

Main routes and secondary routes are usually well signposted, while district and farm roads are signposted with the route number only. Distances are generally indicated at 10 km intervals along main routes, but are not indicated on other routes.

The country's roads are notorious for accidents involving animals, especially kudu. This is usually only a problem in the evening and after dark, making it advisable to slow down or avoid night driving. Warthogs are also a menace, particularly after good rains when the grass on the verges is long.

Motoring hints

Distances between towns are often quite considerable and secondary, district and farm roads often carry little traffic. You should, therefore, be as well prepared as possible to cope in an emergency situation when travelling off the country's main routes. One of the most important rules is: never set off on a journey without a *full* ten litre can of water.

Ensure that your spare tyre is in working order. It is comforting to have two spares and, if this is not possible, carry an inner tube and gaiter so that you can have your tyre repaired at the first opportunity – spares are not always in good supply in small towns.

If unaccustomed to gravel roads, keep the following in mind:

- slow down – 80 km is a reasonable speed;
- keep a regular check on your tyres. Rattles and bumps can disguise a flat tyre until it is too late and your wheel rim is ruined;
- when travelling in the dust of a car ahead or one just past, switch on headlights to make sure you are seen;
- do not take chances and overtake if your vision is impaired by dust from the vehicle ahead – you may be surprised by a donkey cart or a speedy local;
- constantly glance at your side- and rear-view mirrors. Some roads are very lonely and it is easy to forget that other drivers could also be using the road;

- to avoid possible skidding, reduce speed gradually rather than braking suddenly;

- sand thick enough to bog down sedan cars does accumulate on the road verges. Often it is deceptive, so do not take chances by stopping unless you are satisfied that the surface alongside the road is firm;

- concentrate on the road when driving – odd sandy patches, often in riverbeds, could cause you to lose control of your vehicle;

- if a road has not been graded for some time, a fairly thick gravel island may accumulate in the middle of the road – take care and reduce speed should you have to cross this;

- cattle grids are encountered fairly often on the more minor roads. Slow down considerably when approaching these as the road surface just before and after it is often poor and rutted;

- many roads are crossed by barely noticeable river and stream courses which you would probably surmise never carry much water. Causeways are uncommon and after rain the road surface is often washed away, which could be dangerous if travelling at speed and noticed too late.

Tips for four-wheel driving

For the inexperienced, the most important advice is – don't venture into the unknown unless you are well acquainted with your vehicle and know how to use it! On your first outing it is reassuring to be a two-vehicle expedition, accompanied by an experienced off-road driver, giving you the opportunity to get the feel of it and gain experience.

One usually learns by making mistakes. However, the following hints may prove useful:

In sand

- remain in existing tracks, where you will find that the vehicle becomes almost self-steering;

- do not allow yourself to become bogged down to your axles before taking action;

- if you do become bogged down first check that your wheel hubs are actually engaged in four-wheel drive;

- deflate your tyres somewhat before going into heavy sand (although this is not a good idea if you do not have a pump!);
- long, sandy stretches are best tackled in the early morning when the sand is still cool and more compact and able to support a greater weight;
- in the past few years three vehicles have been reduced to smouldering shells on trips through long grass in Bushmanland. This was the result of long grass getting caught under the protection plate and around the driving shaft. Keep a regular check under your car and always carry a fire extinguisher;
- grass seeds can also be a problem by blocking the radiator. With enough seeds gathering, hot air generated by the radiator is not allowed to escape, resulting in overheating.

Rocky terrain

- try to judge the ground clearance of your vehicle – if unsure, slowly edge forward;
- tyre pressure is best left at normal.

The increasing number of four-wheel-drive vehicles has opened up large, unspoilt areas which until a few years ago were closed to tourists. Add to this the growing number of tourists and it is obvious that large areas could become spoilt.

Unfortunately some four-wheel-drive vehicle owners seem to believe that they are free to drive where they choose – without considering the sensitivity of the ecology. For those able to explore remote areas by four-wheel-drive vehicles the most basic rule to observe is: follow existing tracks. To casual tourists much of the Namibian landscape may appear barren, but uniquely adapted plant and animal life exists there. One thoughtless driver could not only scar the landscape for more than three decades but also cause irreversible damage to sensitive ecosystems.

Also bear in mind that having a four-wheel-drive vehicle does not entitle you to drive wherever you desire. Permits are required from the relevant authorities and should you illegally enter an area, you are liable to a heavy fine.

When camping, do not bury refuse as not only does this become exposed by the elements, but broken bottles and cans with jagged edges are dangerous to man and animals.

Trees are scarce in most areas, so take your own supply of wood along. Do not make fires under a tree or on tree roots and never break off seemingly dead branches. Fireplaces dotted around in a small area are unsightly, so rather use existing fireplaces. If you build your own, scrape a hollow in the sand and extinguish the fire properly before breaking up camp.

Human waste should be buried and the paper should preferably be burnt or buried deep enough so that it is not easily uncovered.

Campsites should be chosen with care. Never camp near a waterhole as you may deprive animals of water which is vitally necessary for their survival.

When animals are encountered outside game reserves (eg in the Kao-koveld), never approach too closely and ensure that they can move freely. Some of the river valleys in the north of the country are very narrow and animals trapped by pursuing vehicles are not only poten-tially dangerous to man, but could injure themselves in an attempt to escape.

All rock paintings and archaeological artefacts are protected by law and should never be tampered with in any way or removed. If you come upon something of interest, rather report the site to the State Museum in the Carl List Building, Windhoek.

Maps

Members of the Automobile Association can contact the Association's office in Windhoek at 15 Carl List House, Kaiser Street, Tel (061) 22-4201, for general information, maps and road reports.

The most useful road map is the one issued free of charge by the Directorate of Trade and Tourism, Private Bag 13297, Windhoek 9000. It is usually available at local travel agents and tourist information offices. For those venturing off the beaten track topographical maps are essential and are available from the Surveyor-General, Department of Justice, Private Bag 13267, Windhoek 9000, Tel (061) 38110. Should you be in Windhoek, they are situated in the Justicia Gebou, which is in Kaiser Street, just behind the Nature Conservation reservations office.

Vehicle hire

Sedan cars and four-wheel-drive vehicles can be hired in Windhoek and other major centres from Avis, Budget, Imperial and Kessler. Enquiries should be made regarding drop-off charges if the vehicle is not returned to the depot it was collected from. Budget will supply an extra spare tyre, as well as jerry and water cans at no extra charge, while a full range of camping equipment can be hired from Kessler Car Hire. Owing to the demand for four-wheel-drive vehicles, reservations should be made well in advance. Following is a list of car-rental outlets:

Windhoek (061)

- Avis Rent-a-Car,   Safari Hotel, P O Box 2057, Windhoek 9000, Tel 33166 (a/h 22-2666).
- Budget Rent-a-Car (SWA),   72 Tal St, P O Box 1754, Windhoek 9000, Tel 22-8720/36437 (a/h 22-2666).
- Imperial Car Hire,   43 Stübel St, P O Box 1387, Windhoek 9000, Tel 35819/22-7103 (a/h 22-2666).
- Kessler Car Hire,   cnr Peter Müller and Tal Streets, P O Box 20274, Windhoek 9000, Tel 33451 (a/h 22-2666).
- Trip Car Hire,   P O Box 100, Windhoek 9000, Tel 36880 (a/h 33522).
- Zimmerman Garage,   5 Wright St, P O Box 2672, Windhoek 9000, Tel 37146 (a/h 51578).
- Autodeutsch Camper Hire,   12 Brock St, P O Box 20789, Windhoek 9000, Tel 61221 (a/h 22-2199).

J G Strydom Airport (0626)

- Avis Rent-a-Car,   Tel 271/2.
- Budget Rent-a-Car, Tel 225/251.
- Imperial Car Hire, Tel 278.

Swakopmund (0641)

- Avis Rent-a-Car,   Dolphin Motors, 38 Kaiser Wilhelm St, P O Box 1216, Swakopmund 9000, Tel 2527.
- Budget Rent-a-Car,   Metje & Ziegler Building, 42 Kaiser Wilhelm St, Swakopmund 9000, Tel 2080.

- Imperial Car Hire, Crossroads Garage, Knobloch St, P O Box 748, Swakopmund 9000, Tel 2979.
- Swakopmund Car-a-Van Hire, P O Box 3497, Vineta 9000, Tel 61297.

Katima Mulilo (0020)

- Avis Rent-a-Car, Zambezi Lodge, Katima Mulilo 9000, Tel 203.

Keetmanshoop (0631)

- Budget (Agent), Canyon Hotel, P O Box 950, Keetmanshoop 9000, Tel 3361.
- Avis Rent-a-Car, P O Box 498, Keetmanshoop 9000, Tel 3508.

Lüderitz (06331)

- Avis Rent-a-Car, Grinrod Shipping Office, Hafen Street, P O Box 11, Lüderitz 9000, Tel 2054.

Tsumeb (0671)

- Avis Rent-a-Car, P O Box 284, Tsumeb 9000, Tel 2520.

Walvis Bay (0642)

- Avis Rent-a-Car, Troost Transport, 121 10th St, P O Box 758, Walvis Bay 9000, Tel 5935.
- Budget Rent-a-Car, Rooikop Airport, Tel 2080.
- Imperial Car Rental, Suiwesdienstasie, Tel 5924.

Bus transport

F P Du Toit Transport operates scheduled return *Mainliner* bus services between Windhoek and Walvis Bay and Windhoek and Tsumeb from Monday to Friday, as well as on Sunday. Reservations can be made with Trip Travel in Windhoek, Tel (061) 36880, or appointed travel agents. Reservations for the *Econoliner* service, which operates once weekly to and from Walvis Bay and Windhoek can be made with Woker Travel in Swakopmund (0641) 4950 and with Ritz Reise in Windhoek (061) 36670.

BY AIR

Because of the vast distances to be covered in SWA/Namibia air travel has become increasingly popular. Visitors can make use of scheduled flights or charter aircraft.

Scheduled flights

The country's domestic carrier, Namib Air, has several scheduled flights a week from Windhoek to Upington, Keetmanshoop, Swakopmund, Walvis Bay, Tsumeb, Oshakati, Rundu and Katima Mulilo and back.

Air Cape connections at Walvis Bay link Lüderitz, Alexander Bay and Cape Town.

Aircraft charter

Those with itineraries which do not suit scheduled air routes can consider chartering an aircraft. The following companies operate from Windhoek:

- Hire and Fly
  Eros Airport, P O Box 30320
  Windhoek 9000
  Tel (061) 22-3562/3.
  Operates a fleet of single- and twin-engined aircraft and a Lear Jet. Holders of valid South African aircraft licences can hire the type of aircraft for which they are registered. Their prices are very reasonable and you could be pleasantly surprised upon making an enquiry. Overseas pilots can contact Westair Flying School, P O Box 30320, Windhoek 9000, Tel (061) 37230 to familiarise themselves with local conditions.

- Namib Air
  Eros Airport, P O Box 731
  Windhoek 9000
  Tel (061) 38220.
  Operates a fleet of single- and twin-engined aircraft.

Aircraft maintenance

If you travel to SWA/Namibia in your own aircraft the following addresses could be useful.

- Westair Aviation
  Eros Airport, P O Box 407, Windhoek 9000,
  Tel (061) 37230.

The company offers full service for all types of aircraft and helicopters, i.e. routine maintenance and mandatory periodic inspections (MPI's).

- Radio Repairs
  Thompson Radio (Pty) Ltd, Ausspanplatz, Windhoek 9000.
  Tel (061) 37533.

BY RAIL

Combined goods and passenger train services are operated internally by the National Transport Corporation of SWA/Namibia to and from Windhoek and Swakopmund/.Walvis Bay and Windhoek and Keetmanshoop/Lüderitz.

TOURS AND SAFARIS

Taking advantage of the good roads and excellent accommodation facilities, several scheduled coach tours covering the major tourist attractions are conducted throughout the year, while several safaris are conducted in areas that are not on major tourist routes.

Scheduled and Charter Coach/Minibus Tours

Scheduled tours varying in duration from 4 to 15 days are conducted from Windhoek by the following operators:

- Leisure Tours, Trip Travel (local agent),
  P O Box 100, Windhoek 9000,
  Tel (061) 36880.
- Springbok Atlas Safaris (SWA) (Pty) Ltd,
  P O Box 2058, Windhoek 9000,
  Tel (061) 22-4252/3.

- SWA Safaris (Pty) Ltd,
  P O Box 20373, Windhoek 9000,
  Tel (061) 37567/8/9.
- SAR Travel Bureau,
  P O Box 415, Windhoek 9000,
  Tel (061) 298-2532/34821.

Details about charter tours for small groups can be obtained from:

- Toko Safaris,
  P O Box 5017, Windhoek 9000,
  Tel (061) 22-5539.

Localised Tours

Various operators offer tours of a localised nature.

Visitors flying directly to Etosha in their own or chartered aircraft can make use of the services of an expert guide with transport. The basic duration of the tour is three days and two nights, but it can be extended up to six days. Further details can be obtained from:

- Trip Travel,
  P O Box 100, Windhoek 9000,
  Tel (061) 36880.

A number of tour operators conduct sightseeing tours of Windhoek, Swakopmund and Lüderitz on request.

- Eagle Safaris,
  P O Box 1413, Windhoek 9000,
  Tel (061) 22-2692.
- Charly's Desert Tours,
  P O Box 1400, Swakopmund 9000,
  Tel (0641) 4341.
- Lüderitzbucht Safaris and Tours,
  P O Box 76, Lüderitz 9000,
  Tel (06331) 2719.

Safaris

In order to ensure that safari operators specialising in off-the-beaten-track tours conform to certain minimum requirements local safari undertakings are required to be registered and are also subject to grading.

Factors taken into consideration include conveniences offered by the vehicle (air-conditioning, radio, loudspeakers), the type of tents including the space per person, comfort, furnishing, convenience; all aspects of service to clients, the type of lighting (lanterns, gas or electricity), the neatness of the safari leader and general impressions regarding the serviceability, durability and comfort of vehicles, accommodation and furniture. The maximum number of points is 100 and grading is as follows:

*** 81–100 points
** 56–80 points
* 40–55 points

Further details of safari operations can be obtained from:

- Charly's Desert Tours,
  P O Box 1400, Swakopmund 9000,
  Tel (0641) 4341.
  Safaris are conducted to Etosha, Sossusvlei and Damaraland.

- Desert Adventure Safaris,
  P O Box 339, Swakopmund 9000,
  Tel (0641) 4072.
  Safaris to Damaraland and Kaokoland; backpacking trips along the Kunene River April–October and safaris to Bushmanland May–September.

- Eagle Safaris,
  P O Box 1413, Windhoek 9000,
  Tel (061) 22-2692.
  Specialises in tailormade photographic safaris.

- Ermo Safaris,
  P O Box 27, Kamanjab 9000,
  Tel (0020) 1312.
  Adventure and photographic safaris in the Kaokoveld; guests can be accommodated on the Farm Ermo, bordering on Etosha National Park.

- Moringa Touring,
  P O Box 23044, Windhoek 9000,
  Tel (061) 22-3519.
  Specialises in chartered safari tours for small groups.

- See Africa Tours,
  P O Box 127, Swakopmund, 9000
  Tel (0641) 5243.
  Trips concentrating on the special interests of groups, for example archaeology or geology, are arranged on request.
- Skeleton Coast Safaris,
  P O Box 2195, Windhoek 9000,
  Tel (061) 51269.
  Fly-in safaris are conducted to the Skeleton Coast Park. Two six-day safaris covering Kaokoland and the Skeleton Coast Park and Damaraland and the Skeleton Coast Park are also run.
- Southern Cross Safaris,
  P O Box 20373, Windhoek 9000,
  Tel (061) 37567.
  Safaris to the Namib Desert, Bushmanland, Caprivi.

A number of South African-based companies also conduct safaris and camping tours to SWA/Namibia. Details can be obtained from:

- Afro Ventures Safaris,
  P O Box 2339, Randburg 2125,
  Tel (011) 787-7590.
  Departures from Johannesburg, but tours can be joined in Windhoek.
- Gloriosa Safaris,
  P O Box 212, Walvis Bay 9190
  Tel (0642) 2455.
  Departures from Walvis Bay.
- Karibu Safari,
  P O Box 35196, Northway 4065,
  Tel (031) 83-9774.
  Departures from Durban, but tours can be joined in Johannesburg at no extra cost.
- Namib Wilderness Safaris,
  P O Box 651171, Benmore 2010,
  Tel (011) 884-1458.
  Departures from Windhoek.
- Papadi Tours,
  P O Box 84262, Greenside 2034,
  Tel (011) 782-2565.
  Departures from Johannesburg.

Safaris from SWA/Namibia to Botswana/Okavango Delta

Visitors wishing to join a safari to Botswana from SWA/Namibia can make enquiries with the following operators:

- Botswana/Okavango Delta Fly-in Safaris,
  P O Box 9004, Windhoek 9000,
  Tel (061) 22-5289.

- Charly's Desert Tours,
  P O Box 1400, Swakopmund 9000,
  Tel (0641) 4341.

- Ermo Safaris,
  P O Box 27, Kamanjab 9000,
  Tel (0020) 1312.

- Southern Cross Safaris,
  P O Box 20373, Windhoek 9000,
  Tel (061) 37567.

5 WHERE TO STAY

In SWA/Namibia all accommodation establishments – hotels, pensions, guest farms and caravan parks – are graded. The grading system is different from that used in South Africa and abroad, the highest rating being three stars.

HOTELS AND PENSIONS

The following grading system is applicable to hotels and pensions:

*** a really good hotel (651-750 points) with the following facilities: wall-to-wall carpeting and private bathrooms or showers in at least 75 per cent of the rooms, heating in all rooms and public lounges, three-channel radio and telephone in each room, valets on the premises, a 1:6 ratio of communal bathrooms and toilets to beds in ordinary rooms, à la carte meals available every day, full-time head chef and head waiter, 18 hours floor service a day for light refreshments, at least one permanent reception room, 24-hour reception service, at least one lift if the building has more than three floors, furniture and equipment of a high quality and transport available for guests.

** a good hotel (551–650 points) which has the following: private bathrooms or showers for at least 50 per cent of the rooms, room heating on request, a minimum 1:7 ratio of communal bathrooms and toilets to beds in ordinary rooms, a full-time head chef, 16-hour floor service for light refreshments and 14 hours reception service.

* a standard hotel (400–550 points) (better than the lowest in some other grading systems). Apart from the 71 basic minimum requirements prescribed in terms of the regulations, the following are provided: private bathrooms or showers for at least 25 per cent of the rooms, a ratio of one (or more) communal bathroom(s) and

toilet(s) for every eight other beds and a 16-hour floor service for light refreshments.

The symbol YYY indicates that the establishment is fully licensed, while YY indicates a restaurant licence only.

Most small towns have a hotel, while visitors have a choice of several hotels in the larger centres. The number of graded hotels in the country currently stands at 76. The only local hotel group in the country is Namib Sun Hotels, with hotels in Windhoek, Otjiwarongo, Tsumeb, Swakopmund, Walvis Bay and Keetmanshoop. The Kalahari Sands Hotel in Windhoek is part of Protea Hotels – the only South African hotel group represented in SWA/Namibia.

HOTELS

Town, name and postal address	Telephone	Tariff L Low M Medium H High	Grading	Liquor facilities	Bedrooms available Total no.	With private bath or shower and WC	A la carte restaurant	Telephone in bedroom	Air-conditioning in bedrooms	Garage available or off-street parking	Swimming-pool
ARANOS 9000 Aranos Hotel PO Box 142	(06642) 31	M	★	YYY	11	4	×	×	–	×	×
ARIS Aris Hotel PO Box 5199 Windhoek 9000	(061) 36006	L	★	YYY	5	1	×	–	–	×	×
AROAB 9000 Aroab Hotel PO Box 5	(06352) 27	L	★	YYY	8	8	–	–	–	×	–
ASAB Asab Hotel Private Bag 2036 Mariental 9000	(0668) 15441	L	★	YYY	5	2	–	–	–	–	–

Town, name and postal address	Telephone	Tariff (L Low / M Medium / H High)	Grading	Liquor facilities	Bedrooms available — Total no.	With private bath or shower and WC	A la carte restaurant	Telephone in bedroom	Air-conditioning in bedrooms	Garage available or off-street parking	Swimming-pool
AUS 9000 Bahnhof Hotel PO Box 20	(063332) 44	L	★	YYY	7	3	–	–	–	X	–
BETHANIE 9000 Bethanie Hotel PO Box 13	(06362) 13	M	★	YYY	6	6	–	X	2	X	–
GOAGEB Konkiep Hotel PO Box 90 Bethanie 9000	(06362) 3321	L	–	YYY	5	2	–	–	–	X	–
GOBABIS 9000 Central Hotel PO Box 233	(0681) 2094 2095	M	★	YYY	12	6	X	X	–	X	–
Gobabis Hotel PO Box 474	(0681) 2041 2042	M	★	YYY	12	5	X	4	1	–	–
GOCHAS 9000 Gochas Hotel PO Box 137	(06662) 44	M	★	YYY	8	5	–	X	–	X	–
GROOTFONTEIN 9000 Meteor Hotel PO Box 346	(06731) 2078 2079	M	★	YYY	21	15	X	X	11	X	–
Nord Hotel PO Box 168	(06731) 2049	L	★	YYY	11	3	–	X	–	–	–
GRÜNAU 9000 Grünau Hotel PO Box 2	(0020) 1	L	★	YYY	13	7	–	X	–	X	–
HELMERINGHAUSEN 9000 Helmeringhausen Hotel PO Box 21	(06362) 7	L	★	YYY	10	4	X	–	–	X	–

Town, name and postal address	Telephone	Tariff L Low / M Medium / H High	Grading	Liquor facilities	Bedrooms available Total no.	With private bath or shower and WC	A la carte restaurant	Telephone in bedroom	Air-conditioning in bedrooms	Garage available or off-street parking	Swimming-pool
HENTIESBAAI 9000 Hotel De Duine PO Box 1	(06442) 1	M	★	YYY	11	3	X	–	–	X	–
HOCHFELD Hochfeld Hotel PO Box 454 Okahandja 9000	(06228) Hochfeld 1703	L	★	YYY	5	2	–	–	–	X	–
KALKRAND 9000 Kalkrand Hotel PO Box 5	(06672) 29	L	★	YYY	7	2	–	–	–	–	–
KARASBURG 9000 Kalkfontein Hotel PO Box 205	(06342) 172	M	★	YYY	15	7	–	X	X	X	–
Van Riebeeck Hotel PO Box 87	(06342) 23	L	★	YYY	11	4	–	X	X	X	–
KARIBIB 9000 Hotel Erongoblick PO Box 17	(062252) 9	L	★	YYY	10	3	–	–	–	X	–
Hotel Laszig PO Box 164	(062252) 81	L	★	YYY	10	5	X	X	–	X	–
KEETMANSHOOP 9000 Canyon Hotel PO Box 950	(0631) 3361	H	★★★	YYY	54	54	X	X	X	X	X
Hansa Hotel PO Box 141	(0631) 3344 3345	M	★★	YYY	20	15	X	X	X	X	–
KOËS 9000 Hotel Kalahari PO Box 71	(06322) 14	L	★	YYY	5	2	–	–	–	X	–

36   Namibia

Town, name and postal address	Telephone	Tariff (L Low / M Medium / H High)	Grading	Liquor facilities	Total no.	With private bath or shower and WC	A la carte restaurant	Telephone in bedroom	Air-conditioning in bedrooms	Garage available or off-street parking	Swimming-pool
LEONARDVILLE 9000 Hotel La Ville PO Box 52	(06822) 18	M	★	YYY	8	4	–	4	–	×	–
LÜDERITZ 9000 Bay View Hotel PO Box 100	(06331) 2288	M	★★	YYY	28	28	×	×	–	×	×
Hotel Zum Sperrgebiet PO Box 373	(06331) 2856	H	–	YYY	10	8	–	×	–	–	–
Kapps Hotel PO Box 387	(06331) 2701	M	★	YYY	25	7	×	×	–	×	–
MALTAHÖHE 9000 Maltahöhe Hotel PO Box 20	(06632) 13	M	★	YYY	14	14	×	×	–	×	–
MARIENTAL 9000 Mariental Hotel PO Box 671	(0661) 856	L	★	YYY	18	13	×	14	13	×	–
Sandberg Hotel PO Box 12	(0661) 2291 738	M	★	YYY	22	18	–	14	13	×	–
NOORDOEWER 9000 Suidwes Motel PO Box 1	(0020) 13	M	★	YYY	24	20	×	–	×	×	–
OKAHANDJA 9000 Okahandja Hotel PO Box 770	(06221) 3024	M	★	YYY	13	4	×	–	–	×	–
OMARURU 9000 Central Hotel PO Box 29	(062232) 30	M	★	YYY	12	12	×	–	–	×	×

Town, name and postal address	Telephone	Tariff L Low M Medium H High	Grading	Liquor facilities	Bedrooms available Total no.	With private bath or shower and WC	Facilities A la carte restaurant	Telephone in bedroom	Air-conditioning in bedrooms	Garage available or off-street parking	Swimming-pool
Hotel Staebe PO Box 92	(062232) 35	M	★	YYY	26	22	×	–	–	×	×
OMITARA 9000 Omitara Hotel PO Box 641	(06202) 4	L	★	YYY	5	5	–	–	–	–	–
OSHAKATI 9000 International Guest House PO Box 542	(06752) 75	M	–	YYY	23	20	×	–	×	×	×
OTAVI 9000 Otavi Hotel PO Box 11	(06742) 5	L	★	YYY	10	3	–	×	–	×	–
OTJIWARONGO 9000 Hotel Brumme PO Box 63	(0651) 2420	M	★	YYY	12	4	×	×	–	×	–
Hotel Hamburger Hof PO Box 8	(0651) 2520	H	★★	YYY	28	28	×	×	–	×	–
OUTJO 9000 Hotel Etosha PO Box 31	(06542) 26	L	★	YYY	10	4	×	×	–	–	–
Hotel Onduri PO Box 14	(06542) 14	H	★★	YYY	45	43	×	×	×	×	–
REHOBOTH 9000 Rio Monte Hotel PO Box 3097	(06272) 161	L	★	YYY	10	5	–	–	–	–	–
Suidwes Hotel PO Box 3300	(06272) 238	L	–	YYY	8	8	×	–	–	–	–

Town, name and postal address	Telephone	Tariff L Low M Medium H High	Grading	Liquor facilities	Total no.	With private bath or shower and WC	A la carte restaurant	Telephone in bedroom	Air-conditioning in bedrooms	Garage available or off-street parking	Swimming-pool
REHOBOTH-RAIL 9000 Bahnhof Hotel PO Box 540	(0020) 8550	L	★	YYY	5	2	–	–	–	–	–
RUNDU 9000 Kavango Motel PO Box 203	(067372) 320	M	★ ★	YYY	11	11	×	×	×	×	–
SWAKOPMUND 9000 Burg Hotel Nonidas PO Box 6	(0641) 4544	M	★	YYY	10	2	×	×	–	×	–
Hansa Hotel PO Box 44	(0641) 311	H	★ ★ ★	YYY	35	35	×	×	–	–	–
Hotel Eggers PO Box 13	(0641) 2321	L	★	YYY	13	5	–	×	–	×	–
Hotel Europa Hof PO Box 1333	(0641) 5061 5898	M	★ ★	YYY	28	28	×	×	–	×	–
Hotel Grüner Kranz PO Box 600	(0641) 5016 2039	M	★ ★	YYY	16	16	×	×	–	×	–
Hotel Jay Jay's Restaurant PO Box 835	(0641) 2909	L	★	YYY	12	5	×	–	–	×	–
Hotel Schütze PO Box 634	(0641) 2718	M	★	YYY	13	7	×	×	–	×	–
Pension Dig By See PO Box 1530	(0641) 4130	L	★	–	10	8	–	–	–	×	–
Pension Prinzessin- Rupprecht-Heim PO Box 124	(0641) 2231	L	★	YY	35	30	–	–	–	×	–

Town, name and postal address	Telephone	Tariff (L Low / M Medium / H High)	Grading	Liquor facilities	Bedrooms available — Total no.	Bedrooms available — With private bath or shower and WC	A la carte restaurant	Telephone in bedroom	Air-conditioning in bedrooms	Garage available or off-street parking	Swimming-pool
Pension Rapmund PO Box 425	(0641) 2035	M	★	YY	22	22	–	–	–	×	–
Pension Schweizerhaus PO Box 445	(0641) 2419	M	★	YY	22	22	–	×	–	×	–
Strand Hotel PO Box 20	(0641) 315	H	★★	YYY	42	42	×	×	–	×	–
TSUMEB 9000 Hotel Eckleben PO Box 27	(0671) 3051	M	★★	YYY	19	13	×	×	×	×	–
Minen Hotel PO Box 244	(0671) 3071 3072	M	★★	YYY	38	21	×	×	×	–	–
USAKOS 9000 Usakos Hotel PO Box 129	(062242) 259	M	–	YYY	9	6	×	×	4	×	–
WALVIS BAY 9190 Atlantic Hotel PO Box 46	(0642) 2811 2812	M	★★	YYY	12	12	×	×	–	×	–
Casa Mia Hotel PO Box 1786	(0642) 5975	M	★	YYY	16	16	×	×	–	×	–
Desert Inn Hotel (Narraville) PO Box 8044	(0642) 2053	M	★	YYY	10	2	–	–	–	×	–
Flamingo Hotel PO Box 30	(0642) 3011 3012	M	★	YYY	35	19	×	×	–	×	–
WINDHOEK 9000 Continental Hotel PO Box 977	(061) 37293	M	★★	YYY	70	47	×	×	×	×	–

Town, name and postal address	Telephone	Tariff L Low M Medium H High	Grading	Liquor facilities	Bedrooms available Total no.	With private bath or shower and WC	*A la carte* restaurant	Telephone in bedroom	Air-conditioning in bedrooms	Garage available or off-street parking	Swimming-pool
Hansa Hotel PO Box 5374	(061) 223249	M	★	YYY	10	6	×	×	×	×	–
Hotel Fürstenhof PO Box 316	(061) 37380	H	★★	YYY	18	18	×	×	×	×	–
Hotel Kapps Farm PO Box 5470 (20 km out of town)	(061) 34763 36374	M	★	YYY	5	1	×	–	–	×	×
Hotel Safari PO Box 3900	(061) 38560	H	★★★	YYY	193	193	×	×	×	×	×
Hotel Thüringer Hof PO Box 112	(061) 226031	H	★★	YYY	38	38	×	×	×	×	–
Kalahari Sands Hotel PO Box 2254	(061) 36900	H	★★★	YYY	180	180	×	×	×	×	×
Privat Pension Berger PO Box 5836	(061) 228660	H	★	YY	10	10	–	×	3	×	×
Privat Pension d'Avignon PO Box 3724	(061) 222218	M	★	YY	10	10	–	–	–	×	×
Privat Pension Handke PO Box 20881	(061) 34904	M	★	–	10	9	–	×	–	×	–
South West Star Hotel PO Box 10319 Khomasdal 9000	(061) 224689	L	★	YYY	10	3	–	–	2	×	–
WITVLEI 9000 Witvlei Hotel PO Box 13	(06832) 4	L	★	YYY	6	2	×	–	–	×	–

GUEST OR HOLIDAY FARMS

In recent years the number of guest or holiday farms in SWA/Namibia has grown rapidly and they currently number some 28. The grading system for these establishments is basically the same as for hotels, except that guest and holiday farms which are not fully licensed are exempt from the requirements regarding public conveniences. The maximum award for these farms is a three-star grading:

★★★ excellent (145–180 points)

★★ very good (100–144 points)

★ good (72–99 points)

GUEST FARMS

Nearest town, name and postal address	Telephone	Tariff (L Low, M Medium, H High)	Grading	Liquor facilities	Bedrooms available — Total no.	Bedrooms available — With private bath or shower and WC	Facilities — Hunting	Facilities — Garage	Facilities — Swimming-pool
DAMARALAND Hobatere Lodge c/o Mount Etjo Safari Lodge PO Box 81 Kalkfeld 9000	(06532) 1602	H	★★ ★	YYY	12	12	×	–	×
GOBABIS 9000 Ohlsenhagen PO Box 434	(0688) 11003	L	★★	–	5	–	×	×	×
Steinhausen Private Bag 523 Omitara, 9000	(06202) 3240	MH	★★	YYY	5	2	×	×	×
HELMERINGHAUSEN 9000 Sinclair PO Box 19	(06362) 6503	L	★★	YYY	5	3	×	–	–

Nearest town, name and postal address	Telephone	Tariff (L Low / M Medium / H High)	Grading	Liquor facilities	Bedrooms available — Total no.	Bedrooms available — With private bath or shower and WC	Facilities — Hunting	Facilities — Garage	Facilities — Swimming-pool
KALKFELD 9000 Mount Etjo Safari Lodge PO Box 81	(06532) 1602	MH	★★★	YYY	28	28	X	–	X
KARIBIB Khomas, PO Box 954 Walvis Bay 9190	(0642) 4129 (062252) Tsaobis 4202	M	★★	YYY	6	6	X	X	X
OKAHANDJA 9000 Bergquell PO Box 17	(06228) 82222	M	★★★	YYY	7	4	–	–	X
Moringa PO Box 65	(06228) Wilhelmstal 6111	H	★★	–	5	2	X	X	X
Okatjuru PO Box 207	(06228) Hochfeld 1521	H	★★	YY	5	4	X	X	X
Otjisazu PO Box 149	(06228) 81640	M	★★★	YYY	5	2	X	X	X
Otjisemba PO Box 756	(06228) 82103	H	★★★	YYY	5	5	–	X	X
Wilhelmstal-Nord PO Box 641	(06228) Wilhelmstal 6212	M	★	YYY	5	4	X	X	X
OMARURU 9000 Epako PO Box 108	(062232) 2040	L	★★	YYY	5	2	X	–	X

Nearest town, name and postal address	Telephone	L M H Low, Medium High	Grading	Liquor facilities	Total no.	With private bath or shower and WC	Hunting	Garage	Swimming-pool
		Tariff			Bedrooms available		Facilities		
Immenhof PO Box 250	(06532) 1803	M	★ ★	–	6	3	✕	✕	✕
Otjandaue PO Box 44	(062232) 1203	MH	★ ★	YYY	5	4	✕	✕	✕
Otjumue-Ost PO Box 323	(062232) 1913	L	★	–	5	–	✕	✕	✕
OTAVI 9000 Kupferberg PO Box 255	(06742) 2211	MH	★ ★	–	5	1	–	✕	✕
OUTJO 9000 Bambatsi Holiday Ranch Private Bag 2566	(06542) 1104	LM	★ ★ ★	YYY	10	8	–	✕	✕
Otjitambi Private Bag 2607	(06542) Otjikondo 4402	L	★ ★	YY	7	3	✕	–	✕
TSUMEB 9000 La Rochelle PO Box 194	(0678) 11013	L	★ ★	YYY	5	2	✕	–	✕
USAKOS 9000 Ameib Ranch PO Box 266	(062242) 1111	M	★ ★ ★	YYY	7	6	✕	✕	✕
Wüstenquell PO Box 177	(062242) 1312	H	Pending	YYY	5	4	–	–	–
WINDHOEK 9000 Baumgartsbrunn PO Box 3667	(061) 34542 32623	M	★ ★	YYY	5	5	✕	✕	✕
Bellerode PO Box 5185	(061) 35485	H	★	–	5	–	✕	✕	–

Nearest town, name and postal address	Telephone	L M H Low Medium High	Grading	Liquor facilities	Total no.	With private bath or shower and WC	Hunting	Garage	Swimming-pool
		Tariff			**Bedrooms available**		**Facilities**		
Elisenheim PO Box 3016	(061) 64429	L	★★	YYY	6	3	–	–	✕
Hope PO Box 21768	(0628) Nina 3202	M	★★	YYY	5	5	✕	–	✕
Ibenstein PO Box 20 Dordabis 9000	(0628) Dordabis 8	H	★★	–	5	3	✕	✕	✕
Monte Christo PO Box 5474	(061) 32680	L	★	YY	5	5	✕	✕	✕
Ongoro-Gotjari PO Box 20129	(0628) Seeis 1312	H	★★	YYY	5	3	✕	✕	✕
Silversand Private Bag 13161	(06202) 1102	M	★★	–	5	2	✕	✕	–

PRIVATE AND MUNICIPAL FACILITIES

A number of rest camps, campsites and caravan parks are situated on popular tourist routes in the country. While some facilities have been graded, others are not, but some, nevertheless, offer accommodation of a high standard.

Place	Name and postal address	Telephone	Grade	Licence	Accommodation offered
DAMARALAND	Palmwag Lodge PO Box 1428 Swakopmund 9000	(0641) 4072 or 4950	★★	YY	bungalows campsite

Place	Name and postal address	Telephone	Grade	Licence	Accommodation offered
GOBABIS	Welkom PO Box 450 Gobabis 9000	(0688) 12213	★ ★	–	bungalows
GROOTFONTEIN	Municipality PO Box 23 Grootfontein 9000	(06731) 2040	–	–	campsite
HENTIESBAAI	Swaou-Oord PO Box 82 Hentiesbaai 9000	(06442) 165	★ ★	–	bungalows
KARIBIB	Tsaobis Leopard Nature Park PO Box 143 Karibib 9000	(062252) 1304	★	–	bungalows
KATIMA MULILO	Zambezi Lodge PO Box 98 Katima Mulilo 9000	(0020) Katima Mulilo 6230	–	–	bungalows campsite
KAVANGO	Suclabo Lodge PO Box 6222 Rundu 9000	(067372) 6222	–	–	bungalows
KEETMANSHOOP	Municipality Private Bag 2125 Keetmanshoop 9000	(0631) 2657	–	–	campsite
KHORIXAS	PO Box 2 Khorixas 9000	(0020) Khorixas 196	★ ★	–	bungalows campsite
LÜDERITZ	Namib Tours PO Box 377 Lüderitz 9000	(06331) 2475	–	–	bungalows
OMARURU	Municipality PO Box 14 Omaruru 9000	(062232) 28	–	–	bungalows campsite
OTAVI	Municipality PO Box 59 Otavi 9000	(06741) 22	–	–	bungalows campsite
OTJIWARONGO	Municipality Private Bag 2209 Otjiwarongo 9000	(0651) 2231	★	–	campsite
OUTJO	Municipality PO Box 51 Outjo 9000	(06542) 13 205	★	–	bungalows campsite

Place	Name and postal address	Telephone	Grade	Licence	Accommodation offered
REHOBOTH	Reho Spa Recreation Resort Private Bag 2500 Rehoboth 9000	(06272) 774	–	–	bungalows campsite
SWAKOPMUND	Mile 4 Caravan Park PO Box 3452 Vineta 9000	(0641) 61781 62901	–	–	campsite
	Swakopmund Restcamp The Head: Tourism Swakopmund Municipality Private Bag 5017 Swakopmund 9000	(0641) 2588	–	–	flats, chalets, cabins
TSUMEB	Municipality PO Box 275 Tsumeb 9000	(0671) 3056	–	–	campsite
UIS	The Secretary Imkor Club Uis 9000	(062262) 30	–	–	campsite
USAKOS	Ameib Ranch PO Box 266 Usakos 9000	(062242) 1111	–	–	campsite no caravans
	Wüstenquell PO Box 177 Usakos 9000	(062242) 1312	Pending	–	campsite
WALVIS BAY	Municipality PO Box 86 Walvis Bay 9190	(0642) 5981	★★	–	campsite
WINDHOEK	Safari Hotel PO Box 3900 Windhoek 9000	(061) 38560	–	–	campsite caravans to hire

DIRECTORATE OF NATURE CONSERVATION REST CAMPS AND RESORTS

Following is a list of accommodation in the game parks and resorts of the SWA/Namibia Government. All reservations must be made through the reservations office next to the main post office in Kaiser Street, Windhoek. The postal address is Private Bag 13267, Windhoek 9000,

Tel (061) 26975. Reservations are accepted Mondays to Fridays from 08h00 to 13h00 and 14h00 to 15h00, while payments are only accepted from 08h00 to 13h00. The office is closed on Saturdays. The reservations office and the resorts accept credit cards for payment.

Resort/Park	Accommodation	Facilities
Ai-Ais	flats bungalows campsite	shop restaurant filling station swimming pool thermal hall
Daan Viljoen	bungalows campsites	shop restaurant swimming pool
Etosha Okaukuejo Camp	bungalows bus quarters tents* campsites	shop restaurant filling station swimming pool
Etosha Halali Camp	bungalows dormitory bus quarters tents* campsite	shop restaurant petrol swimming pool
Etosha Namutoni Camp	rooms in fort bus quarters mobile homes campsite	shop restaurant filling station swimming pool
Gross Barmen	bungalows campsite	shop restaurant filling station swimming pool thermal pool
Hardap	bungalows dormitory campsite	shop restaurant filling station swimming pool
Kaudom Kaudom Camp	rustic huts campsite no caravans	no

Communal ablution facilities and field kitchens are available at all campsites unless otherwise indicated.
* To be phased out.

Resort/Park	Accommodation*	Facilities
Kaudom Sikereti Camp	rustic huts campsite no caravans	no
Lüderitz	campsite	no
Namib-Naukluft Naukluft	campsite	no
Namib-Naukluft Sesriem	campsite	filling station cooldrinks
Namib-Naukluft Namib Desert	campsites no water or ablutions	no
National West Coast Mile 14	campsite	no
National West Coast Mile 72	campsite	filling station
National West Coast Mile 108	campsite	filling station
National West Coast Jakkalsputz	campsite	no
Popa Falls	rustic huts campsite	kiosk
Skeleton Coast Terrace Bay	double rooms	shop restaurant filling station
Skeleton Coast Torra Bay †	campsite	shop petrol
Von Bach	campsite only drinking water and toilets	no
Waterberg	bungalows campsite	shop restaurant filling station swimming pool

* Communal ablution facilities and field kitchens are available at all campsites unless otherwise indicated.
† Facilities of the shop and petrol are only available during school holidays.

Regional notes
on
places of interest

6 SOUTH

AI-AIS AND FISH RIVER CANYON

Approaching from the south via Noordoewer, the turnoff from the B1
to the Fish River Canyon is signposted 37 km north of Noordoewer,
from where it is a further 82 km to Ai-Ais. When approaching via
Upington and Karasburg, Ai-Ais is best reached by taking the signposted turnoff on the B1 31 km south of Grünau, Ai-Ais being 73 km
on. This route can also be used by visitors travelling from the north.
Alternatively, Ai-Ais can be reached by turning onto route 28 at Seeheim, enabling you to visit the main viewpoint on the way.

The Fish River Canyon is one of the great natural wonders of Africa
and the second largest canyon in the world. The canyon forms part of
the Fish River Canyon Conservation Area, which was originally proclaimed a reserve in 1969. The well-known resort Ai-Ais is situated
about 80 km from the northern viewpoint.

Accommodation at Ai-Ais includes luxury flats as well as camping
and caravan sites. Other facilities include a shop where basic commodities, liquor and souvenirs can be purchased, a licensed restaurant,
a communal spa complex, open-air swimming pool and tennis courts,
and a filling station.

Backpackers may cover the 85 km hike between the northernmost
viewpoint and Ai-Ais over four or five days. No facilities have been
provided and you can enjoy total wilderness. The trail is usually booked
up well in advance and reservations must be made well in advance at
the DNC office in Windhoek. Owing to excessive summer temperatures
and the danger of flash floods, the trail is only open between 1 May
and 31 August.

The main viewpoint over the Fish River Canyon, 80 km north of Ai-
Ais, offers visitors awe-inspiring vistas of the canyon, which was formed
over a period of tens of millions of years by the relentless forces of

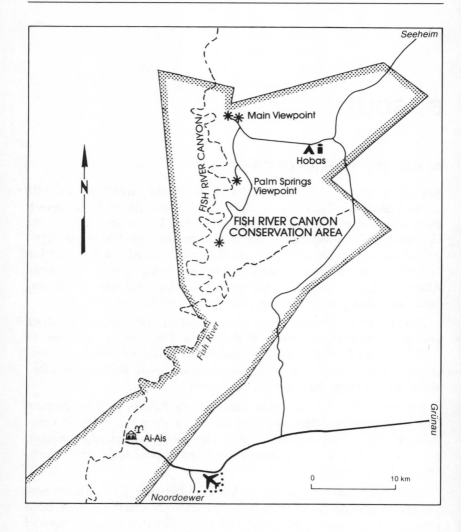

erosion. Situated immediately west of the main viewpoint in Hell's Bend – a classical example of a meander – which originated when the river was still young. The 161 km long canyon is up to 27 km wide in places, while its depth is between 457 m and 549 m.

Looking down into the canyon, its various geological formations can be seen clearly. The dark, steep slopes leading up from the riverbed were originally sandstone, shale and lavas deposited about 1 800 million years ago. During deep burial about 1 300–1 000 million years ago these deposits were intensely compressed and folded. At the same time they were heated to over 600°C and became metamorphosed, a process by which they recrystallised and changed appearance. Together with intrusive granites of the area these rocks form the Namaqualand Metamorphic Complex. The dark lines that cut these rocks are fractures filled with lava that never reached the surface. Referred to as dolerite, these were formed 900 million years ago. The first major period of erosion began soon after this, exposing all the above rock types and levelling them into a vast peneplain which, some 650 million years ago, became the floor of a shallow sea that covered the flat southern part of SWA/Namibia. Sediments of the Nama Group were deposited in this sea. You will notice the almost horizontal contact line between the Namaqualand Metamorphic Complex and the overlying, flat layers of the Nama Group. In geological terms this is known as an unconformity – a term used to refer to a break in the geological record, during which time the deformed strata were exposed and eroded.

The base of the Nama Group is only a few metres thick and consists of a small-pebble conglomerate. Above this are 150–200 m of black limestones, grits and sandstones. These rocks are capped by 10 m of shale and sandstone. Fracturing of the crust about 500 million years ago enabled a north–south valley to form in the region of the Fish River. Slow erosion gradually removed the uppermost parts of the Nama Group. Then, about 300 million years ago, during the Dwyka Ice Age, southward-moving glaciers deepened the north–south valley. Another period of fracturing deepened the valley even further. These younger fractures, or faults, penetrate deep into the earth. Groundwater circulating in the faults emerges at the surface as hot springs – the best known being Ai-Ais and the Sulphur Spring 16 km south of the main viewpoint. Incision by the Fish River is relatively recent and most of the striking features of the canyon developed over the past 50 million years.

Another perspective of the canyon is gained by following the road to the Sulphur Springs lookout point. Although fairly rocky, it is generally kept in good condition and suitable for sedan cars.

The terrain between Ai-Ais and the main viewpoint is mainly level, with scattered mountains and ridges. The vegetation has been classified as Dwarf Shrub Savanna (Giess Vegetation Type 9) with trees such as quiver tree (29), shepherd's tree (122) and jacket-plum (433). Other plants occurring commonly on the plains include *Euphorbia, Rhigozum* and *Hoodia* species. The dominant grasses are *Stipagrostis uniplumis* and *S. ciliata.*

Trees along the river include camel thorn (168), sweet thorn (172), wild tamarisk (487), buffalo-thorn (447) and ebony tree (598). The plains are the habitat of springbok, while Hartmann's mountain zebra, klipspringer, chacma baboon and rock dassie prefer the more rocky areas. Leopard also occur, but on account of their solitary nature and shy behaviour are unlikely to be encountered.

To date more than 60 bird species have been recorded at Ai-Ais. The riverine bush supports the largest number of species and here you should keep an eye open for swallowtailed bee-eater (445), dusky sunbird (788) and blackchested prinia (685). Purple gallinule (223) are common in the reedbeds bordering pools, while moorhen (226) are less numerous. Less common species recorded at or near Ai-Ais include scimitarbilled woodhoopoe (454), yellowbellied eremomela (653) and brubru (741).

Ai-Ais is a Khoekhoen name which is translated as "fire-water" (that is, hot as fire or scalding hot). It is certain that the spring was known for thousands of years to the Stone Age people who lived in the area, as well as the pastoralists who settled here much later, before it was "discovered" in 1850 by a Nama shepherd searching for stray stock. The spring was visited by farmers of the area and during the Nama War of 1903–7 it was used as a base camp by the German forces. When the South African forces under General Louis Botha invaded South West Africa in 1915 German soldiers allegedly sought refuge here to recover from their wounds. After World War I the South West Africa Administration leased the spring to a Karasburg entrepreneur, who provided basic facilities. In 1962 the canyon was proclaimed a national monument and seven years later a conservation area. The modern rest camp complex was opened officially on 16 March 1971, but almost a year later the Fish River came down in flood, causing extensive damage to the complex. Floods in 1974 and 1988 also forced the resort to be closed for some time. In 1987 the Fish River Canyon Conservation Area was enlarged when state land west of the canyon, including the rugged Hunsberge, was incorporated into the existing conservation area. Extensive improvements to the rest camp were carried out during 1987–8.

Depending on demand, sightseeing flights lasting about 30 minutes can be arranged over the canyon during the peak tourist season. Enquiries can be made at Ai-Ais.

KEETMANSHOOP

For those travelling by road from either the Cape or the Transvaal, Keetmanshoop is the first major SWA/Namibian town on the route further north.

Keetmanshoop, originally a Nama settlement on the banks of the Swartmodder River, was known as *Nugoaes* (translated as "black mud")

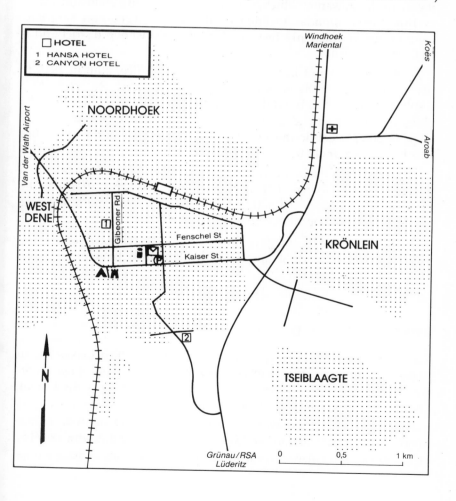

– a reference to the river, which only flows after very good rain. In 1866 a Rhenish mission station was established and named after Johann Keetman, a prosperous German industrialist and chairman of the Rhenish Missionary Society, who made funds available for the establishment of the mission. The first missionary, Johan Schröder, set about building a church, but in 1890 the building was swept away when the Swartmodder River flooded its banks. A new church, built on higher ground, was completed in 1895 and remained in use until 1930. The church was declared a national monument in 1978 and was acquired subsequently by the Keetmanshoop Municipality for use as a museum. The theme of the museum, which is open from 08h00 to 12h00 and 16h00 to 18h00 from Monday to Friday and 08h00 to 12h00 on Saturday, concentrates on the early history of the Keetmanshoop district and is well worth a visit.

Another building of interest is the Old Post Office, built in 1910 to plans drawn up by the government architect, Gottlieb Redecker. As a result of a decision to build the post office on a single erf, not two, the plans had to be amended, and because Kaiser Street ran at a slight angle to other streets in the vicinity, the northern wall of the post office was built at an angle too.

The attractive façade incorporates a prominent pointed gable with a wide, rectangular tower where a telegraph mast was once attached. The building was proclaimed a national monument in 1987 and now serves as offices for the Southern Tourist Forum and Namib Air.

Other interesting buildings in the town include Schutzenhaus (1907) in Gibeon Street, the old hospital, also known as Johanniter House (1913) and the German Evangelical Lutheran Church (1935) on the corner of Kaiser Street and Third Avenue.

KOKERBOOMWOUD

This dense stand of about 250 quiver trees (29), which makes for an unusual "forest", is situated on the farm Gariganus, some 14 km northeast of Keetmanshoop. The turnoff to the forest is signposted along route 29 (C18) between Keetmanshoop and Koës.

The branches of these trees were hollowed out by the San for use as quivers for their arrows – hence the name. The quiver tree, a member of the genus *Aloe*, usually reaches a height of 3–5 m, although trees occasionally grow up to 8 m high. They occur from Namaqualand in the north-western Cape to the Brandberg and the bright yellow flowers are particularly attractive during June and July.

GELLAP OST KARAKUL FARM

Those interested in finding out more about karakul farming should visit the experimental farm north-west of Keetmanshoop. Leave Keetmanshoop on the D609 to the J G van der Wath Airport, continuing for about 16 km to the signposted turnoff. The farm is open from Monday to Friday for the periods 1 March to 15 April, 1 June to 15 July and 15 September to 20 October only.

Gellap Ost was established in the late 1930s. Research on the 13 700 ha farm centres on the improvement of the pattern and quality of the coats of karakul sheep, as well as the improvement of pastures.

Today, Maltahöhe is the centre of the country's karakul breeding region. The first karakul sheep imported into the country arrived at Swakopmund from Vienna in 1907, following a visit by a prominent fur trader, Paul Albert Thorer, to Bokhara in Central Asia, where the karakul sheep originate. On his return to Germany, Thorer began promoting the exportation of karakul sheep to German colonies. The initial consignment of 12 sheep to this country was followed by the arrival of 22 rams and 252 ewes from Bokhara early in 1909. A breeding and experimental centre was established after World War I at Neudam, east of Windhoek, to improve the quality of local pelts. Among the achievements of the Neudam experimental farm are its success in breeding a pure white pelt and one with a shallow "water silk" curl pattern. Breeders were also anxious to improve the quality of their pelts and the SWA Karakul Breeders Association was founded as early as 1919. Karakul pelts from SWA/Namibia are marketed internationally under the name Swakara. Although the Soviet Union and Afghanistan are the world's two largest producers of karakul, Swakara is internationally recognised as the best quality karakul fur.

The sheep are almost exclusively bred for their pelts, which are used for fashion garments. The lambs are slaughtered within 24 hours of birth; about 25 pelts are required to manufacture a jacket and 32 for a coat. Most pelts are sold at the London Fur Fair, which holds auctions in February, July, September and November each year. The main buyers of Swakara pelts are Italy, Spain and West Germany (in that order), but pelts are also bought by Canada, the USA and Japan. Black Swakara pelts are the most popular, followed by grey, white, brown and variegated pelts.

The fortunes of this industry are closely linked to factors such as international economic conditions, changing fashions and local climatic conditions. Consequently the number of sheep and pelts varies considerably from year to year. In 1986, for example, only 770 000 pelts were produced because of the drought and a decline in pelt prices, compared with 3,2 million pelts in 1973.

Karakul sheep are a hardy breed, well suited to the southern parts of the country. When pelt prices are low, a large percentage of the lamb is raised for mutton. In addition to pelts and mutton, the stomach linings of lambs are used in the cheese manufacturing process, while several pharmaceutical products are manufactured from the carcass. Karakul wool is much in demand, especially for manufacturing carpets.

BRUKKAROS

Brukkaros, which dominates the landscape west of the main road between Keetmanshoop and Mariental, is reached by turning off the B1 onto route 98 (signposted Berseba) just south of Tses, 80 km north of Keetmanshoop. Some 36 km on, about 1 km before reaching the settlement of Berseba, you turn onto the D3904 (signposted Brukkaros). From here the road continues for 12 km, although those in sedan cars are advised to look for a suitable parking place after 10 km, when the road narrows into a steep track.

At present (1988) permits are not required to explore the area and no facilities are provided. You are free to camp wherever you choose, the best site being amongst the boulders at the end of the road. If you intend spending a night here, ensure that you are self-sufficient in respect of water and firewood.

From the end of the road a well-constructed path takes you into the crater via the eroded southern rim – an easy half-hour walk. This path was constructed in 1930 when the Smithsonian Institute established a station on the western rim of the crater from which to observe the sun's surface. Once inside the crater you can follow this path, which continues up a valley towards the western rim, reaching the old observation station after about one hour. A short scramble brings you to the edge of the rim and a wonderful view of the surrounding plains, with the drainage lines radiating from Brukkaros. Although there are other vantage points from the crater rim, this is probably the best one and the heat, with not much shade to be found, will deter most hikers. However, if you have the time it is interesting to explore the crater floor with its numerous quiver trees (29).

On account of its prominent position, rising some 650 m above the surrounding plains, the mountain has also served various other purposes. Early in the century a heliograph station was established on the eastern side of the rim by the Germans, while more recently (as you will probably have noticed) a VHF radio mast was erected on the northern rim of the mountain.

The Nama name, *Geitsigubeb*, refers to the mountain's apparent resemblance to a large leather apron worn by Khoikhoi women around their waist. The German name, *Brukkaros*, is derived from the Khoikhoi name and is said to be a combination of a German adaptation of the Afrikaans name for trousers (*broek*) and *karos*, which means leather apron.

A surprising feature of Brukkaros is the absence of lava, despite its volcanic origin. The evolution of Brukkaros began 80 million years ago with the intrusion of the kimberlite-like magma (molten rock) into rocks about 1 km below the earth's surface. This magma must have encountered underground water, which would have turned to steam immediately, the extremely high pressure causing the overlying rocks to bulge up into a dome 400 m high and 10 km across. More magma was then able to intrude higher into the centre of the dome, where it encountered underground water. This time the cover of overlying rock was thinner and the superheated steam blew out the centre of the dome in a huge explosion. As the underground water was able to drain into the resulting crater it encountered more intruding magma. This resulted in further explosions from successively deeper and deeper levels in the crater. In the end, rocks from as deep as 2 km within the earth crust were being blasted out in the crater.

The highly shattered ejected rock fragments built up a rim of rubble and ash around the crater. Once explosive volcanism ceased, rain began to wash the fine material in the ash rim back into the crater, where it built up layers of sediment on the floor of the crater lake which had formed in the meantime. Numerous hot springs occurred around the edge of this lake, and in bubbling up through the sediment, they deposited large quantities of fine-grained quartz, which gradually cemented the sediments into hard, extremely weather-resistant rocks. Volcanism was very short-lived, possibly lasting only a year or two, but sedimentation could have lasted hundreds of thousands of years. Subsequent erosion gradually removed the surrounding rocks, leaving the cemented, weather-resistant crater-lake sediments, once located down in the throat of the dead volcano, standing high above the centre of the dome that formed when the first magma intruded.

Berseba, the settlement about 10 km south of Brukkaros, was founded in 1850 by the Rhenish missionary, Samuel Hahn. It takes its name from the biblical Berseba (Gen. 21:31) which means "well of the oath".

MUKUROB

Travelling along the B1 you reach the small railway siding of Asab, 98 km south of Mariental. Here you have the option of a short detour to the site of what used to be one of the country's best known landmarks, Mukurob. For centuries this fascinating rock pinnacle balanced precariously on a narrow "neck" and base of shale. Sadly, in early December 1988 it succumbed to the elements and tumbled down, shattering into pieces, but a brief visit is still recommended. Turn onto route 1066 which is followed for 12 km, before turning right onto route 620 to reach the site, which has been fenced in, less than 10 km on.

The pinnacle was a relic which resisted the erosion of the Weissrand Plateau which lies immediately to the east. The upper 9,4 m of the "head" consisted of sandstone, followed by a 3 m layer of conglomerate.

The origin of Mukurob can best be understood when surveying the landscape east of the formation. As a result of the erosion of the softer shale and vertical seams, the sandstone escarpment of the Weissrand Plateau has been broken down into large blocks which mostly collapsed, though Mukurob defied the elements for much longer. Some 200 m north-west of the formation are two low koppies with debris which appear to be other relic columns which have tumbled down.

Although the Khoekhoen name *Mukurob* is commonly associated with the English name, The Finger of God, the names bear no relation to each other, as Mukurob is said to mean "look at the ankle" – an apparent reference to the narrow neck between the pedestal and the crown. It is also known as the *Vingerklip* (Afrikaans) and, on account of its resemblance to the face and headdress of a Herero woman, as the *Hererovrou*.

According to a popular legend the name means "now you can see" (*mu-kuro*). This legend relates how the Nama and the Herero were in perpetual rivalry over who was in possession of the best pastures. The Nama told the Herero they could continue boasting, as they had a rock in their area which could not be matched. To this the Herero retorted "we will easily pull over that little rock". Ten oxen were slaughtered, thongs were made and attached to the neck of the formation and a large number of Herero tried in vain to pull over the rock. The Nama jeered, saying *Mu-Kuro – now you can see*.

Mukurob was 34 m high, the height to the base of the head being almost 22 m. The head, with an estimated weight of 637 tons, was supported by a neck which was 3,6 m long, between 1,8 and 3,6 m broad and almost 1,5 m wide. According to calculations the head exerted pressure of some 11,75 kg per 1 cm^2 on the neck.

GIBEON

Gibeon railway station, on the B1 63 km south of Mariental, is usually passed by unnoticed. However, of interest here is a small graveyard which testifies to one of the bloodiest battles of the 1914–15 German South West African campaign. The graveyard is reached by taking the turnoff to the station and leaving your vehicle near the station building. Cross the railway line opposite the station building to the graveyard.

During the battle fought here on 27 April 1915 between a 1 500 strong force under Brigadier-General Sir Duncan McKenzie and a German force of 800 men, commanded by General Von Kleist, 29 South Africans were killed or died of wounds and 66 wounded. The German losses were 12 dead and 30 wounded, while 188 German soldiers were taken prisoner of war. Two field guns, four machine guns, a train, wagons with supplies and a quantity of ammunition were also captured by the Union of South Africa Defence Force. The battle resulted in a proclamation the following day by General Jan Smuts, who commanded the Southern Force, that enemy territory south of Gibeon was under control of the Union of South Africa Defence Force.

The settlement of Gibeon is reached by taking the signposted turnoff opposite the Gibeon station and travelling about 9 km on. The town has an interesting history, but as none of the historic buildings has remained, a detour is not recommended. The spring around which the settlement grew was originally known to the Nama as *Gorego-re-Abes*, or the drinking place of the zebras. As with several other settlements in the south of the country, Gibeon was founded by the Rhenish Mission. A mission station was established in 1863 by missionary J Knauer and named after the biblical Gibeon (Josh. 10:2). The first church was built in 1876, but a few years later the mission station was destroyed. However, it was rebuilt later.

In 1894 Gibeon was declared a district, with the settlement as district town, and a military post was established in the same year on the orders of Major Theodor Leutwein. While the fort was being built non-commissioned officer Bahr and 14 troopers were temporarily accommodated in the mission church. After the 1893–4 war against Hendrik Witbooi, Senior Lieutenant Von Burgsdorff was appointed district commander or *Bezirksampt* of the Gibeon district. On 4 October 1904 he was murdered at Mariental after riding unarmed to Hendrik Witbooi's settlement at Rietmond in an unsuccessful final attempt to persuade him not to go to war. Following Von Burgsdorff's murder the whites in the area sought refuge in the fort, which unfortunately has been demolished since.

In the late 1890s De Beers Consolidated Mines Limited explored the Gibeon area, following the discovery of kimberlite pipes. Despite the absence of diamonds hopeful explorers persisted and in 1902 the Gibeon Syndicate was formed. Two years later the syndicate changed its name to the Gibeon Schurf- und Handelsgesellschaft, but in 1910 abandoned its search.

GIBEON METEORITES

Today you are unlikely to come across a meteorite here, but Gibeon has attracted world-wide attention because one of the most extensive meteorite showers in the world is known to have fallen in the area. The "Gibeon Shower" is estimated to have occurred over an area of some 20 000 km^2 with the highest concentration falling in the Gibeon/Amalia area, covering approximately 2 500 km^2. It has been suggested that the shower was due to the meteors remaining together after a violent explosion, an unusual occurrence, and striking the earth's atmosphere as a group after a relatively long journey through outer space.

Thirty-seven fragments, with a total mass of 12,6 tons, of the "Gibeon Shower" were brought to Windhoek between 1911 and 1913 by the state geologist of the German Imperial Government, Dr P Range. They were given to the *Landesmuseum* in Windhoek for safekeeping as a temporary measure and after World War I transferred to the Zoo Garden (now Verwoerd Park) in the city. In April 1975 they were moved to the Alte Feste to be catalogued and have remained there ever since, although it is planned to display them once again in the Verwoerd Park. Four of the original meteorites found by Dr Range were made available to museums and institutions in South Africa and abroad, leaving 33 of the original 37 in Windhoek. The average weight of the meteorites in the collection is 348,5 kg, while the total mass is 11,5 tons and the heaviest meteorite is 555,7 kg.

Some 77 Gibeon meteorites with a total weight of 21 tons have been recovered to date and can be seen in various museums throughout the world, including the British, Budapest and Prague museums as well as the Washington and New York museums of natural history. The largest known Gibeon meteorite, one of 650 kg, was donated to the South African Museum in Cape Town.

The meteorites consist of 90–95 per cent iron, 7,7–8,18 per cent nickel (the Hoba meteorite near Grootfontein, by comparison, contains 16 per cent nickel), up to 0,6 per cent cobalt and as much as 0,06 per cent phosphorus as well as carbon, sulphur, chrome and copper. Other trace elements include zinc, gallium, germanium, iridium and platinum.

The bubbly surface, melting seams and cavities have led scientists to believe that the appearance of the meteorites is primarily due to atmospheric transformation at low temperatures following the breakup of the parent body. On account of their dense and pure metallic structure, the arid climate of the Gibeon area and their relatively young age, only minor corrosion took place after the meteorites struck the earth.

OLD GERMAN FORT NEAR SEEHEIM

The turnoff to the railway siding of Seeheim (signposted Visrivier Afgronde, Ai-Ais, Grünau) is passed on the B4, about 40 km west of Keetmanshoop. Continue for 1,5 km on the B4 to reach the bridge over the Fish River, where there is a viewpoint. Some 11 km further, on the farm Naiams, a national monument signboard marks the starting point of a 1 km walk (or drive, if you are in a four-wheel-drive vehicle) to an old German fort dating back to 1905–6. After passing through the gate opposite the Naiams farmhouse, turn left and follow the track into the valley, passing the ruins on your right, and continue slightly uphill until you reach the fort on your left. Natural slabs and rocks from the area were used in the construction, making the fort blend in very well with the surroundings.

The fort was built to protect traffic on the road between Keetmanshoop and Lüderitz against attacks by bands of raiding Nama. Travellers were particularly vulnerable in the narrow defile and at the nearby waterhole, and a small contingent of German *Schutztruppe* was stationed here. On the way up to the fort the tracks of the original road can still be seen and nearby the fort are the graves of two *Schutztruppe*.

NAUTE DAM

The turnoff to the Naute Dam is signposted on the B4 32 km west of Keetmanshoop, from where it is approximately 18 km to the dam. Situated in the Löwen River, a tributary of the Fish River, the dam has a capacity of 84 million m³. The dam, in glorious surroundings, is popular with water sports enthusiasts and freshwater anglers. At present (1988) no overnight camping is permitted at the dam, which is open daily between 09h00 and 17h00. Plans are, however, underway to develop a recreation resort on 5 ha set aside for this purpose, while the DNC has been allocated 17 000 ha for development as a game park.

BETHANIE

Bethanie is reached 25 km north of Goageb, and the turnoff is signposted 100 km west of Keetmanshoop on route B4 between Keetmanshoop and Lüderitz. The town is not situated on a major route, but if you are travelling between Goageb and Helmeringhausen on route 31 (C14), do plan to spend at least an hour here.

A mission station to serve the Nama was established here in 1814 by the German missionary Heinrich Schmelen of the London Missionary Society. Known as *Uigantes* to the !Aman Nama who had settled in the area around 1804, the station was first named Klipfontein, but was soon renamed Bethanien.

In 1822 inter-tribal conflicts forced Schmelen to abandon Bethanien and his attempts in 1823, 1827 and 1828 to re-establish the mission station failed, not only because of the inter-tribal friction, but also because of drought and locust plagues. After 14 years' service, Schmelen left Bethanie. Following the transfer of the rights of the London Missionary Society to the Rhenish Missionary Society in 1840, the Rev Hans Knudsen was sent to Bethanie in 1842.

In the main street (Keetmanshoop Street) you will see the Joseph Fredericks House, erected in 1883 by Captain Joseph Fredericks as a dwelling and council chamber. The first protection treaty between the Germans and the Bethanien Nama was signed in this house by Captain Fredericks and the German Consul General, Dr Friedrich Nachtigal, in October 1884. The house was declared a national monument in 1951 and the Nama Administration plans to use the building as offices.

The turnoff to Schmelen House in the grounds of the Evangelical Lutheran Church, is signposted on Keetmanshoop Street, opposite Joseph Fredericks House. Shortly after turning into Quellen Street you will see the Rhenish Mission Church on your right. The church was inaugurated on 30 May 1899 as a replacement for the original twin-tower mission church.

Schmelen House is reached by turning left into the grounds of the Evangelical Lutheran Church.

The house, originally built by Schmelen in 1814, was burnt down after he left the mission station, but later rebuilt by missionary Knudsen, and the stone walls are now the only part dating from Schmelen's time. It was declared a national monument in 1952, and houses an interesting photographic display on the history of the mission station and the surrounding area. The key to the house can be obtained either from the vicarage opposite or from the hotel in the town.

In the nearby graveyard, the graves of several of the missionaries who served the Bethanie parish can be seen. Also to be seen is the old limestone church built in 1859 by missionary Hermann Kreft. The church was originally built with a twin tower, but unfortunately the towers became derelict and had to be demolished. Following the inauguration of a new church the building was used as a school, a purpose it fulfilled until about 1970 when a new school was built. The building, one of the oldest churches in the country, has since fallen into disrepair, but plans are afoot to renovate it and to rebuild the towers.

ROOIPUNT

Rooipunt, well off the beaten track, is only worth visiting if you are particularly interested in the way of life of the early inhabitants of the area. Not only must you have at least half a day free, but it is also essential to have a four-wheel-drive vehicle. If you are determined to visit the farm, contact Mr Willem de Vries, Tel (06362) 81, in Bethanie for the necessary permission. You could perhaps ask him to accompany you (for a fee) as it will save you time in locating the sites and he will also be able to tell you some interesting stories about his pioneering days – he was the first white farmer to settle in the area.

From the B4 Rooipunt is reached by turning onto the D459 (signposted Rosh Pinah), a few kilometres west of Goageb. Continue along this road (ignore the D446 signposted to Rosh Pinah 10 km on) for 28 km until turning right onto a farm road signposted Haaswater. Keep to the left when, 3 km on, the road divides into three. From here it is another 10 km, keeping to the right of the farmhouse passed 6 km after the split, before you pass through the Rooipunt farm gate. Continue for 6 km to the farmhouse, where it is advisable to park your car and proceed on foot to the rock engravings, about a 1 km walk there and back.

Follow the track leading past the windmill and up the hill. Once at the top of the hill veer slightly to the right and make your way towards the prominent tree in the river valley. Look carefully at the flat rock slabs on the edge of the river, to the right of the tree. Three unusual engravings depicting bulbous plants are to be found here. Other engravings, including some of zebra, rhino and giraffe, as well as battle shields, can be seen on the rock in the riverbed, provided the rock shelf has not been covered with sand. Sadly, they have been defaced by more recent "artists".

Return to the farmhouse, from where you can continue to the music stones. Follow the track which crosses the riverbed behind the homestead to the left of the farmhouse, and continue for about 100 m along the southern bank until you reach blackish, slab-like rocks with conspicuous white hollows. It has been suggested that these rocks served as a musical instrument to earlier inhabitants whose origin has not yet been determined. Judging by the depth of the white indentations in the black limestone rocks, it seems likely that they were used over a long period. Pick up one of the round river stones (they give the best sound) and try to play a tune by striking different hollows in quick succession, much like a xylophone. The upper slab rests on a slightly larger base, and the narrow gap between the two slabs is thought to act as a resonator when the rock is struck.

AUS

The terrain of the World War I prisoner-of-war camp at Aus is reached by turning off the B4 into Aus. Turn left at the T-junction as you enter the village and travel for about 3 km until you reach the road signposted to Rosh Pinah. Ignore the the turnoff and continue straight ahead for another 0,6 km before turning right, from where it is a short distance to a clearing where a national monuments plaque on a large boulder serves as a marker.

On 9 July 1915 the German forces in South West Africa, who were assembled at Khorab just north of Otavi, surrendered to the forces of the Union of South Africa. Two prisoner-of-war camps were originally established – at Okanjande near Otjiwarongo for officers of the active German forces and police, and at Aus for non-commissioned officers and other personnel.

At first glance Aus seems a most unlikely place for a prisoner-of-war camp. The town was, however, of great strategic significance, as well as being one of the two important stations on the Lüderitz–Keetmanshoop railway line. As there was no railway link between the Union of South Africa and South West Africa at the time and the railway line between Lüderitz and Keetmanshoop had been repaired only as far as Aus, the town was a logical choice from an economic point of view. Food and equipment for a camp could be shipped with little effort from Cape Town to Lüderitz and transported from there to Aus. By August 1915, 1 552 prisoners of war, as well as 600 guards of the South African Veteran Regiment (SAVR) (later known as the Protectorate Garrison Regiment), were settled in Aus, where bell tents housed the men. The tents offered little protection against the elements and with the extremes of temperature, conditions soon became unbearable. No attempt to improve conditions was made by the Union and the prisoners of war were left to their own devices. They improved their own lot by making bricks in the camp and building their own houses and by April 1916 it was reported that tents were no longer used. These bricks were also sold to the SAVR at 10 shillings per 1 000.

The houses were ingeniously constructed – even tins were put to use, flattened out and joined together to make tiled roofs. Unfortunately, the elements have almost completely destroyed any record of these unique buildings and you will have to use your imagination when visiting the site. However, the local community has expressed interest in reconstructing some of the houses, which were generally one-roomed, some semi-detached, giving the impression of a small, closed neighbourhood. You will notice that in one building style the floor was well below ground level, with the roof just visible above the ground. From archive records it is apparent that the Germans were proud of their houses, making themselves as comfortable as possible, and some even constructed attractive front gables, while others just kept gardens.

Initially, the lack of water supply to the camp was a cause of dissatisfaction but within a few months a pipeline was installed and showers and laundry facilities were provided. By February 1919 three boreholes sunk in the camp supplied water. At first, no cooking facilities were available to the prisoners, but in February 1916 the medical officer, Captain Joubert, mentioned that the prisoners had built a few stoves.

The garrison stationed at Aus were not very happy with their living and working quarters, but made no attempt to improve the situation. An offer of building material for the construction of barracks was turned down because the men would rather suffer in their tents than live in barracks. Some of the men constructed unsightly shacks from sacking which provided inadequate protection against the elements. Eventually, however, in the second half of 1918, barracks were constructed – those for A, B and D companies to the east of Maxim Koppie, and C company south of the railway line and prisoner-of-war camp.

A copy of the book *Aus 1915-1919* will enhance your visit to the camp. Although it is only available in Afrikaans, the map at the back of the book will help you to orientate yourself. An interesting feature you will notice on the map is the extensive tramway stretching over almost 5 km around the camp, which was completed in February 1917. It was supplied by the Department of Railways and Harbours of the Union of South Africa.

Generally the physical condition of the prisoners of war was good and it improved when they were able to benefit from their garden produce. In total, 65 prisoners of war (4,1 percent) compared to 60 members of the garrison (8,3 per cent) died in the camp. Most deaths – 59 prisoners of war and 50 members of the garrison – were caused by an influenza epidemic during October and November 1918.

With the signing of the Treaty of Versailles at the end of the war, the first two groups of men eventually left the camp on 19 and 20 April 1919. Others followed slowly and when the last group left on 13 May 1919, the camp was officially closed.

WILD HORSES OF THE NAMIB

Travelling westwards from Aus you enter Diamond Area 1, about 11,5 km on. The road forms the southern boundary of the Namib–Naukluft Park. The area is strictly controlled by Consolidated Diamond Mines (CDM) and you may not leave the road under any circumstances! Although there are no signposts indicating that you are entering the *Sperrgebiet* (German for "forbidden territory"), a fence demarcates the eastern boundary. A roadsign here warns you against the danger of horses, so keep an eye out for the legendary wild horses of the Namib. Be especially careful if you are travelling this section after dark as the horses often lie on the road at night.

Continuing through the wide open plains of this almost untouched land, you pass Garub, where you are most likely to see some of the wild horses. Their numbers depend on the condition of the veld, the average being about 150–160. The horses have adapted themselves to the harsh desert conditions and have been observed to drink only once in five days during arid periods. By slowing down, they sweat less, and consequently are able to reduce the number of drinking trips, leaving more grazing time. The horses, however, have only one water supply, on which they depend entirely. They must visit Garub, where water is pumped from the borehole for their sole benefit.

There are several theories on the origin of these horses – perhaps the only wild desert-dwelling horses in the world. It has been suggested that they once belonged to surrounding farms from where they ran wild into the desert. The most popular theory is that they are descendants of horses owned by Baron von Wolf of Duwisib (see pp 83–85). As Garub lies some 160 km south-west of Duwisib, this seems an unlikely explanation. Another theory is that they are descendants of the horses left behind when the German *Schutztruppe* abandoned Aus during the South West African campaign in 1915. According to one Mr Fritz Bolz his father caught some of the horses and on one a regimental number had been tattooed on the inner lip. During March 1987 16 horses were captured, of which 10 were transported to Onderstepoort Veterinary Research Institute near Pretoria in South Africa where a research project will attempt to determine their origin. It is hoped to tame the remaining six horses and use them as patrol horses in Etosha National Park.

If you see the area for the first time during a dry period, you will find it difficult to believe that the horses are able to survive in their harsh surroundings. However, when the area does receive rain the horses graze in beautiful fields of grass and build up reserves to carry the stronger and fitter animals through the lean years. Another factor which is to the advantage of the horses in this dry environment is that it is almost parasite free. The horses are also protected by living within the restrictions of Diamond Area 1 – keeping poachers and horse thieves at bay.

LÜDERITZ

Although Lüderitz is not on any through route a detour to this picturesque coastal town is rewarding. The most direct approach is from Keetmanshoop along the B4. Motorists are, however, cautioned to drive with care on the gravel section (103 km) between Goageb and Aus. A particularly enjoyable scenic drive for visitors approaching from the north is via Helmeringhausen along route 35 (C13), which joins the trunk road (B4) at Aus. The final 122 km from Aus is along a tarred road and does not offer any alternative routes as you are passing through the Diamond Area, where no deviations from the main road are permitted.

When travelling to Lüderitz plan to reach the town as early as possible because sandstorms on the last stretch of the road are fairly common in the afternoon and can "sandblast" your vehicle.

There are three hotels in the town as well as bungalows/beach houses at Ostend. The latter were managed for a number of years by the DNC, but since August 1988 the rest camp has been privately managed. A caravan and camping site on Shark Island caters for those preferring more basic facilities.

After having travelled a fair distance to Lüderitz you will enjoy relaxing in this town for a few days. Plan for at least two days, as a one-night stopover will not allow sufficient time!

Some of the sights in Lüderitz are described below.

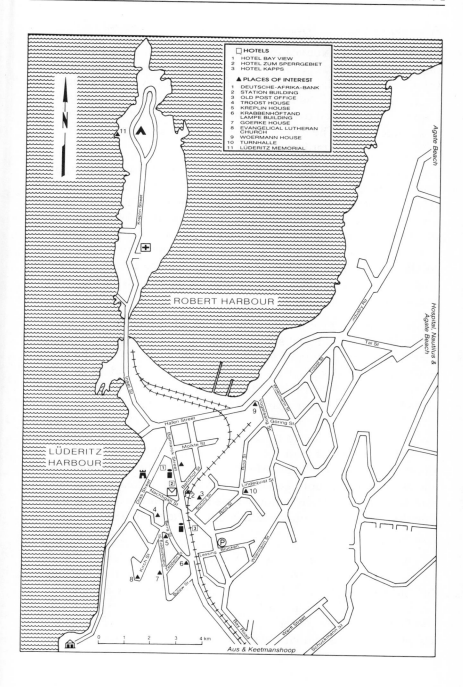

HOTELS
1 HOTEL BAY VIEW
2 HOTEL ZUM SPERRGEBIET
3 HOTEL KAPPS

▲ PLACES OF INTEREST
1 DEUTSCHE-AFRIKA-BANK
2 STATION BUILDING
3 OLD POST OFFICE
4 TROOST HOUSE
5 KREPLIN HOUSE
6 KRABBENHÖFTAND
  LAMPE BUILDING
7 GOERKE HOUSE
8 EVANGELICAL LUTHERAN
  CHURCH
9 WOERMANN HOUSE
10 TURNHALLE
11 LÜDERITZ MEMORIAL

ROBERT HARBOUR

LÜDERITZ HARBOUR

Agate Beach

Hospital, Nautilus & Agate Beach

Aus & Keetmanshoop

A walking tour

The beautiful Art Nouveau and German Imperial Style buildings will undoubtedly impress you and only by walking will you truly experience the German colonial atmosphere of yesteryear. A walking tour, with brief descriptions of the buildings, is given here. However, should you require more detailed coverage, contact Lüderitzbucht Safaris and Tours to arrange a tour. The buildings described here correspond to the numbers on the map, starting in the centre of the town.

1 Deutsche-Afrika-Bank Built in 1907 by the Bause brothers, an attractive feature here is the lower storey and one corner of the upper storey, which are constructed from stone. You will notice that the builders favoured a more decorative style than used in Woermann House (9). They incorporated a belltower and Renaissance-style gable, and although the building is not situated on a corner plot, it was set back to allow the corner to be built in the Wilhelminische style. The bank was established in 1905 as a private bank with its headquarters in Hamburg.

2 Station Building Still the focal point of the town, this building, although not the original station building, is particularly interesting in that it is a combination of various building styles. Lohse, the government architect, designed the building, with the building division of Metje & Ziegler responsible for the construction. The building was completed in 1914 – seven years after the railway line between Lüderitz and Aus was completed. This railway line was initially constructed because it was quicker to transport troops and military equipment directly from Lüderitz than via Swakopmund, which became important during the Nama rebellions. After the discovery of diamonds in Lüderitz the railway traffic, both goods and passengers, increased dramatically, and the original station building became inadequate. The German Imperial Government authorised this new building in 1912.

3 Old Post Office The offices of the Directorate of Nature Conservation are housed here today. Oswald Reinhardt, the railway commissioner of the southern line, drew up the original plans for this building but his successor, Rukwied, changed the design to include an upper storey with a tower. The public clock was placed on the tower and it rang for the first time on New Year's Eve 1908. However, in 1912 the clock was transferred to the church tower.

4 Troost House You are now in the "Altstadt Area", which is the older area of the town. This semi-detached house, in typical colonial style, dates back to 1909. It was built by Hermann Metje for Edmund Troost, who himself never occupied the house. Architecturally it blends in well with its neighbours, especially the house to the south, also built by Hermann Metje.

5 Kreplin House Dating back to the close of 1909, this impressive double-storeyed house with its symmetrical façade belonged to Emil Kreplin, a manager of the railway branch at Lüderitz and later director of a diamond company and the first mayor of the town. It was built by Friedrich Kramer, and, together with Woermann House in Swakopmund, is one of the few examples belonging to the second period of the Wilhelminische style.

6 Krabbenhöft and Lampe Building This shop with adjoining residence was built in 1909–10 by Friedrich Kramer after he completed Kreplin House (5). The building was owned by the trading firm of Krabbenhöft and Lampe, who also had branches in Gibeon, Helmeringhausen and Keetmanshoop. The double-storeyed house, with its symmetrical façade, reflects the building style of the neo-Renaissance. It is noticeable, though, that the windows of the first storey are not positioned directly above the arches on the ground floor.

7 Goerke House The house is situated on Diamond Hill, from where you have a good view of the town, including the Evangelical Lutheran Church (8). Hans Goerke had this German colonial style house built in 1909 and occupied the elaborate building until his return to Germany at the end of February 1912. At the time, Goerke was manager and shareholder of three different companies, but had been a store inspector in the *Schutztruppe*. It is not known who the architect of the house was, but unique to this building is the eye-catching sundial – a Wilhelminische decoration not known in this country at the time.

Consolidated Diamond Mines (CDM) became the owner of the building in April 1920 and in February 1944 the South West Africa Administration bought the house. During this period the magistrate occupied the building, hence another name by which the building is known – Old Magistrate's Residency. CDM, the present owner of Goerke House, once again purchased the property in February 1983 and has restored the building to its former glory. Today the house serves as a guest house for CDM officials and visitors, and when occupied is closed to the public. Otherwise it can be visited on weekdays between 14h00 and 15h00 and on Saturdays between 10h30 and 11h30 (enquire at the CDM office for confirmation). It is closed on Sundays and public holidays.

8 Evangelical Lutheran Church (also known as the *Felsenkirche* – the church on the rocks). Initially, the population of Lüderitz was too small to justify a Lutheran congregation and although the first requests were made in 1906, it only came into being three years later. This was a result of the growth of the settlement, with several military regiments being stationed here during the Nama rebellions of 1904–7, as well as the discovery of diamonds and the completion of the railway to the interior.

A minister arrived from Germany in December 1909 and a parsonage was built by Heinrich Bause the following year. Heinrich's brother, Albert, was responsible for the design and construction of the church. The foundation stone was laid on 19 November 1911 and on 4 August 1912 the building was consecrated. Donations from Germany covered most of the building costs (46 300 Mark). One of the beautiful stained glass windows, the altar window, was donated by Kaiser Wilhelm II and the altar bible by his wife.

Strangely, the architecture of the church is not in keeping with the German neo-Gothic building style of the time but more closely related to Victorian Gothic. This is said to be because the Bause brothers came to SWA/Namibia from the Cape, where they were influenced by the Cape Victorian building style.

The church is normally kept locked but is open to the public on Saturdays and Sundays at 18h00 when the bells are rung. However, you can visit it at other times – the best time being at sunset – by making arrangements with church council members (contact the Tourist Information Office).

9 Woermann House The Woermann Line was entrusted with transporting German troops to Lüderitz and found it necessary to establish offices in the town. Friedrich Höft drew up the plans, which were approved in 1906. Before construction could commence the hill on the site had to be levelled and rock broken up here was used in the foundations and ground floor. The design of the house is simple, but the inclusion of a water condenser – then a technical innovation – made the building unusual.

10 Turnhalle This large rectangular building dates back to 1912–13, when it served as a gymnasium. Albert Bause, a member of the gymnasium, was the builder. The simple lines of the building are broken by a curvilinear gable on the façade with a matching semi-circular window. Large rectangular windows, separated by pillars, interrupt the monotony of the side walls and allow light into the building.

Exploring the Lüderitz Peninsula

There are several delightful bays waiting to be explored and an outing can be combined with a beach walk and a picnic lunch, so set aside the best part of a day. The turnoff to the various bays is at the southern end of the town. The first is Radford Bay, which is named after the first white settler, David Radford, who lived here in a house constructed from jetsam. Radford sold dried fish and shark-liver oil to Cape-bound ships and exchanged ostrich feathers for fresh water with northward-bound ships, as no water was available at Lüderitz. He also obtained water by collecting dew, and from Khoikhoi women who carried it in ostrich eggshells and seal-bladder skins from a distant waterhole.

Fishermen are usually well rewarded here.

Continue to Second Lagoon, where oyster cultivation is taking place. The coastline from Second Lagoon to the harbour is likely to be the most rewarding for birdwatchers. Greater flamingo (96) is the most obvious species but your chances of spotting them depends on the tide.

A few kilometres beyond Second Lagoon the road forks, the turnoff to your left leading to Grosse Bucht (Large Bay). With the exception of Agate Beach, this 2 km long beach is one of the few sandy bays in the area open to the public and is therefore popular with bathers, fishermen and walkers. Picnic facilities have been provided.

The road leading northwards from Grosse Bucht gives access to a number of bays and from the cliffs on the western side of Guano Bay you have a good view of Halifax Island. Continuing to Dias Point, you pass a grave with a wooden cross which simply reads "George Pond of London, died here of hunger and thirst 1906."

A short distance further you pass the lighthouse, which dates back to around 1910. Dias Point is reached by way of a wooden bridge across

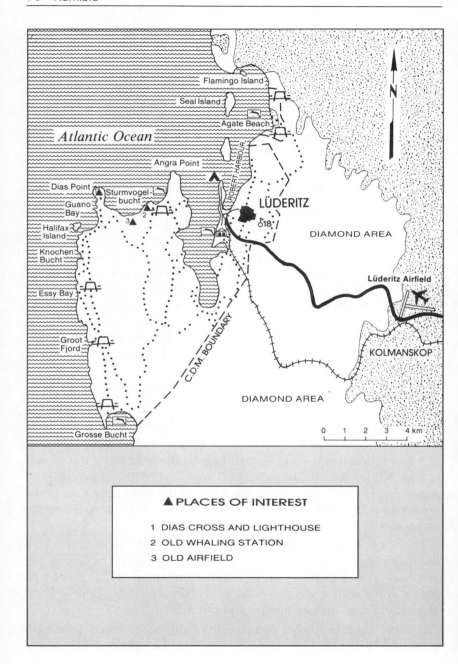

Atlantic Ocean

Flamingo Island
Seal Island
Agate Beach
Angra Point
Dias Point
Sturmvogel-bucht
Guano Bay
Halifax Island
Knochen Bucht
Essy Bay
Groot Fjord
Grosse Bucht
LÜDERITZ
ROBERT HARBOUR
DIAMOND AREA
Lüderitz Airfield
KOLMANSKOP
C.D.M. BOUNDARY
DIAMOND AREA

0 1 2 3 4 km

N

▲ PLACES OF INTEREST

1 DIAS CROSS AND LIGHTHOUSE
2 OLD WHALING STATION
3 OLD AIRFIELD

the rocky gulley. The bridge was built in 1911 to facilitate access to the steam-operated foghorn which was originally on the point.

Bartolomeu Dias, on his southward journey, was the first recorded white man to have sheltered in the protected bay at Lüderitz. With his three ships he entered the bay on Christmas 1487 and gave it the name of Angra das Voltas before continuing south to become the first navigator to round the Cape. On his return journey in July the following year, Dias renamed the bay Golfo de São Cristovão (it changed its name again to Angra Pequena) and erected a stone cross on Dias Point on 25 July 1488. Fragments of the cross were taken to Cape Town in 1856. A cross of Karibib marble bearing no resemblance to the original was erected in 1929. During the Dias '88 Festival a replica of Dias's original cross made of Namib dolerite was unveiled – five centuries later.

From Dias Point the road takes you past a long-abandoned landing strip and a short detour leads to Sturmvögelbucht (*Sturmvögel* is the German for "petrel", a seabird which visits the coast in summer). Here the remains of the old German whaling station, dating back to about 1913, can be seen rusting away.

The adjacent Griffith Bay takes its name from an American ship's officer who was buried here by David Radford. During the American Civil War Griffith sought refuge at Angra Pequena, but was shot as a traitor when another ship arrived. The bay affords a magnificent view of the town across the lagoon.

Returning to town, you rejoin the main access road which takes you past Second Lagoon and Radford Bay once again. Back in town, follow Bismarck Street into Hafen Street, where you turn right into Insel Street. A short distance further you cross onto Shark or Haifisch Island by way of a causeway. A plaque on the island reminds one of the founder of SWA/Namibia's oldest harbour town – the German merchant Adolf Lüderitz.

Heinrich Vogelsang, agent of Adolf Lüderitz, landed at Angra Pequena on 9 April 1883 to establish a trading station. After negotiating with the Bethanien Khoikhoi chief, Joseph Fredericks, he purchased the land within an 8 km radius of Angra Pequena, which in April 1884 became part of the protectorate of the German Empire – the beginning of German control in South West Africa.

Adolf Lüderitz himself arrived at Angra Pequena in October 1883, but perished three years later when he ignored advice not to sail in a small boat from the Orange River mouth to Angra Pequena. The town was named Lüderitzbucht in honour of the merchant from Bremen whose trading venture never succeeded. Finally, Agate Beach is also worth a visit. This long, sandy beach, about 8 km out of town, is well signposted from the turnoff at the junction of Hafen and Tal streets. Do not be too enthusiastic about finding agates here, though, and take care to remain on the hard-surface roads. Picnic facilities are provided.

Kolmanskop

The ghost town of Kolmanskop, 10 km east of Lüderitz, can only be visited by obtaining a permit from the CDM office in Lüderitz (next to the old power station) and joining a guided tour. Permits are only valid for the day for which they are issued. Tours are conducted on weekdays and Saturdays from 9h30 to 10h30 and, if there are sufficient people, from 10h45 to 11h45. By special arrangement tours are also conducted from 08h30 to 09h30. After the tour you can enjoy refreshments at the tearoom.

Kolmanskop is said to be named after a transport driver on the route between Lüderitz and Keetmanshoop, Johny Kolman or Coleman. He regularly camped near a *koppie* (hillock) which was named Kolmans-kuppe after he had had to be rescued there when his oxen disappeared during a vicious sandstorm.

August Stauch established his headquarters at Kolmanskop after one of his labourers found a diamond in April 1908, at Grasplatz. Kolmanskop subsequently became the centre of the diamond mining industry, and CDM had their headquarters here until 1943, when they moved to Oranjemund. Initially, prefabricated wooden buildings clad with corrugated iron were shipped from Germany, but in time these were replaced with some fine, solid structures. The double-storeyed houses of the manager and mining engineer were especially elaborate. The lemonade and sodawater factory must have been popular not only for refreshing drinks but also for the blocks of ice which were supplied to all households free of charge.

The availability of fresh water was every bit as much a problem at Kolmanskop as it had been for the settlers at Lüderitz. Although a pump station at Garub, some 100 km away, did supply some water, the town was also dependent on barrels of water shipped to Lüderitz from Cape

Town and hauled through the sand by two mules. Condensers were used to make seawater drinkable and a 28 km long pipeline from Elisabethbucht supplied the washing and treatment plants of the mining operations with seawater.

In 1950 all mining operations ceased at Kolmanskop. The last person left the town six years later, and the buildings were abandoned to the elements. April 1983 marked the 75th anniversary of the discovery of diamonds in the town and to celebrate the occasion CDM restored certain buildings, including the casino, skittle alley and the retail shop.

A yacht trip

These trips are offered daily, weather permitting, from Robert Harbour and should not be missed. Trips last between two-and-a-half and three hours, depending on the weather. If the weather is favourable you may get a close-up view of the penguin colony on Halifax Island. The trip affords you beautiful views of Lüderitz and its numerous bays and dusky dolphins are frequently seen playing near the bow of the yacht. Trips usually commence fairly early in the morning with the time depending on the season. Details can be obtained from Lüderitzbucht Safaris and Tours.

The museum

The theme of the museum focuses on the early days of Lüderitz and the surrounding Namib Desert. It is open between 16h00 and 18h00 on Tuesdays, Thursdays and Saturdays and can also be visited by arrangement with the curatrix, Mrs Dyck, Tel 2628. Although small, the museum is well worth a visit.

Crayfish factories

Crayfishing is one of the major industries of Lüderitz and during the season, which extends from 1 November to 30 April, the factories can be visited by arrangement with the management. Enquiries about the best times to visit the factories can be made at Lüderitz Buchhandlung and Lüderitzbucht Safaris and Tours.

Crayfishing

If you are trying your hand at crayfishing remember that no crayfish may be caught in the reserve area between Dias Point and Agate Beach. The minimum length is 6,5 cm and only five crayfish are permitted per person. The season extends from 1 November to 30 April. (Check at the Sea Fisheries office that these and other regulations are still current.)

Angling

There are several rewarding angling spots along the peninsula where stumpnose and harder can be caught. Make enquiries with the Directorate of Sea Fisheries if you are not familiar with local regulations.

Oyster culture and seaweed operations

A visit to various operations of the Taurus Company can be arranged by telephoning (06331) 2674. The company's activities include the commercial utilisation of seaweed, the production of agar-agar from locally collected seaweed and the cultivation of oysters.

Karakul carpet weavery

Guided tours are conducted around the factory in the Krabbenhöft and Lampe Building from Monday to Friday from 08h00 to 13h00 and 14h00 to 17h00. You will see how the karakul wool is first handspun and then handwoven into rugs.

Digging for desert roses

Lüderitz is well known for its desert roses – crystals of gypsum and calcium sulphate salts occurring in the desert sand, developing under damp, moist conditions. Until fairly recently the collection of desert roses was prohibited, but after obtaining a permit from the DNC offices visitors may now search for these beautiful rosette-like crystals. Collectors are limited to three sand roses or a total weight of 1,5 kg and spades or other hard implements may not be used as they will damage concealed sand roses. Collectors are allowed two hours, and must restore the area to the satisfaction of the nature conservator.

Excursions offered by tour operators in Lüderitz

At present (1988), Lüderitzbucht Safaris and Tours is the only tour company operating in Lüderitz. They offer an excellent service, with tours ranging from Lüderitz on foot to overnight tours exploring the south of the country. Day trips to the Koichab Pan area in Diamond Area 2 are also conducted. Access to this area is controlled strictly and it can only be visited by way of an organised tour, which should be booked at least two weeks in advance, as arrangements must be made for a Nature Conservation officer to accompany the tour.

Where to eat in Lüderitz

- *Bay-View Hotel* (hotel guests only), seafood
  Diaz Street, Tel 2288

- *Casanova Inn Restaurant*, steaks and seafood
  Diaz Street, Tel 2855

- *Franzls Restaurant*, German home-cooking and seafood
  Tal Street, Tel 2292

- *Kapps Hotel Diningroom and Boat Restaurant* (hotel guests only), seafood
  Bay Road, Tel 2701

- *Strand Restaurant*, seafood
  Ostend, Tel 2752

HELMERINGHAUSEN

The small settlement of Helmeringhausen is, in fact, nothing more than a farm with a general dealer store, petrol station and hotel. From the south it can be reached either via Aus (route 35 [C13]) or Goageb and Bethanie (route 31 [C14]), while the main approach from the north is route 31 (C14) from Maltahöhe. Alternatively it can be approached from Sesriem via Duwisib along routes 826 and 831 which join route 31 (C14) 60 km north of Helmeringhausen.

Petrol is available at Helmeringhausen from Monday to Saturday, from 8h00 to 18h00 only.

Adjacent to the Helmeringhausen Hotel is an interesting open-air farm museum with a large number of old farming implements on display. Among the displays are an old fire engine used at Lüderitz and an ox-wagon used to transport building material and furniture from Lüderitz to Duwisib. The key to the museum, which was established in 1984 by the Helmeringhausen Farmers Association, can be obtained from the hotel. It is intended to make a small explanatory pamphlet available.

About 19 km south of Helmeringhausen on route 31 (C14), the turn-off to the graveyard on the farm Mooifontein is signposted. Unlike most others in the country, the graveyard is not only of historic but also of architectural interest. One kilometre after taking the turnoff you reach the farmhouse, where you follow the road to the left of the reservoir – the graveyard is about 1 km on, in the riverbed.

Mooifontein was originally known as Chamis and during the German colonial period a military station was established here. In 1899 a wooden, prefabricated house was shipped from Germany to Lüderitz, from where it was transported by ox-wagon to Chamis. This prefabricated house, erected on the northern bank of the Konkiep River, served as barracks and mess for the German troops for a number of years. It was later replaced by a permanent double-storeyed structure, which was converted to the single-storey house today serving as the farmhouse.

The graveyard is surrounded by an attractive stone wall, which forms a half-circle on one side. The graves of German troops and NCOs who died during the wars with the Nama are alongside the wall, their tombstones in recesses in the wall. In the centre of the graveyard is a memorial in the form of a chapel. Also of interest are the heavy iron gates forged from the rims of ox-wagon wheels.

MALTAHÖHE

Maltahöhe, 111 km west of Mariental, can be reached along any of a number of routes, the most direct being route 34 (C19) from Mariental, which gives access to Sesriem and Naukluft along routes 36 and 14/2 (C14) respectively. From the south the town can be approached either from Aus along route 35 (C13) or from Goageb along route 31 (C14), via Helmeringhausen.

Named after Malta von Burgsdorff, the wife of the commander of the garrison at Gibeon, the town was established in 1900.

More than 40 graves of German *Schutztruppe* who died in active service or in the numerous battles during the campaign against Hendrik Witbooi in 1894 and the Nama rebellion of 1903–7 can be seen in the graveyard to the east of the town.

North of Maltahöhe, route 14/2 (C14) passes through the farm Nomtsas, where a national monument sign indicates the turnoff to the graveyard of SWA/Namibia's pioneer wool farmer, Ernst Hermann. An employee of the Deutsche Kolonialgesellschaft, Hermann started the first wool farming operation in the country at Kubub (at Aus). After Kubub was destroyed by Hendrik Witbooi in 1893, Hermann continued the operation at Nomtsas, which, with an area of more than 100 000 ha, became the largest sheep farm in the country.

In 1904 Hermann and others were murdered by Nama and buried in the graveyard. Alongside the graveyard the remains of Hermann's house and the shearing sheds can be seen. The original waterhole, which is still in use today, can also be seen nearby.

SCHLOSS DUWISIB

The imposing Schloss Duwisib, south-west of Maltahöhe, is a complete surprise to the unsuspecting traveller.

If you are travelling south from Sesriem, Duwisib can be reached by taking the D826 from Sesriem to Helmeringhausen – the castle is 162 km from Sesriem. However, visitors travelling on route 31 (C14) between Helmeringhausen and Maltahöhe can reach the castle by turning onto route 831, 62 km north of Helmeringhausen (signposted D831) – 25 km on you turn left onto the D826, which is followed for about 15 km to the entrance gate of Duwisib. At present (1988) the castle is open daily between 08h00 and 17h00 and entry is free.

The castle, its contents and 50 ha of surrounding land were bought by the DNC in the late seventies with a view to providing tourist accommodation. On account of the limited number of guests that can be accommodated it is planned to provide additional accommodation, as well as a restaurant. Although the furniture has been removed for restoration and storage until the completion of the restoration/expansion project, Duwisib is worth a visit if you are travelling by.

The schloss was built in 1908–9 by Captain Hans-Heinrich von Wolf and his wife Jayta. Von Wolf, a member of the Saxon nobility, was born in Dresden on 11 January 1873. After completing school he followed in the footsteps of his father and entered military service. He became an artillery captain in the Royal Saxon army at Königsbrück, Dresden, and in 1904 was sent to South West to serve with the *Schutztruppe*. As a result of a tactical error during a battle with rebellious Nama, Von Wolf lost several field guns – a mistake which greatly disturbed him.

Following the end of hostilities in 1907, Von Wolf returned to Germany and married Jayta Humphries, the stepdaughter of the American consul in Dresden. The couple decided to settle in South West and by the end of 1907 they owned eight farms with an area of 140 000 ha in the Maltahöhe district.

Von Wolf envisaged a home similar to the castles built during that time by the *Schutztruppe* at Gibeon, Namutoni and Windhoek, and the renowned architect August Sander was commissioned in 1908 to design a building which would simultaneously be a home and a fortress.

Stone for the schloss came from a quarry some 3 km from the building site, while other material was imported from Germany via Lüderitzbucht. One can only appreciate the ambitiousness of this project when considering the logistics of transporting all the material (except the stone) overland by ox-wagon. Twenty ox-wagons were used on the 640 km jouney, half of which was across the Namib Desert. Skilled craftsmen also came from abroad – stonemasons and builders from Italy and carpenters from Sweden, Denmark and Ireland. The combined efforts of these craftsmen resulted in a building which has been described as surpassing any comparable project in taste, craftsmanship – and expense.

Duwisib consists of 22 rooms arranged in a U-shape, the open end of which has been closed with a high wall. From the entrance you pass through an arch into the main hall or *Rittersaal*. A narrow wooden staircase in the hall leads up to a minstrels' gallery and the *Herrenzimmer* – a room reserved exclusively for men. Back downstairs, the main hall is flanked by sitting rooms, both with beautifully embellished fireplaces. In a country as hot as SWA/Namibia you may be surprised to see fireplaces in most rooms. However, the thick stone walls, small windows and the south-west aspect necessitated this, especially during the winter when the castle became extremely cold. During summer, however, it remained pleasantly cool. Central to the design of Duwisib is the way it was built to withstand any attack, and most of the rooms have embrasures, not windows. Further evidence of this is the well, now concealed by a flowerbed, inside the courtyard.

The schloss was lavishly furnished with family heirlooms and fine furnishings and fittings which Von Wolf bought during a visit to Germany in 1908. The walls of the castle were decorated with paintings, etchings and family portraits as well as swords and rifles. Several of the paintings and etchings reflected Von Wolf's passion for horses.

The couple's passion for horses took them on a journey to England in August 1914 to buy horses for their stud. However, as a result of the outbreak of World War I their ship was diverted to South America. In Rio de Janeiro his American wife succeeded in obtaining a berth on a Dutch vessel bound for Scandinavia, but Von Wolf and a companion were smuggled on board as stowaways. From Scandinavia they travelled to Germany, where he joined the army, only to be killed in 1916 in the battle of the Somme in France. His wife never returned to Duwisib and the property was eventually sold to a Swedish family. The company Duwisib (Pty) Ltd purchased the farm in 1937.

However, Duwisib is not the only reminder of Von Wolf. It is not known what happened to his horses after he was killed and according to one theory the wild horses of the Namib (see p 69) are descendants of Von Wolf's stud.

MARIENTAL

Mariental, on the main route between Windhoek and South Africa (B1), is 261 km south of Windhoek and 221 km north of Keetmanshoop. At an altitude of 1 100 m above sea level, the town is the centre of the largest district in SWA/Namibia.

Before the arrival of white settlers the site of the present town was known to the Khoikhoi as *Zaragaebis* – a word meaning "dusty" or "dirty face". The name has its origin in the heavy dust storms which often occur here in summer.

Hermann Brandt was the first farmer to settle in the area, after purchasing a farm in 1890 from the Nama chief Hendrik Witbooi. Brandt named the farm Enkelkameeldoring ("solitary camel thorn"), but three years later renamed it Mariental, in honour of his wife, when he married Anna-Maria Mahler. The name is translated as "Mary's dale".

In 1894 the district of Gibeon was proclaimed with the town of Gibeon, 60 km south of Mariental, as the administrative centre. A non-commissioned officer and 14 soldiers were stationed here and in the following year a police station was established on the farm Mariental. During the Nama rising of 1903–7 about 40 whites were murdered in the vicinity of Mariental. In 1905 the farm Koichas was sold to Police Sergeant E Stumpfe at 5 cents a hectare. In April 1912 Stumpfe gave 70 ha of his farm to the German railway authorities. Two months later the railway-building commando of the line between Windhoek and Keetmanshoop moved to Mariental and built the station building, naming it Mariental (though it was situated on Koichas farm). In 1914 Stumpfe requested the German Administration to establish a village at Mariental, but in the following year the country was placed under military control, following the surrender of the German forces. In 1919 Stumpfe donated land to the Dutch Reformed Church and repeated his request to the military magistrate at Gibeon. The cornerstone of the first Dutch Reformed Church in the country was laid on 11 September 1920 and the town was proclaimed two months later.

HARDAP RECREATION RESORT

Hardap Recreation Resort, on the northern banks of SWA/Namibia's largest dam, is open throughout the year and is a popular overnight stop. The turnoff to the resort is signposted 15 km north of Mariental on the B1. The entrance gate is reached 6 km on and the resort office 2,5 km further.

Overnight visitors may enter the resort at any time – bungalow keys

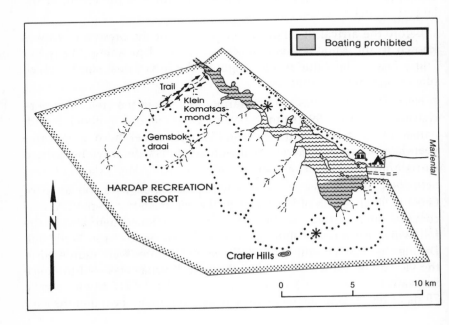

are handed to late arrivals at the entry gate. Provided your accommodation and entry fees have been paid in full, you may also leave the resort at any time. Day visitors are admitted between sunrise and sunset, but must leave the resort before 23h00.

Accommodation facilities include bungalows, dormitories and rooms, as well as caravan/camping sites. The restaurant on the edge of the dam affords diners a magnificent view over the large expanse of water. Adjoining the restaurant is a shop which stocks groceries, frozen fish from the dam, souvenirs and liquor. Other facilities include a swimming pool ingeniously protected by a natural cliff, tennis courts, a playground for children and a filling station.

The resort is popular for boating, windsurfing and angling. Seven fish species as well as a mudfish hybrid occur in the dam. Among the angling species are small-mouth yellowfish, carp, barbel, mud mullet, mudfish and blue kurper. Fishing licences can be obtained from the tourist office or any magistrate's office. Fishing from the dam shore is restricted to special angling and day camping sites on the north-eastern bank. Angling from boats is permitted except in the areas indicated on the resort map obtainable from the tourist office. Angling is also permitted in the river below the dam wall.

Some of the fish species occurring in the dam and in the country's major rivers such as the Fish, Kunene and Kavango can be viewed in the aquarium adjacent to the tourist office. It is the only public freshwater aquarium in the country but unfortunately the tanks are unlabelled, making identification of the various species difficult for the novice. There are also displays on some biological aspects of fish and a distribution map of freshwater fish in SWA/Namibia. Entry is free.

Below the dam wall is the Fresh Water Fish Institute of the Department of Agriculture and Nature Conservation, where research is carried out into various aspects of fish production, breeding and conservation problems. The Department of Agriculture and Nature Conservation controls the distribution of freshwater fish in the country and fish fingerlings can be obtained from the Institute. Hardap Dam is the first in a series of state dams where commercial harvesting of freshwater fish has been given out on tender to a private entrepreneur. The effect of commercial fishing on the fish population of the dam is monitored regularly.

The suitability of the area for a dam to harness the water of the Fish

River was realised as early as 1897 by a German professor. After various investigations, construction finally commenced in 1960 and the dam was completed three years later. Behind the 39 m high dam wall, which stretches between two koppies over a distance of 865 m, lies a vast man-made lake with a capacity of 323 million m^3 and a surface area of 25 km^2. Up to 5 500 m^3 of water can be discharged per second via the four radial gates in the spillway.

The Hardap Game Reserve is divided into two sections by the dam, covering 1 848 and 23 420 ha. The larger area on the southern and western side of the dam is reached by crossing the dam wall. A network of roads covering 82 km leads the visitor to viewpoints overlooking the dam and the appropriately named Crater Hills, and the more energetic can explore the park by way of a circular trail of either 9 km or 15 km.

The topography of the reserve consists of wide plains interspersed with rondavel-type koppies and stony ridges, especially near the upper reaches of the dam.

The vegetation of the reserve has been classified as Dwarf Shrub Savanna (Giess Vegetation Type 9) with scattered trees such as camel thorn (168), which occurs mainly in the river courses, wild green-hair tree (214) and buffalo-thorn (447). In some localities gabbabos (*Catophractes alexandri*) forms dense stands. The most important grasses are of the genera *Stipagrostis, Eragrostis* and *Aristida*.

Among the game reintroduced into the reserve are gemsbok, kudu, red hartebeest, springbok, Hartmann's mountain zebra, eland and ostrich. Cheetah used to occur naturally, but under ideal conditions their numbers increased so much to the detriment of the game that they were removed.

Owing to the diverse habitat types some 260 bird species have been recorded. As the perimeter of the dam consists mainly of krantzes which rise up to 30 m above the water level, there are few sandy "beaches". The numbers of white pelican (49) fluctuate with the availability of water elsewhere, but you could see up to a thousand. Keep an eye open for osprey (170) between October and April. Species which can be spotted here far out of their normal range include Goliath heron (64), greenbacked heron (74), kelp gull (312) and Caspian tern (322). You might also be surprised to record the fantailed cisticola (664) here. This species, which favours wet grassland, is largely limited to the northeastern part of the country.

The dam is also the habitat of whitebreasted (55) and reed (58) cormorant, darter (60), African spoonbill (95), Egyptian goose (102), South African shelduck (103), spurwinged goose (116) and redknobbed coot (228). You might also be fortunate enough to hear the challenging cry of the African fish eagle (148).

Kori bustard (230) and doublebanded courser (301) are two of the birds that can be spotted during game drives, but bird-watching is generally most rewarding in the reedbeds along the Fish River and the dense stands of camel (168) and sweet (172) thorn below the dam wall.

Unless the water level of the dam is very high a visit to the Voël-paradys (Bird Paradise) is not worth while. The alluring name refers to a large stand of dead camel thorn trees a few minutes' walk from the parking area. These trees died off after the dam filled up to capacity in 1963, attracting large numbers of whitebreasted cormorants (55). The roosting sites were, however, abandoned when the water level dropped.

STAMPRIETFONTEIN TO GOCHAS

A signpost 10 km north of Mariental indicates the turnoff onto route 5/1 (C20) to Stampriet, 54 km on. The area, with its artesian wells, is an important fruit and vegetable growing centre.

Just outside Stamprietfontein you turn onto route 33 (C15) (signposted Gochas) and about 20 km on you pass the farm Gross Nabas. Here a fairly inconspicuous monument on the left-hand side of the road serves as a reminder of one of the bloodiest battles fought during the Nama rebellion. During the battle fought here between 2 and 4 January 1905 the Witbooi Nama inflicted heavy losses on a German force under *Oberleutnant* Von Burgsdorff. About 24,5 km on a granite monument to the left of the road marks the spot where a German patrol of 14 men was killed when a surprise attack was launched on them on 4 March 1905.

The turnoff to Gochas is 24 km further on and at the far end of the four-way crossing, on the right-hand side of the road, the grave of the first missionary of Gochas, Heinrich Rust, can be seen under a large camel thorn tree. The village is reached by taking the signposted turnoff at the four-way intersection and then turning right again a few hundred metres on.

Gochas, on the banks of the Auob River, takes its name from a

Khoekhoen word translated as "place of many !go-bushes" – a reference to the candle thorn (170). After Gibeon was declared a district in 1894, a non-commissioned officer and three soliders were stationed at Gochas to maintain law and order. A fort was completed in 1897, but unfortunately the building has long since disappeared.

In the cemetery, a short distance beyond the post office in the village, the graves of a large number of soldiers killed in the numerous battles along the Auob and in the vicinity with the Witbooi Nama and the tribe of Simon Koper can be seen.

Two monuments, 10 km and 13,7 km south-west of Gochas, on the farm Haruchas, are further reminders of the battles fought here on 3 and 5 January 1905 between the German forces under *Hauptmann* Eugen Stuhlmann and the Nama tribe of Simon Koper.

KALAHARI GEMSBOK NATIONAL PARK

The Kalahari Gemsbok National Park, although in South Africa, is included here as it offers an exciting alternative to the usual direct routes between SWA/Namibia and South Africa. The main approaches from South Africa are either via Kuruman (from Johannesburg) or Upington (from Cape Town) through the Twee Rivieren gate. From SWA/Namibia the route is via Stamprietfontein and Gochas to Mata Mata along route 33 (C15). *N.B. The Auob gate at Mata Mata is closed for thoroughfare to and from SWA/Namibia – visitors must sleep overnight in the park.*

Accommodation is provided in the Mata Mata, Nossob and Twee Rivieren rest camps. Facilities in Mata Mata and Nossob comprise self-contained cottages and cottages with communal bathroom and kitchen facilities (all with crockery and cutlery provided). The modern rest camp at Twee Rivieren comprises 22 cottages, a *lapa* where breakfasts and *à la carte* dinners are served and a swimming pool. Campsites with ablutions are available at all three rest camps for those preferring more basic facilities.

The information office in Nossob camp is well worth a visit and will enhance your appreciation and understanding of this fascinating area considerably.

All three camps have shops where non-perishables, soft drinks, liquor, cigarettes and curios can be purchased. Bread cannot be purchased in the park, while frozen meat, eggs and margarine are obtainable at Twee Rivieren camp only. Petrol and diesel are available at all three camps.

Reservations for accommodation must be made with the Chief Director, National Parks Board, P O Box 787, Pretoria 0001, Tel (012) 44-1191 or with the Reservations Office, National Parks Board, P O Box 7400, Roggebaai 8012, Tel (021) 419-5365.

The park falls within a malaria epidemic area and visitors are strongly advised to take the necessary precautions.

Visitors can explore the park by way of the more than 400 km of roads which, with the exception of the road through the dune veld, are confined to the beds of the Auob and Nossob rivers. The roads are well maintained, but on account of soft sand on road edges it is not advisable to pull off the road other than at designated places. A number of shady picnic sites allow you to have a pleasant break on your game-viewing drives. Do remember, though, to keep a wary eye open for potentially dangerous animals.

Covering 9 591 m², the Kalahari Gemsbok National Park is contiguous to the 27 100 km² Gemsbok National Park in Botswana. Situated in a semi-desert region, the park is characterised by long, parallel north-west/south-west trending dunes of red and white sands. The red sand dunes are particularly well developed in the south of the park, reaching up to 15 m in height. The Auob and the Nossob rivers which flow through the park are usually dry and only come down in flood perhaps once in 30 years. Twee Rivieren is the meeting place of the two rivers – hence the name.

The vegetation of the area between the riverbeds, known as the inner veld, consists of grasses such as *Stipagrostis* species and *Eragrostis leh-manniana* with scattered trees, such as shepherd's tree (122), candle thorn (170) and silver cluster-leaf (551). The vegetation along the river-beds is much more prolific, the most common species being camel (168) and black (176) thorn, raisin bush (*Grewia* spp.) and driedoring (*Rhigozum trichotomum*).

The park is the habitat of animal species typical of the dry western region of southern Africa. About 90 per cent of the animals in the park occur either in the river valleys or around the few scattered pans. As there is no fence between the two parks, the animals move freely between the park and the adjoining Gemsbok National Park in Botswana, especially during droughts when large numbers of blue wildebeest, eland and red hartebeest migrate in search of grazing and water. Consequently the numbers of game can vary considerably. Springbok and gemsbok are distributed widely and are encountered most frequently, while blue wildebeest occur in more specific localities. Eland favour the sand dune areas while red hartebeest are restricted almost exclusively to the Nossob River, especially its northern reaches. Smaller antelope are represented by steenbok and duiker.

Predators include lion, cheetah, leopard, wild dog, spotted hyaena, brown hyaena and black-backed jackal. Your best chances of seeing these animals are either early morning or late afternoon, although you may spot lion at waterholes during the day.

To date some 238 bird species, including 44 birds of prey, have been recorded in the park. The large variety of raptors is due to the absence of persecution and the abundance of food. The enormous nests of the sociable weaver (800) are a familiar sight in the Kalahari. Depending on the space available in the host tree, the number of sociable weavers in a nest varies between 2 and 500. Those interested in bird-watching are advised to obtain a copy of *A Revised Checklist of Birds in the Kalahari Gemsbok National Park* by M G L Mills published in *Koedoe* 19 (1976) – the Journal for Scientific Research in the National Parks of South Africa.

7 CENTRAL

REHOBOTH

Rehoboth, the administrative centre of the Rehoboth Gebiet (District), is reached 87 km south of Windhoek along the B1.

The town is usually by-passed, as many tourists are unaware of the spa complex at the thermal spring (originally known as *Aris*, a Khoe-khoen name meaning "smoke", which refers to the steam rising off the spring on cold winter mornings). Amenities include a warm-water swimming pool, thermal bath with a temperature of 39°C, bungalows, cafeteria and caravan/camping sites.

Also of interest is the Rehoboth Museum, established in December 1986. Adjacent to the post office, the museum is housed in the residence of the town's first postmaster, which dates back to 1903. Displays include an interesting photographic collection from the years 1893–6, the vegetation of the Rehoboth Gebiet, archaeology and relics from the area. Plans are underway to create an open-air museum at a Late Iron Age site near the village and the staff can direct you to other places of interest off the well-known tourist routes.

Of late the Rehoboth Government has become increasingly involved in developing the area's tourist potential and although most projects are still in their planning stages details can be obtained by telephoning (06272) 4.

Like so many towns in SWA/Namibia, Rehoboth developed around a mission station, established here in 1844 by the Rhenish missionary Heinrich Kleinschmidt. The mission station was abandoned in 1864, but was rebuilt when the Basters under Hermanus van Wyk settled here around 1870.

The Rehoboth Gebiet has been set aside for the Basters, a group of mixed European/Khoikhoi blood. They originated in the Cape, from where they gradually migrated northwards, settling along the Orange River towards the end of the 18th century. Following legislation passed in 1865 which required all settlers to prove their right over property, a large number of Basters migrated northwards and eventually settled at Rehoboth around 1870.

The Basters are proud of their heritage and although the name (meaning half-caste) is considered derogatory elsewhere, they insist on being called Basters.

WINDHOEK

Windhoek, capital city of SWA/Namibia, is situated in the country's central region – approximately 1 500 km from Cape Town via Vioolsdrif and 1 800 km from Johannesburg via Upington and Grünau.

For visitors arriving at the J G Strijdom Airport, Windhoek is the starting point of tours to various exciting destinations. Although 42 km east of the city, a regular bus service operates between the airport and the city centre, while some hotels also provide transport for guests.

The city is renowned for its blend of German colonial and modern buildings, the annual Windhoek Carnival and traditional German dishes and confectionery, not forgetting the beer! Although a city, it has retained its *Gemütlichkeit* and warm atmosphere.

Windhoek offers visitors all the necessary amenities, sport and recreation facilities, restaurants and a wide choice of accommodation ranging from top-class hotels to congenial *pensions* (guest houses). Some of the sights in and around Windhoek are described below.

A walking tour

Although some of the attractive buildings from the German colonial era have sadly had to make way for "modern" structures, a two- to three-hour walking tour of the city will take you back through the city's history over the past century. Numbers marked on the map correspond to the following text.

1 Old Business Façades, Kaiser Street Opposite the Verwoerd Park are three eye-catching buildings designed by Willi Sander which can best be viewed, especially during weekdays, from the raised walkway outside the park. To the right (next to the SWA Building Society) is Erkrath Building, built in 1910, with business premises downstairs and a residence upstairs – a common feature of buildings of this period.

Gathemann House, next door, dates back to 1913 and also had a

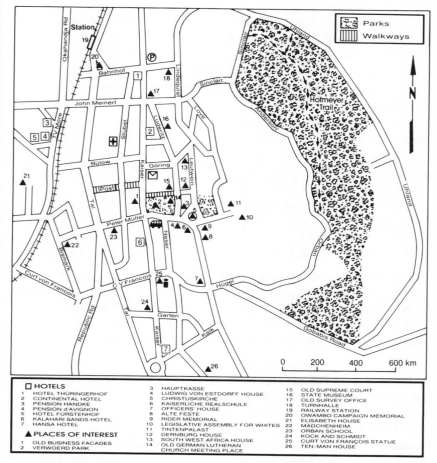

□ HOTELS		
1 HOTEL THÜRINGERHOF	3 HAUPTKASSE	15 OLD SUPREME COURT
2 CONTINENTAL HOTEL	4 LUDWIG VON ESTDORFF HOUSE	16 STATE MUSEUM
3 PENSION HANDKE	5 CHRISTUSKIRCHE	17 OLD SURVEY OFFICE
4 PENSION d'AVIGNON	6 KAISERLICHE REALSCHULE	18 TURNHALLE
5 HOTEL FÜRSTENHOF	7 OFFICERS' HOUSE	19 RAILWAY STATION
6 KALAHARI SANDS HOTEL	8 ALTE FESTE	20 OWAMBO CAMPAIGN MEMORIAL
7 HANSA HOTEL	9 RIDER MEMORIAL	21 ELISABETH HOUSE
	10 LEGISLATIVE ASSEMBLY FOR WHITES	22 MADCHENHEIM
▲ PLACES OF INTEREST	11 TINTENPALAST	23 ORBAN SCHOOL
	12 DERNBURG HOUSE	24 KOCK AND SCHMIDT
1 OLD BUSINESS FACADES	13 SOUTH WEST AFRICA HOUSE	25 CURT VON FRANÇOIS STATUE
2 VERWOERD PARK	14 OLD GERMAN LUTHERAN	26 TEN-MAN HOUSE
	CHURCH MEETING PLACE	

residence above the business premises. Heinrich Gathemann, then mayor of Klein Windhoek, commissioned the building, which has an unusually steep roof – a European technique to prevent snow from collecting!

Gathemann also had business premises next door, where in 1920 he converted the Hotel Kronprinz into what we see today (except for the restaurant upstairs, which is a more recent innovation). The name Kronprinz and the year, 1902, can still be seen on the single-storey section of the building, now a separate shop.

2 Verwoerd Park (also known as Zoo Park) Besides the shady trees, cool stream, pond and attractive gardens which make the park an inviting resting spot, two interesting features should not be missed here. An unobtrusive glass-topped structure near the centre entrance on Kaiser Street marks the spot where remains of a prehistoric elephant were uncovered. The remains date back some 5 000 years to when the area was a marsh, and quartz tools which were probably used to slaughter the elephant at this spot can be seen amongst the bones.

Looking south, an obelisk-shaped memorial crowned by a golden eagle – the *Kriegerdenkmal* (Soldiers' Memorial) – attracts attention. This memorial was unveiled on 5 April 1897 in honour of members of the German *Schutztruppe* who died during the war of 1893–4 against the renowned Nama chief, Hendrik Witbooi.

There is also the possibility that some of the Gibeon meteorites will once again be exhibited in the park. They were kept here from the end of World War I until April 1975 when they were moved to the Alte Feste, where they have remained, for cataloguing. (Refer to page 63.)

3 Hauptkasse (Old Receiver of Revenue) Dating back to 1898–9, this building on the corner of Peter Müller and Lüderitz streets formed part of the core of old Windhoek. Besides serving its original purpose as the offices of the Receiver of Revenue, it was also used as officers' quarters and a school hostel, and now provides offices for the Department of Agriculture.

4 Ludwig von Estorff House Built in 1891 to serve as the military artisans' canteen, the building style was very simple and the outside walls were left unplastered until 1910. During alterations between 1898 and 1902, the shady veranda was added. Ludwig von Estorff, a commander of the *Schutztruppe*, resided here during the period 1902–10. Over the years the building served various purposes – residence for senior officers, hostel, trade school and finally, in 1984, the reference library was moved here.

5 Christuskirche Gottlieb Redecker was the architect of the Evangelical Lutheran Church, which was built as a symbol of gratitude for peace at the conclusion of various wars against the indigenous people of SWA/Namibia in 1907. The cornerstone of the church was laid in 1907 and the building was consecrated on 16 October 1910. The design of the church is based on that of a basilica with influences of the neo-Gothic and Art Nouveau styles and it is built from local sandstone.

The church contains elements which are the same as those of the

Evangelical Lutheran churches of Lüderitz and Swakopmund. As in the Lüderitz church, the stained glass altar windows were donated by Kaiser Wilhelm II and the altar bible by his wife, Augusta. The brass bells were cast by the firm Schilling in Apolda, as were those of the Evangelical Lutheran Church in Swakopmund.

The poor acoustics and ventilation of the building have been improved, while the terrazzo floor, which replaced a cement floor, and the tiled roof are also later improvements to the original building.

If you are interested in entering the church, obtain the key from church offices at 12 Peter Müller Street – you pass by there on your way up to the church.

6 "Kaiserliche Realschule" Built in 1907–8, a primary school opened its doors here in January 1909 with 74 pupils, housed in three classrooms. In 1912–13 the school was cleverly enlarged by building additional classrooms off the central hall. The turret, part of the original building, was an important feature as it improved ventilation through the wooden slats. The enlarged building became the first German High School in Windhoek and has in the course of time also served as the English School and a German Primary School before it was converted into a cultural centre.

7 Officers' House (today offices of the Ombudsman) Restoration of this beautiful house, erected in 1906–7, was completed in 1987. Gottlieb Redecker drew up the plans after returning from a year's visit to Germany and the decorative brickwork around the windows, arches and doorway are characteristic of the Putz architecture fashionable in Germany at that time. This was the first building of this style in the country (though Redecker's design included a relatively steep roof with eaves, which was not in keeping with the typical style in Germany). Provision was also made for stables, which today serve as a garage and outbuilding.

8 Alte Feste When Curt von François arrived in the country in 1889, he decided to establish the headquarters of the *Schutztruppe* in Windhoek. He drew up the plans and in October 1890 construction commenced on what is today the oldest surviving building in Windhoek. Although the fort is strategically positioned, it was never put to the test in any battles.

The historical section of the State Museum is housed here today and can be visited from 08h00 to 18h00 on weekdays, from 10h00 to 12h45 and 15h00 to 18h00 on Saturdays, and on Sundays and on public holidays it is open from 11h00 to 12h30 and 15h00 to 18h00. Displays concentrate on the country's history from the arrival of the first missionaries to the end of German administration.

A narrow-gauge train, including the engine and coaches, which has been positioned down the side of the building, is also of interest here.

At present (1988) the Gibeon Meteorites are displayed in the courtyard of the fort. For more information, refer to page 62.

9 The Rider Memorial Unveiled on 27 January 1912 (the birthday of Kaiser Wilhelm II), the memorial, which realistically depicts a mounted soldier of the period, honours those killed in the Nama and Herero wars of 1903–7. Colonel von Estorff promoted the idea of a monument and launched a public fund-raising campaign, while Adolf Kürle of Berlin was given the commission.

10 Legislative Assembly for Whites This modern building (1964) is approached along the avenue between the Alte Feste and the gardens of the Tintenpalast. Murals and works of art in copper, ceramics, paint, wood and marble on each floor depict various aspects of the country's minerals, fishing industry, agriculture, history and nature. When not in session, guided tours of about 30 minutes are conducted at 10h00, 11h00, 12h00, 14h00 and 15h00, weekdays only.

11 Tintenpalast Adjacent to the Legislative Assembly for Whites is the Tintenpalast, which dates back to 1912–13. Built as administrative offices for the German Colonial Government, it has been appropriately named the Ink Palace – a reference to the large volume of writing which took place here.

When, in 1910, Governor von Schuckmann announced that a new administrative building was to be erected on the hill behind the magistrate's court, he met with some opposition. The townsfolk were of the opinion that the building should be in the centre of town and raised every conceivable argument to further their case.

Once again, Gottlieb Redecker was the architect and he had the difficult task of designing a building which would not exceed the limited building funds. This he achieved by keeping the structure as simple and functional as possible.

The building was completed in November 1913 and the local authority (*Landesrat*) held its first meeting here on 11 May 1914, only to be disbanded in July the following year with the surrender of the German forces to the South African Union forces. The National Assembly met here from its inception in 1985 to February 1989, when it dissolved in view of UN-supervised elections scheduled for November 1989.

You will welcome the well-kept gardens below the Tintenpalast, where it is pleasant to rest on the grass lawn under one of the many shady trees.

12 Dernburg House This building was erected to house the German Secretary of State, Dr Dernburg, who visited the country in July 1908. After his departure it was used as offices for the governor.

13 South West Africa House Continuing down Park Street, the Administrator-General's official residence is to your right. In 1958 the former Colonial Governor's residence was demolished to make way for this palatial building, residence of the Administrator, and, since 1977, the Administrator-General. It is not open to the public.

A reminder of the Colonial Governor's residence is the retaining wall of the garden in Lüderitz Street, which was not demolished with the rest of the building.

14 Old German Lutheran Church meeting place This is one of the earlier buildings of the city, dating back to 1896. It was built by Tünschel and Wilke Company for the German Lutheran Church, who met here until 1910 when the Christuskirche was completed. The building is still owned by the parish who, as you will notice from the paintings on the outside, have their nursery school here.

15 Old Supreme Court (*Obergericht*) The old Supreme Court, facing the nursery school, was originally erected by the government builder, Carl Ludwig, as his home. However, his stately style was not to the liking of the Governor and his contract was not renewed after its three-year period. He therefore never occupied his home and it was utilised as the magistrate's and supreme courts. Today the State Conservatorium occupies this building, as well as other similar buildings in the area.

Other places of interest

As you will notice from the map, Windhoek in its earlier days was centred around the area described above. There are, of course, other interesting buildings and places worth visiting but these are not included in the walking tour as it would then become too tiring, especially if you are not used to the climate.

16 State Museum Opening times are as follows: weekdays 09h00 to 18h00; Saturdays 10h00 to 12h45 and 15h00 to 18h00; Sundays & public holidays 11h00 to 12h30 and 15h00 to 18h00. A visit to the museum at the start of your SWA/Namibia tour will give you some valuable background information, as the exhibits concentrate on the natural history and the early inhabitants of the country.

17 Old Survey Offices (*Oude Voorpost*) Dating back to 1902, this functional building was constructed by the German Government to house the survey office, which consisted of a large drawing office and a fireproof archive where the maps were stored, as well as rooms for the survey equipment. During 1907 and 1909 expansions were necessary to the original building, but it has now stood empty for a number of years and at present (1988) is being restored.

18 Turnhalle or Gymnasium The architect Otto Busch drew up the plans for the practice hall of the Windhoek Gymnasium Club, which had been formed in 1899. Originally the building, completed in 1903, consisted of a single storey but it was expanded to the present double storey in 1912–13.

The first sitting of the Constitutional Conference on independence for SWA/Namibia took place here on 1 September 1975 – for this reason it is better known as the Turnhalle Conference.

19 Railway Station The middle and southern wings of Windhoek's station building date back to 1912, when it became necessary to replace the ten-year old prefabricated building which became inadequate with the increased traffic on completion of the line to Keetmanshoop. Although it is uncertain who was responsible for the design, the attractive building is an amalgamation of various building styles and the only complaint at the time was that it lacked a restaurant.

The South African Railways added the northern wing in 1929 but cleverly retained the original building style, making the extension hardly distinguishable.

"Poor Old Joe", a locomotive imported from Germany and assembled in Swakopmund in 1899, is positioned in the parking area outside the station building. When coupled back to back with another locomotive it was known as a "Zwilling" (*zwei* meaning two in German). These locomotives could also be used separately (then referred to as "Illing"), and over 100 were employed in the country by 1906.

20 Owambo Campaign Memorial Opposite the station, a stone obelisk erected in 1919 is a reminder of the turbulent history of the country. It is set amongst tall palm trees and jacarandas, which create an attractive picture in spring.

21 Elisabeth House During the 73 years Elisabeth House served as a maternity home a total of 12 669 births were registered here. The inauguration took place on 24 April 1908, two years after the Deutsche Kolonialgesellschaft decided to collect money for a maternity home in Windhoek. The building was named after Countess Elisabeth zu Mecklenburg, honorary secretary of what later became known as the *Frauverein vom Roten Kreutz für Deutsche Uber See* and wife of Count Johan Albrecht zu Mecklenburg, who was president of the Deutsche Kolonialgesellschaft at that time.

Provision was made by architect Redecker for four maternity wards, a sisters' ward, a large communal dining/living room, kitchen, store room and operating theatre.

The growing population of Windhoek necessitated the enlargement of the maternity hospital and in 1914–15 the Sander annex to the south of Elisabeth House was added. It remained in use as a maternity hospital until 1981, when it became the property of the Academy. The old Elisabeth House is today used as a theatre while the Sander annex is used as offices. *Sjordes* or lunch-hour concerts ranging from poetry readings to folk songs are staged regularly at the Space Theatre and should not be missed. The entrance fee covers a mug of beer or a glass of wine and a snack.

22 Mädchenheim This stately building, dating back to 1914, was originally designed as a boarding school for girls, but never served this purpose. It was initially used as a secondary school after the school in Leutwein Street was vacated. After 1915 it was used as a state boarding school for the Orban School lower down in Peter Müller Street. In later years the building was enlarged on several occasions and today serves as a pre-primary state school.

23 Orban School By 1911 the growing number of pupils in Windhoek made a new school necessary and a design competition was held. Of the 14 architectural designs submitted, the one by Willi Sander was selected the winning entry and on 20 April 1912 the school was opened officially. The building today forms part of the conservatoire of the Administration for Whites and the modern block, quite out of tone with the rest of the building, was added in 1987.

24 Kock & Schmidt Still impressive almost 90 years after it was erected, this building was designed by Willi Sander and, as with the Gathemann buildings further north in Kaiser Street, the living quarters were built above the business. The business of Kock & Schmidt has been operating from here since 1910, making it one of the oldest businesses in the city – it has also remained in the same family over the years.

25 Curt von François Statue This statue of Windhoek's founder is the work of Hennie Potgieter and was unveiled on 19 October 1965. On this occasion, the 75th anniversary of Windhoek's founding, the town was proclaimed a city.

26 Ten-Man House Adolf Matheis was responsible for this H-shaped building which was completed in 1906. As the name describes, ten unmarried administration officials were housed in the almost fort-like building. The military tone was, however, lightened by wide verandas and the relief work on the towers, with their decorative turrets. Each of the four corners contained one-bedroom flats with bathrooms, while one-bedroom flats without bathrooms were in the centre of the H.

Hofmeyer Walk

Allow about an hour for this interesting walk, with its splendid views of the Klein Windhoek Valley. Vegetation typical of the area can be seen along the trail, which is particularly attractive during autumn when the red flowers of *Aloe littoralis* add a colourful splash to the surroundings. A large variety of birds, including sunbirds, mousebirds and bulbuls, are attracted by the nectar of the flowers. Although the path is well kept, it is advisable to don a pair of comfortable walking shoes.

Bird-watching at Avis Dam

Situated on the eastern outskirts of Windhoek, off the road to the J G Strijdom Airport, Avis Dam offers excellent opportunities for bird-watching. The best time of the year is prior to the first heavy summer rains, when 100–120 species can be ticked in a single day. The dam is

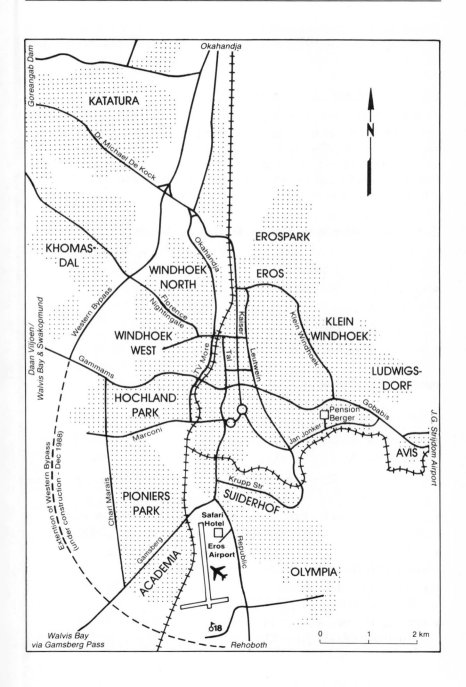

leased to the Wildlife Society of Namibia and plans are afoot to build a floating bird island and to construct walking trails around the dam and on adjacent land.

Goreangab Dam north-west of the city

The dam is popular with local windsurfers and sailboaters, though swimming in the dam is strictly prohibited. Picnic and braai facilities are also provided. The dam is reached by leaving Windhoek along the Okahandja road (B1), the turnoff being signposted opposite the Van Eck power station on the northern outskirts of the city. From here it is a further 7,5 km to the dam.

Excursions offered by tour operators in Windhoek

The following tour operators can be contacted should you wish to join a guided bus tour of the city:

- Eagle Safaris, Tel 22-2692
- Springbok Atlas Safaris, Tel 22-4252/3
- SWA Safaris, Tel 3-7567/8/9
- Toko Safaris, Tel 22-5539

Where to eat in Windhoek

- *Alla Pergola*, steaks and seafood,
  59 Farm Nuabamis, Brakwater, Tel 6-4550
- *Bacher's Braai*, rump steaks and seafood,
  Eros Shopping Centre, Klein Windhoek Road, Tel 3-3997
- *Café Restaurant Schneider*, cakes, lunches, light meals (closed evenings),
  Jack Levinson Arcade, Kaiser Street, Tel 22-6304
- *Central Café*, cakes, light meals (daytime), continental cuisine (evenings), Jack Levinson Arcade, Kaiser Street, Tel 22-2659
- *Continental Hotel – Linger Longer Restaurant*, à la carte,
  Kaiser Street, Tel 3-7293
- *El Toro*, spareribs, steaks,
  4 Rehobotherweg, Tel 22-2797
- *Fürstenhof Hotel*, international cuisine,
  4 Romberg Street, Tel 3-7380

- *Garden Restaurant*, pizzas, steaks and German dishes,
  25 Garden Street, Tel 22-7858
- *Gathemann Restaurant*, continental cuisine,
  Kaiser Street, Tel 22-3853
- *Gert Klause*, German dishes,
  90 Stübel Street, Tel 3-5706
- *Gourmet's Inn*, international dishes,
  195 Jan Jonker Street, Tel 3-2360
- *Kaiserkrone Restaurant and Café Terrassen*, cakes, lunches, light meals
  (daytime), wide variety of meat dishes (evenings),
  Kaiserkrone Centre, Post Street, Tel 22-2779
- *Kalahari Sands – Bauernstube*, light meals, lunches, salads, meat dishes,
  Kaiser Street, Tel 3-6900
- *Kalahari Sands – Moringa Room*, international dishes,
  Kaiser Street, Tel 3-6900
- *La Cave Restaurant*, à la carte,
  Carl List Building, Peter Müller Street, Tel 22-4173
- *Micado Restaurant*, à la carte,
  Stübel Street, Tel 3-4028
- *Okambihi Restaurant*, steaks and vegetarian platter,
  A Wesel Street, Northern Industrial Area, Tel 6-3204
- *Restaurant Alt Windhoek*, steaks, à la carte
  Bülow Street (opposite Swabank), Tel 22-3602
- *Safari Motel*, steakhouse and restaurant with à la carte menu,
  Republic Road, Tel 3-8560
- *Sam's Restaurant and Grill*, pizza, pasta, steaks,
  90 Gobabis Street, Klein Windhoek, Tel 22-8820
- *Sardegna*, pizzas, pasta and Italian ice-cream,
  39 Kaiser Street, Tel 22-5600
- *Seoul House*, Korean and Chinese dishes,
  Ausspannplatz (next to Standard Bank), Tel 3-4691
- *Thüringerhof Hotel – Jagerstube Restaurant*, continental dishes,
  Kaiser Street, Tel 22-6031
- *Yang Tze Restaurant*, Chinese dishes,
  106 Gobabis Road, Tel 3-4779

KHOMAS HOCHLAND

The Khomas Hochland, an upland region forming part of the interior plateau of central SWA/Namibia, lies between 1 750 m and over 2 000 m above sea level. Extending eastwards from the Great Escarpment to the Windhoek area, it is a deeply dissected terrain with abundant seasonal river valleys, sharp ridges and rolling hills. The similarity in altitude of many hill tops in the Khomas Hochland points to the existence of a former erosion surface in the geological past. The Khomas Hochland summit levels are close to a surface formed during Karoo times, some 180–300 million years ago, which has subsequently been exhumed and modified by erosion during the last 100 million years after the break-up of West Gondwana.

The Khomas Hochland consists of mica schists of the Kuiseb Formation, which is Late Precambrian in age. Some 650 to 750 million years ago sediments accumulated on the floor of a sea. These sediments were subsequently metamorphosed during a mountain-building phase to form schists which, in turn, were folded and tilted some 500 to 600 million years ago. This mountain chain was reduced to the "roots", as we see it today, during several major erosion periods in the geological past.

From Windhoek the adventurous traveller has a choice of three routes via the Khomas Hochland and the Namib Desert to the coast, namely the Bosua, Us and Gamsberg passes. It is advisable to enquire about the condition of the road after heavy rain at either the Automobile Association (AA) or the Department of Transport. Petrol is not available along any of the routes, so ensure that you have a full tank when setting off.

Bosua Pass

This direct route to Swakopmund through the Namib Desert is the most northerly of the three passes. On account of its steep gradient (1:5) caravans are not permitted and the pass is best travelled from east to west.

In Windhoek, take the turnoff signposted Daan Viljoen at the Curt von François and Republiek roads intersection. Follow this road out of the city, to reach the turnoff to the Daan Viljoen Game Reserve after 14 km. Ignore the signpost further on to the Matchless Mine, which is closed to the public. Your route lies straight ahead.

Archaeological excavations here and at several other sites in the Kho-mas Hochland have provided evidence of indigenous copper smelting between 200 and 300 years ago. Large-scale commercial exploitation of the mine dates back to 1856, when the Walvisch Bay Mining Company began exploiting copper deposits in central SWA/Namibia. The first manager of the mine was the renowned traveller, explorer and trader, Charles John Andersson, who supervised the mining operations between 1856 and 1858. The company abandoned its mining operations in 1860 and some four decades passed by before the mine attracted renewed interest in 1902 when a subsidiary of the Deutsche Kolon-ialgesellschaft sank trial shafts. No ore was mined and the mine was abandoned shortly afterwards. In the late 1960s an extensive drilling programme was carried out by Tsumeb Corporation Limited, resulting in the mining of copper and sulphur between 1970 and 1983, when the mine was closed owing to the fall in the early 1980s of world copper prices.

Sixteen km on, you pass the derelict, ghostly looking Liebig House, which was built around 1912 on the farm Neu-Heusis for the director of the Deutsche Farmgesellschaft, Dr R Hartig. The farm was acquired in 1908 as headquarters for the company, which had also purchased other farms for cattle breeding.

Stop here, and take a stroll through the unusual colonial double-storey house where, with a little imagination, you will be able to picture the once lavish life-style of the occupants. A fountain in the large room downstairs must have been the focal point of the entertainment area, while a row of beautifully patterned tiles decorates some of the walls. On proceeding upstairs one is forced to envy past occupants the ex-pansive view they awakened to each morning.

Further west, at Karanab, you pass the ruins of the Von François Fort, named after Major Curt von François, the founder of Windhoek. Together with a force of 21 men, disguised as a scientific expedition to conceal their military objective, Von François landed in Walvis Bay in June 1889 and made his temporary headquarters at Tsaobis, south-west of Otjimbingwe. In the following year Von François moved his head-quarters to the present-day Windhoek and established a series of mil-itary posts. This one was built to protect the route between Swakopmund and Windhoek, but later served as a *Trockenposten* (drying-out post) for German troops guilty of liquor abuse.

The fort, constructed of flat stones from the area, blends in so well with the surroundings that unless you keep your eyes peeled you will spot it only at the last minute. Mortar used in the construction of the fort has not withstood the weathering of the years, revealing how stones were skilfully placed on top of each other to form the walls. Looking through the "windows" you will have a view of the Heusis River Valley and the surrounding hills, underlining the strategic position of the fort.

Us Pass

From Windhoek the Us Pass (gradient 1:10) is reached by following Republiek Road in a southerly direction to the southern end of the town. Ignore the turnoff to the left (signposted Rehoboth and RSA) and continue into Gamsberg Road (signposted Academia and Pioniers Park). A signpost 3 km on, reading Walvisbaai oor Gamsberg, confirms that you are heading in the correct direction. The D1982, which leads over the Us Pass, is reached 32 km further and 145 km on you enter the Namib–Naukluft Park, from where it is another 114 km to Walvis Bay.

Gamsberg Pass

Of the three Khomas Hochland routes to the coast, the route via the Gamsberg Pass, also known as the Garden Route of SWA/Namibia, is the most popular. The mountain is said to derive its name from the Khoekhoen name *gan*, meaning "shut" or "closed" – a reference to the fact that the mountain obscures one's view.

From Windhoek the directions for this route are the same as those for the Us Pass. About 32 km out of Windhoek you turn left, continuing on route 49 (C26) (signposted Walvis Bay via Gamsberg Pass).

As you travel further west the scenery is increasingly dominated by the 2 347 m high Gamsberg, a large tabletop mountain. Rising some 500 m above the Khomas Hochland, the mountain consists of granite 1 000 million years old, with a conspicuous horizontal capping of weather-resistant sandstone. The capping, 25 m thick, was formed about 200 million years ago when this area, and indeed most of southern Africa, was covered by sediments washed into a sea that covered large parts of the old supercontinent, Gondwana. Gamsberg has been protected from the ravages of subsequent erosion by its capping of sandstone.

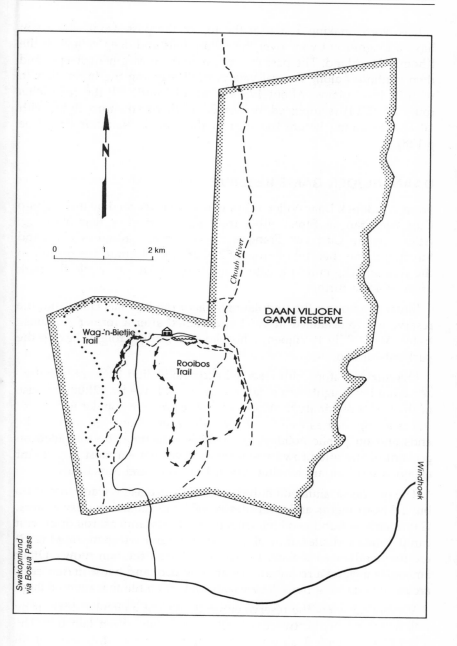

It is worth making a stop at the top of the pass, from where you have a magnificent view over the rolling hills and deep valleys of the Khomas Hochland. The pass snakes down the escarpment steeply and then continues along several valleys until reaching the Inner Namib, with its level plains. About 175 km out of Windhoek the road joins route 36 (C14) (signposted Walvis Bay) where you turn right, with 10 km remaining before the start of the Namib–Naukluft Park (see p 128).

DAAN VILJOEN GAME RESERVE

From Windhoek Daan Viljoen Game Reserve is reached by turning into Curt von François Street either from Kaiser Street or Republiekweg. After a while Curt von François Street becomes Khomas Hochland Street and you then follow route 52 (C28) for 14 km to the turnoff to the reserve. The entrance gate is reached 1,5 km on, while the park office is 4 km further.

Situated amongst the undulating hills of the Khomas Hochland, the reserve was proclaimed in 1962 and named after a former Administrator, Mr D T du P Viljoen, who played a leading role in having the park established.

Overnight visitors with reserved accommodation may enter the reserve until midnight, while day visitors must leave by 22h00. Because of the park's proximity to Windhoek, it is extremely popular with tourists as a stop-over as well as with Windhoekers. However, over weekends and on public holidays the park is sometimes best avoided on account of the often rowdy behaviour of visitors – a most unpleasant experience if you are looking forward to peace and tranquillity.

The rest camp, situated on the banks of the Augeigas Dam, comprises bungalows, caravan and campsites as well as picnic sites for day visitors. Game such as eland and blue wildebeest often wander through the rest camp, while redbilled francolin (194) and helmeted guineafowl (203) are frequently seen looking for scraps amongst the bungalows. Other amenities include a restaurant, swimming pool and two entertainment areas, suitable for groups. There is, however, no filling station or shop.

Visitors can view the reserve either by way of a circular drive or by following one of the two day walks which have been laid out. The 3 km Wag 'n Bietjie Trail is ideal for family groups or those seeking an easy ramble. The route starts near the park office, from where it follows the Augeigas River upstream for 1,5 km to the Stengel and Koch und Schultheiss dams. The same route is followed back. The 9 km Rooibos Trail follows a more strenuous, circular route which starts near the swimming pool and ends at the restaurant. However, as there are no dangerous predators you may also follow any of the numerous game tracks criss-crossing the park. Provided you remain downwind of game you stand the chance of approaching fairly closely. The DNC plans to establish a two-day overnight trail in the reserve.

Permits to fish in the dam at the rest camp, which is stocked with barbel, kurper and black bass, can be obtained at the park office.

Daan Viljoen Game Reserve lies within the Highland Savanna Veld Type (Giess Vegetation Type 8). The hills are open with scattered mountain thorn (171), Namibian resin tree (369) and red bushwillow (532), known locally as koedoebos. Other species include candle thorn (170), wild camphor bush (733) and *Elephantorrhiza suffruticosa* – locally known as looiwortelbos. Dense stands of camel thorn (168), sweet thorn (172), karree (386) and buffalo-thorn (447) occur in the valleys, while *Antephora, Enneapogon,* and *Stipagrostis* are the main grass genera. The green-flowered *Aloe viridiflora,* which normally grows singly, is en-demic to the central part of the country and can be seen in the reserve. Another species endemic to the central highlands and growing in the reserve is *Euphorbia avasmontana.*

Daan Viljoen is the habitat of mammal species typical of the Khomas Hochland such as eland, gemsbok, Hartmann's mountain zebra, blue wildebeest, red hartebeest, springbok and kudu. Smaller species here include klipspringer, steenbok, rock dassie and chacma baboon.

To date more than 200 bird species have been recorded in the reserve and if you are experienced you should be able to tick between 60 and 90 species in a day – among them several South West "specials" such as Monteiro's hornbill (462), rockrunner (662) and whitetailed shrike (752). Species recorded infrequently in the central highlands include greenbacked heron (74) and pintailed whydah (860).

Those not familiar with birdwatching will find the guide, *Birds of Daan Viljoen Game Park,* a great help. A short description of species likely to be seen, accompanied by colour photographs, a description of the habitat types of the reserve and a checklist are given. The guide is sold at the park office.

VON BACH RECREATION RESORT

The turnoff to Von Bach Recreation Resort is signposted about 3,5 km south of Okahandja on the B1, from where it is short distance along a gravel road to the entrance gate.

Facilities at the dam include picnic sites near the entrance gate for day visitors and camping facilities for overnight visitors on the south-eastern banks of the dam. Unlike most other resorts managed by the DNC, there is no restaurant, shop or filling station – only ablutions, fireplaces and drinking water are available. The resort is open throughout the year, from sunrise to sunset.

The dam is situated in the north-eastern outliers of the Auas Mountains, in the upper reaches of the Swakop River drainage system. Covering some 4 285 ha, the reserve is divided into two unequal parts when the dam is full – the south-eastern part covers approximately two-thirds of the area and the north-western section the remainder. The terrain is extremely hilly, the highest point being about 300 m above the dam wall in the south-western corner.

Work on the dam started in 1968 and was completed two years later. It is the main storage dam supplying water to Windhoek and forms part of the first phase of the Eastern National Water Carrier System which was designed to meet the projected water requirements of the central areas of the country. The dam has a storage capacity of 54 million m^3 and an assured yield of 4 million m^3 a year.

The vegetation falls within the Thornbush Savanna (Giess Vegetation Type 7) with ringwood tree (136), blue thorn (164), black thorn (176) and red bushwillow (532). In the rivercourse below the dam wall good specimens of camel (168) and sweet (172) thorn will be seen.

When the reserve was proclaimed only a few kudu and a troop of baboons occurred naturally in the area. Hartmann's mountain zebra, springbok, eland and ostriches were reintroduced later. Opportunities for game viewing are limited, though, as the only tourist road is the one leading to the camping area on the south-eastern banks of the dam.

A variety of aquatic sports – waterskiing, windsurfing and yachting – are enjoyed here. The dam is also popular with anglers and has been stocked with large-mouth bass, blue kurper and small-mouth yellowfish, while carp and barbel also occur. Angling permits can be purchased from the office at the entrance gate.

OKAHANDJA

Okahandja is still the administrative centre of the Herero people, despite its distance from the Herero tribal areas, and much of the early history of this pleasant little town is closely connected with that of the Herero. In 1843 Carl Hugo Hahn and Heinrich Kleinschmidt, two missionaries of the Rheinische Missiongesellschaft, visited the spring at Okahandja with a view to establishing a mission station for the Herero. Okahandja met with their requirements and they named it Schmelens Verwachting, after Heinrich Schmelen of the London Missionary Society, who had visited the area 16 years earlier.

Friedrich Kolbe, the first missionary to settle in Okahandja, arrived here in 1849, but after three months he abandoned the mission station as a result of the reign of terror of the Nama leader, Jonker Afrikaner, and the station was only re-opened when peace returned to the area.

A small koppie, about 600 m north of the turnoff to Gross Barmen on the B2, marks the site of Moordkoppie. Here, on 23 August 1850, a large number of followers of the Herero chief Kahitjenne were murdered by Namas under the command of Jonker Afrikaner. The site was declared a national monument in 1972, but is fenced off, unfortunately, and not signposted.

Several monuments and places of interest can be seen in Church Street, which runs parallel to Main Street. At the southern end of Church Street is the Rhenish Mission Church, which was built between 1871 and 1876 by the missionaries P H Diehl and J Irle. The church was in use up to 1952 and declared a national monument 20 years later. The graves of several German soldiers, missionaries and Herero leaders, including those of Trougoth and Willem Maharero, can be seen in the church graveyard.

Immediately opposite the church are the graves of Jonker Afrikaner, captain of the Afrikaner Nama tribe until his death in 1861, and of the Herero chiefs Clemens Kapuuo and Hosea Kutako. Chief Clemens Kapuuo, the first President of the Democratic Turnhalle Alliance, was assassinated in Katutura, Windhoek in 1978. Chief Hosea Kutako is considered the father of black nationalism in this country and made the first direct petition to the United Nations against South African rule in South West Africa. To demonstrate his commitment to unity, Kutako chose to be buried near a former enemy of the Herero people, Jonker

Afrikaner, and not, as is customary, in the cemetery of his ancestors.

About 600 m further north along Church Street a signpost slightly obscured by trees indicates the footpath to the communal grave of Tjamuaha, Maharero and Samuel Maharero. On the weekend either before or after 23 August each year the Red Flag Hereros pay homage to their forefathers and the stately procession from the Tjamuaha complex to the graves of Afrikaner, Kutako and Kapuuo has become a well-known event on the Okahandja calendar.

GROSS BARMEN

The turnoff to Gross Barmen is well signposted on the B1 bypassing Okahandja. From the turnoff it is 24 km along a tarred road to the resort south-west of Okahandja, on the banks of a tributary of the Swakop River.

Gross Barmen is well known for its thermal spring and visitors have a choice of swimming either in the cooled mineral water of the outdoor swimming pool, which is open to all visitors, or in the glass-enclosed thermal hall which is for the exclusive use of overnight visitors. The fountain or "eye" which feeds the two pools can be seen between the outdoor pool and the restaurant complex. The water temperature of the fountain is about 65°C, compared with about 41°C and 29°C for the pool in the thermal hall and the outdoor pool, respectively.

Other facilities include tennis courts and a children's playground.

Accommodation, built around a dam, comprises luxury units and bungalows. Camping and caravan sites are also available. There is a restaurant, a shop selling souvenirs, groceries and liquor, and a filling station.

The surrounding hillsides and the dam offer good opportunities for bird-watching. A path has been cut through the dense reedbeds alongside the dam and numerous wooden benches make excellent vantage points over the dam. Those in want of more strenuous exercise can either walk along the river or among the rocky outcrops. However, no trails have been laid out.

Gross Barmen is a popular overnight stop and visitors with reserved accommodation may enter the resort any time. Provided you have paid the necessary entrance fees you may also leave at any time. Day visitors, however, are admitted only between sunrise and sunset, and must leave the resort before 23h00.

Originally known as Otjikango, a Herero word meaning "a spring flowing weakly through rocky ground", the resort is built on the site of the first Rhenish mission station for the Herero in SWA/Namibia.

The mission station was founded in October 1844 by Carl Hugo Hahn and Heinrich Kleinschmidt, after the spring they had visited at Okahandja months earlier had almost dried up. Five days after their arrival at Okahandja Jonker Afrikaner arrived unexpectedly and, on learning of their plight, encouraged them to settle at Otjikango. The station was named Neu-Barmen after the headquarters of the Rhenish Missionary Society at Barmen in Germany. The name was later changed to Gross Barmen.

The mission station had to be abandoned on several occasions as it was situated in the line of attack between the warring Herero and Nama tribes, and after 1890 no more missionaries were stationed here, as Gross Barmen became a branch of the mission station at Okahandja. Sadly, all that remains is the ruins of the church and the mission house. The site is marked by a solitary palm tree west of the dam.

OTJIMBINGWE

Otjimbingwe is not on any of the main routes and a visit to this historic settlement, once the "capital" of the country, requires a special detour. On the Okahandja/Swakopmund road (B2) turnoffs are signposted at Wilhelmstal and Karibib, from where Otjimbingwe is approximately 67 km and 55 km, respectively.

Situated at the junction of the Swakop and the Omusema rivers, the Herero name is translated as "place of refreshment" – a reference to the spring in the Omusema River.

On account of its strategic position, halfway between Windhoek and Walvis Bay on the old ox-wagon route, Otjimbingwe developed into the most important settlement in the country after Reichs-Kommissar Heinrich Göring decided on Otjimbingwe as the administrative seat of Deutsch-Südwestafrika.

The Rhenish missionary, Johannes Rath, established a mission station for the Herero here in 1849. Following the discovery of copper deposits in the area, the Walvisch Bay Mining Company (WBM) made Otjimbingwe its headquarters in 1854. In the same year a trading store was established where arms, ammunition and liquor were sold on credit or bartered with the Herero and Nama, and Otjimbingwe soon degenerated into a den of iniquity. When the copper boom came to an end in 1860 the explorer, Charles John Andersson, bought the WBM Company's assets in Otjimbingwe and established his headquarters here. The store was later purchased by Eduard Hälbich. Although not a national monument, the building serves its original purpose to this day.

The Rhenish church at Otjimbingwe, still in use, dates back to 1867, although the tower was only added in 1899. It is the oldest church built for the Herero. Although the Herero Chief, Zeraua, was not a follower of the Christian faith, he offered to have 10 000 bricks made for the church. On more than one occasion the church, with its thick walls, served as a refuge for women and children during attacks by the Nama on Otjimbingwe.

Two other historic monuments can also be seen in Otjimbingwe – the old powder magazine and the wind motor. The powder magazine was erected in 1872 by the Missionshandelsgesellschaft to protect its trading venture against the Nama who frequently attacked Otjimbingwe. Since the 1860s an increasing number of unscrupulous traders dealing in liquor, arms and ammunition had been active in the area, which seriously interfered with missionary work at Otjimbingwe. In an attempt to counteract this situation, the Missionshandelsgesellschaft was founded in Germany in January 1871 to promote trade. Otjimbingwe served as the local headquarters, while branches were established at Okahandja and Rehoboth. Nine years later the Handelsgesellschaft suffered financial problems following the start of the second Nama–Herero war and in 1882 the tower passed into the hands of the firm Hälbich. No less than 30 attacks were made against the 8 m high tower – none of which was successful.

Facing the tower you will notice the old wind motor, erected in 1896 by the Hälbich family to generate power for the machinery in the adjoining wagon factory, on your right. Power was derived from the 9 m diameter windmill wheel, which turned a driving shaft attached to a gear on the ground. From here a belt ran to a long horizontal driving shaft inside the building, where several belts turned a variety of machines. The 8 hp motor generated power for, amongst others, a band saw, turntable and iron drill, and also supplied the settlement with water from a nearby fountain.

The first post office in SWA/Namibia, housed in a tiny hut in the vicinity of the trading store, was opened in Otjimbingwe in July 1888 – a week after the country joined the Universal Postal Union on 1 July 1888.

The Germans transferred their headquarters to Windhoek towards the close of 1890 and the settlement lost its importance when the railway line, following a more northerly route between Windhoek and Swakopmund, was completed early this century.

Today, Otjimbingwe seems an unlikely place to have served as the country's administrative centre.

OMARURU

Omaruru is situated 55 km north of Karibib and 135 km south-west of Otjiwarongo. The main approaches from these two towns are along route 2/3 (C33) and route 2/4 (C33), respectively.

In 1870 the Swedish trader and hunter, Axel Eriksson, made Omaruru the headquarters of his trading ventures and in the same year a mission station was established on the shady banks of the Omaruru River.

Omaruru is a Herero word, translated as "bitter thick-milk", a reference to milk produced by cows grazing on the bitterbush (*Pechuel-loeschae leubnitziae*). These bushes remain green long after most other vegetation has become unpalatable and the meat and milk of animals which feed on the bitterbush becomes temporarily bitter.

Reminders of the early history of the town include the *Franketurm* or Franke Tower, the adjacent battlefield and the old mission house.

The Franke Tower can be reached by taking the signposted turnoff near the southern end of the town or by turning into Hospital Street from the Main Road. The tower, which was declared a national monument in 1963, was erected by the residents of Omaruru in 1908 to honour Captain Victor Franke. Captain Franke had been engaged in suppressing a Bondelswarts uprising in Gibeon when, in January 1904, he heard that Okahandja and Omaruru were being besieged by the Herero. After gaining permission from Governor Leutwein he and his company started marching north. Nineteen and a half days later, after covering roughly 900 km, they had freed both Okahandja and Omaruru. The task of relieving the besieged Omaruru proved to be a difficult one, as the German troops were greatly outnumbered. On 4 February 1904 Captain Franke led a cavalry charge, causing the Herero chief,

Manassa, and his followers to flee. After this battle, Franke's outstanding achievement as a soldier was recognised when he was awarded the *Pour le Mérite* – the highest German military honour – which he received from the Kaiser himself.

The tower is kept locked but on your way there call at either the Central Hotel in Main Street or at Hotel Staebe in Monument Street, where you can collect the keys. In the grounds around the tower is a cannon used during the battle which claimed the lives of about 100 Herero and 9 Germans. Adjacent to the tower is part of the battlefield, declared a national monument in 1972, where the Herero were defeated.

Another monument to be seen in the town is the old mission house – the oldest house in Omaruru. The building, of raw clay bricks, was completed in 1872 by the Rhenish missionary Gottlieb Viehe, who had established a mission station in Omaruru two years earlier. In this house, in 1874, Viehe translated the New Testament, the liturgy, prayers and the catechisms into Herero. In the years following the house served several purposes, including that of a temporary military post, and several highly placed officials, including the special envoy of the Cape Government, W C Palgrave, and *Hauptmann* C von François, held meetings with local Herero chiefs here.

Opposite the mission house is the old graveyard where a number of Germans and the Herero chief, Wilhelm Zeraua, have been buried. On the weekend usually before 10 October each year the Herero pay homage to their leader and the colourful procession from the Ozonde residential area to the graveyard and back is worth seeing if you are in the area. Unfortunately the graveyard has been neglected over the years and is normally kept locked.

PAULA'S CAVE

Despite the prominent roadsign just south of Omaruru indicating the turnoff to the cave (signposted Paula's Cave and Krantzberg Mine), this detour is not recommended. Unfortunately fires made in the cave to smoke out wasps and bees have damaged the rock paintings, which were declared a national monument in 1951 – amongst the first monuments to be proclaimed in the country. In addition, the 3 km walk from the parking area, where the path to the cave is signposted, is not well marked.

EPAKO GUEST FARM

Leaving Omaruru on route 2/4 (C33) to Kalkfeld, Epako is reached by taking a turnoff to the left immediately after crossing the railway line on route 2/4. This farm, combined with Tjirundu to the west, covers approximately 11 000 ha. Undulating hills and mountains cover a third of the area, while the remainder is fairly level.

Sight-seeing tours are conducted from the farmhouse. Game which might be spotted includes blue and black wildebeest, impala and black-faced impala, eland, giraffe, Burchell's zebra and red hartebeest. There is also a variety of birdlife to entertain the bird-watchers. Walking and horseriding excursions can be arranged.

Well-preserved rock engravings, as well as some weathered rock paintings, can be seen on the farm. Interesting rock formations, which are especially photogenic in the early morning or late evening, can also be visited.

Facilities for visitors consist of seven double rooms with bathrooms. Full board is available and the farm has a restricted liquor licence. There is also a swimming pool for guests to cool down in.

Epako is primarily a hunting farm and reservations should be made at least one month in advance by writing to P O Box 108, Omaruru 9000, Tel (062232) 2040.

ETEMBA GUEST FARM

The turnoff to Etemba is signposted shortly before the southern entrance to Omaruru, where you turn onto the D2315 (also signposted Paula's Cave and Krantzberg Mine). The turnoff is indicated further along the D2315.

Etemba takes its name from a Herero word meaning "halting place" – it was a favourite resting place of travellers between Swakopmund and Omaruru, as water was always available in the sandy riverbed of the Omaruru River.

Following the severe drought of the early 1980s, the guest farm was forced to close at the end of 1984 when the boreholes on the farm ran dry. It was re-opened to tourists in January 1988 and facilities offered include fully equipped bungalows, a swimming pool, a restaurant and campsites with ablutions.

The main attraction on the farm, north of the main Erongo massif, is the numerous rock paintings. Especially interesting are the rock paintings in Etemba Cave and it is easy to understand why this cave, with its beautiful view of the Omaruru River, was chosen to house this "gallery". There are also various other rock painting sites in the area and the map obtainable from the farm will help you to locate them.

Also not to be missed is the Mushroom Rock, where the erosive action of the elements has created this delicate balance of a boulder resting, seemingly precariously though, on a smaller base.

Reservations can be addressed to P O Box 174, Omaruru 9000, Tel (062232) 1720.

ANIBIB GUEST FARM

Anibib, about 52 km west of Omaruru, on the northern perimeter of the Erongo Mountains, is best approached by turning onto route 2315 (signposted Paula's Cave, Krantzberg Mine) just south of Omaruru. The turnoff to the guest farm is indicated along route D2315.

Judging by the number of paintings on the farm, Anibib must have been very popular with the earlier inhabitants of the area. It is said to boast one of the largest collections of rock paintings in SWA/Namibia, as well as the greatest concentration of different animals in a variety of positions. Human figures have also been portrayed in interesting positions. The paintings occur over an area of about 2 000 ha and most are well preserved. The paintings on Anibib and other nearby sites are described in detail in the book *Anibib and Omandumba, and Other Erongo Sites* by the Abbé Breuil.

Anibib caters mainly for day visitors and can only accommodate four overnight visitors (full board if desired), so book well in advance by writing to P O Box 184, Omaruru 9000, Tel (062232) 1711.

A maximum of two guided tours for parties consisting of not more than six people are conducted daily. (A fee is charged.) Besides the beautiful scenery, these tours also afford you a glimpse into the way of life of the earlier inhabitants of the area. Stone Age tools, including grinding stones, have been left untouched, as have beads and ostrich egg shells. The guided tour ensures that the paintings and artefacts are not damaged, and also helps visitors to leave the farm with a deeper insight into the early inhabitants.

KARIBIB

The small town of Karibib, 100 km west of Okahandja on the main route to Swakopmund (B2), is easily passed through, but if you are interested in historic buildings you would do well to stop here for a while.

When entering the town from Okahandja, the first building of interest is the bakery and baker's quarters, which were built in 1913 as a hotel – one of six hotels in Karibib during the German colonial period. In the 1950s the main building of the old hotel was converted into a bakery, a purpose which it still serves today.

A little further on, the Rösemann Building, one of the oldest buildings in Karibib, will attract your attention. Although the building has been altered on numerous occasions since it was first built around 1900, the façade has remained virtually unchanged. Towards the end of 1900 the building became the headquarters of the trading firm Rösemann and Kronewitter. In those days trains on the Windhoek–Swakopmund line only travelled during daytime, with the result that accommodation was much in demand in Karibib, which is exactly half-way. Small wonder, then, that this building too was converted into a hotel by the end of 1900.

Opposite the Rösemann Building is the station building, which was completed in April 1901 and also served as a post office.

The firm of E Hälbich & Co, established at Otjimbingwe 27 years earlier, was moved to Karibib in 1900. Continuing downstreet, on the left-hand side you will see the historic Hälbich property, comprising four buildings.

Adjacent to the Hälbich property is Haus Woll, which is easily mistaken for a church. The building dates back to the beginning of the century, when it was used by a certain George Woll partly as a shop and partially as living quarters. The granite building reflects the typical style of the German colonial period.

Karibib is also renowned for its high-quality marble, which has been quarried near the town since 1904. Karibib marble, considered the hardest in the world, has been used for the wall panels in the Legislative Assembly for Whites in Windhoek, the floors of the extensions to the Parliament buildings in Cape Town and at Frankfurt Airport.

About 100 tons of marble is processed at the plant, Marmorwerke, each month. The marble is quarried in the hills 10 km south-west of the town and transported to the marble works in 20 ton blocks. Here it is cut into blocks of varying sizes by the largest granite saw in Africa, before it is again cut into smaller blocks and finally washed and polished. Floor and bathroom tiles are particularly in demand, while a variety of ornaments and tombstones are also manufactured.

In July 1985, gold was discovered on the farm Navachab, south-west of Karibib, and two years later the Anglo American Corporation of South Africa and Consolidated Diamond Mines announced that they were to develop the mine.

It is estimated that the mine will produce 62 500 ounces of gold during its lifespan of 13 years. However, there is a possibility that the operation could be extended. The ore is low grade, about 2–3 grams a ton, and about 750 000 tons of rock will be treated annually.

USAKOS

Usakos, on the southern bank of the Khan River, is 148 km east of Swakopmund on the B2. Tourists usually pass through the town without realising the important role Usakos played in the history of the railways in this country.

The town developed around the railway workshops which were built here early this century to serve locomotives on the narrow-gauge Otavi Line. By 1907 Usakos boasted two hotels and a population of 300 and in time the workshops were rivalled only by those at De Aar in South Africa. In 1960 the steam locomotives were replaced by diesel engines and a modern workshop was opened in Windhoek, resulting in the depopulation of Usakos. However, more recently this trend has been reversed and the commissioning of a gold mine in the hills south-east of Usakos is likely to attract more people and revive business in the town.

Reminders of the heyday of the railway era in Usakos are the water tower south of the railway line and the locomotive in front of the station.

This locomotive, No. 40, is one of three Henschel heavy-duty locomotives built in 1912 by the firm of Henschel and Son in Casel, Germany. They were used on the narrow-gauge (600 mm) Otavi line between Kranzberg, about 20 km west of Karibib, and Tsumeb and

Grootfontein until 1960 when the line was standardised with a 1,067 m track. The Henschel heavy-duty locomotives were originally manufactured with a steam dome and a sand dome, but for practical purposes the latter was removed and sand boxes were fitted onto the locomotive's running boards. Locomotive No 41 can be seen in front of the Otjiwarongo station.

AMEIB GUEST RANCH

The turnoff to Ameib Guest Ranch is signposted on the Swakopmund side of Usakos. Continue for roughly 13 km on the D1935 before turning right onto the D1937, which is followed for about 16 km.

Ameib, on the southern edge of the Erongo Mountains, is best known for the rock paintings in Phillip's Cave and the Bulls' Party rock formations.

Fully inclusive accommodation is available in the guest house, or, for those preferring something more basic, a campsite with ablutions is provided. Be warned, though – camping tariffs are extremely high when compared to those of other campsites. Caravans are not permitted. Day visitors are also welcomed, but once again the entry fee is high.

In addition to the numerous rock paintings in the Erongo Mountains, the fascinating rock formations are also a great attraction. The Bulls' Party is probably one of the best examples. This collection of more-or-less round boulders is positioned in such a way as to create the impression of a number of bulls engaged in conversation – hence the name. Endless hours can be spent exploring the area but the heat usually becomes unbearable amongst the granite boulders at midday. Pleasant lunch spots can be found here in the coolness of some of the towering boulders. A stream, which rises among the jumble of rocks at Bulls' Party, trickles over the boulders for a short distance before disappearing into the sand. Tempting as it may be, the management of Ameib have requested visitors not to cool off in the water.

A nearby rocky outcrop has appropriately been named the Elephant Head, and it is fun to do some exploring and rock scrambling here. Keep an eye open for an enormous, 16 m high boulder which seems as though it has just come to rest.

A national monument on the ranch, Phillip's Cave, is the other attraction not to be missed. The walk from the car park to the cave is most enjoyable provided you set off early in the morning or in the late afternoon, but should not be attempted by the unfit. About 45–60 minutes should be allowed each way.

On entering Phillip's Cave you will be struck by the painting of a large white elephant on the wall facing you. Other animals you will be able to distinguish include giraffe, zebra and ostrich, as well as a red antelope superimposed on the elephant. There are also several figures in various postures. These paintings were described in detail in the Abbé Breuil's book *Phillip Cave*. However, his theories on the Mediterranean origin and age of the paintings have been rejected by later archaeologists.

TREKKOPJE

A road sign, Trekkopje, 65 km west of Usakos along the B2, indicates the turnoff to the military cemetery. Turn in here and continue along the gravel road towards the railway line, which is crossed after less than 1 km. After crossing the railway line turn right and follow the road to the fenced graveyard marked by a large tree, almost opposite the old station building.

German and South African soldiers killed in the Battle of Trekkopje, which took place on 26 April 1915, are buried here.

Following the occupation of Swakopmund by South African forces in January 1915 the retreating Germans destroyed the Otavi Line between Swakopmund and Usakos, as well as the State Line as far as Welwitch, 62 km east of Swakopmund. While engaged in rebuilding the Otavi Line between Swakopmund and Usakos to the 1,067 m Cape gauge, the construction camp of the South African Engineering Corps was attacked by the Germans at Trekkopje. Of significance in this clash is that armoured vehicles were used for the first time by the South African Forces. Although the South Africans were outnumbered, they defeated the Germans with the assistance of Rolls Royce-powered armoured cars with revolving machine-gun turrets.

RÖSSING URANIUM MINE

The Rössing Uranium Mine, 56 km east of Swakopmund, can be visited only by joining a bus tour. Tours are conducted on Fridays only, leaving at 08h00 from the parking area below Café Anton and returning at 13h30. Reservations can be made with the Swakopmund Museum.

The discovery of uranium was made in the 1920s by a prospector, Captain Peter Louw. A company, G P Louw (Pty) Ltd, later obtained a concession over an area of 1 000 km², but various attempts to interest mining companies failed. In the mid-1960s a subsidiary of Rio Tinto Zinc, Rio Tinto Management Services South Africa Ltd, took an option on the concession.

After four years of extensive geophysical and geological surveys, Rössing Uranium Ltd was established in 1970 and exploitation of the ore body began, though full production was not reached until 1978.

The uranium deposit, the largest of its kind in the world, is a low-grade deposit contained in tough, abrasive granite known as alaskite. It has been calculated that the uranium deposit here is about 3 km long and 1 km wide.

The geological history of the Rössing deposits goes back some 1 700 million years, when the Namib Desert was part of the sea. Sediments from higher-lying areas were deposited on the sea bed, causing its subsidence and further accumulation of deposits which sank deep into the earth's crust. As a result of stress, the rocks were folded and metamorphosed, underlying molten matter was forced upwards and became embedded in the sedimentary rock. The uranium minerals – uraninite and beta-uranophone crystals – are found in these granites.

Each week about 1 000 000 tons of rock are recovered from the open pit, which is mined in 15 m deep benches and has an average slope of 45°. For this, 270 tons of explosives are used per week and once the rock has been blasted it is loaded into 150-ton trucks and transported to two crushers with a capacity of 40 000 tons a day. After two more crushing stages, the particles of rock undergo a complex series of processes involving grinding, leaching, the separation of sand and slime and the thickening of the slime.

This is followed by several recovery stages until a yellow paste, ammonium diuranate, is recovered on rotating drum filters. In the final stage the yellow paste, also known as yellow cake, is dried and roasted at a temperature of more than 600°C to form uranium oxide. The uranium oxide (U_3O_8) is then loaded into steel drums for export overseas, where it is further processed.

The open pit will eventually cover 5 km² and although it will be impossible to conceal the fact that the mine once existed when it is closed down, Rössing has a decommissioning plan which will reduce its negative environmental impact. All mine structures will be removed, waste material will be buried under a layer of rock, and landscaping will attempt to re-arrange rock as naturally as possible. The area will also be fenced off.

REGIMENTAL BADGES

Another reminder of the South West Africa Campaign during World War I can be viewed by turning off the B2 47 km east of Swakopmund – the turnoff is indicated by a national monument sign. Follow the track to the railway line (about 1 km), from where it is a short distance on foot to the raised platform from which you will have a splendid view over the regimental insignia of the 2nd Durban Light Infantry, laid out in stones.

Some of the South African soldiers assigned to patrol the railway line to ensure that it was not sabotaged by the Germans occupied themselves by skilfully setting out their names, initials or regimental signs. There are a number of these insignia along the railway line – the best known being the 27 m by 12 m badge of the 2nd Durban Light Infantry. White quartz chips and dark brown rocks were contrasted to portray details which are still clearly visible today. Further to the right is the incomplete thistle of the Transvaal Scottish Regiment, where one is just able to make out the Gaelic motto *Alba nam buadh*.

WINDHOEK TO BOTSWANA VIA GOBABIS AND BUITEPOS

Travelling eastwards from Windhoek along route B6, the turnoff to Dordabis (route 15 [C23]) is signposted after about 24 km. Some 66 km along this road brings you to Dordabis, where karakul carpet weaving can be seen on the farm Ibenstein. The weavery is open from Monday to Friday from 08h00 to 12h00 and from 14h30 to 18h00, but appointments must be made beforehand by phoning Dordabis (0020) 13.

Although hot during the summer, Gobabis, which is reached 205 km east of Windhoek, is a pleasant town. It is popularly accepted that the name of the town means "place of the elephants", but according to

Raper (1987) it is a Khoekhoen name meaning "place of arguing or discussing". The town is the centre of one of the most important cattle ranching areas in the country. It also serves as administrative centre for the country's smallest population group, the Tswana, numbering about 10 000 people.

The town grew up around the mission station established here in 1856 by the Rhenish missionary Eggers. In 1865 he was driven out of the mission station when he tried to establish peace between the Khauas Khoikhoi and the Damara. Missionary work was resumed only in 1876, but the missionaries were later again forced to abandon the mission station when hostilities broke out between the Khauas Khoikhoi and the Herero. A military unit under the command of Lieutenant Lampe occupied Gobabis in March 1895 on the orders of Major Theodor Leutwein and in May the following year a rebellion by the Herero and Khauas Khoikhoi was put down. Shortly afterwards work on a sturdy fort commenced and the building was completed in 1897. Unfortunately the building was later demolished.

The old hospital or lazarette is the only building in the town dating back to this era. At present it is not open to the public, but plans are underway to establish a museum there. It is reached by travelling along Church Street and then turning into Lieutenant Lampe Street, which is followed to the junction with Lazarette Street on the southern edge of the town. The lazarette, a national monument, is immediately opposite the junction.

The remaining 121 km to Buitepos, the border post on the SWA/ Namibia border with Botswana, is along a gravel road. From Buitepos it is about 480 km to Maun, the gateway to the Okavango Delta. The condition of this road is generally poor and at least 8–10 hours should be allowed for the journey between Buitepos and Maun. A two-vehicle party is advisable.

8 NAMIB DESERT

NAMIB-NAUKLUFT PARK

Covering nearly 5 million hectares, the Namib–Naukluft Park is the largest game park in Africa and the fourth largest in the world. For the purposes of this book the park is divided into four sections: the Naukluft section, the sanddune desert stretching south of the Kuiseb River to Lüderitz, the gravel plains of the Central Namib between the Kuiseb and Swakop rivers, and Sandwich.

Naukluft

The Naukluft section of the park can be approached along several routes, the entrance gate to the park being on the D854, about 10 km south-west of Büllsport. The D854 can be joined either along route 36 between Solitaire and Maltahöhe, which gives access to Sesriem and Sossusvlei, or along route 14/2 (C14) between Solitaire, Büllsport and Maltahöhe. The park office is about 12 km beyond the entrance gate.

Facilities at Naukluft consist of campsites only. Situated by the Naukluft River, the four sites each have a fireplace, cement table and benches, as well as an ablution block with hot water and refuse bins. Groups must consist of at least three people and are limited to eight people per site. As only 32 people are permitted altogether, it is advisable to book well in advance, especially during school holidays and over weekends. Reservations can only be made at the DNC offices in Windhoek and day visitors are not allowed.

The topography of the Naukluft complex does not lend itself to cars and the only way visitors can explore the park is on foot. There are two circular day trails to be attempted, so remember to take sturdy walking shoes, a hat, sunscreen cream, daypack for carrying lunch, trail snacks and at least two litres of water per person. The Waterkloof Trail starts at the campsite and can be completed in five or six hours, while

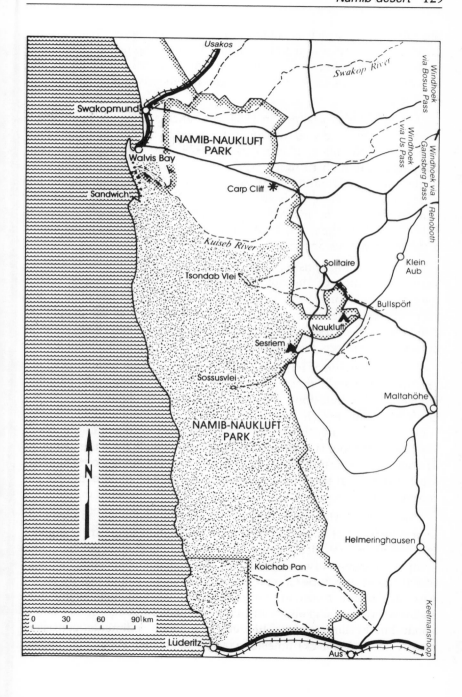

the Olive Trail, which is signposted about 3 km before reaching the park office, requires four to five hours. Trailists should be fit and take sufficient water along with them. An eight-day trail (although shorter variations are possible) with overnight facilities is due to be opened during 1989.

Naukluft was proclaimed in 1964 as a sanctuary for the Hartmann's mountain zebra and was subsequently joined to the Namib Desert Park to form the Namib–Naukluft Park in 1979. The Naukluft Mountains are part of the high-rising escarpment which marks the western edge of the interior highlands of SWA/Namibia. The flat, plateau-like top of the mountain complex is separated from the adjacent highland plateau to the south by impressive near-vertical cliffs (Johann Albrechts Felsen), while in the north-west and west its highest peaks loom almost a thousand metres above the plains of the Namib.

The plateau top consists mainly of dolomite and limestone formations. Dissolution of the dolomite and limestone by meteoric waters over many millennia has given rise to karstification of the plateau and an extensive underground drainage system. In some of the deeply incised kloofs discharge from this underground water reservoir occurs as crystal-clear springs and streams.

Tufa, also known as fountain stone or waterfall limestone formations, are associated with these springs and streams. These soft, or semi-friable, porous limestone deposits are formed by evaporation of the calcium carbonate-rich stream water that filters through the dolomite rocks. A particularly impressive tufa formation with inviting pools in the Naukluft Kloof is reached after a 20 minute walk from the campsite. The widespread distribution of these tufa deposits throughout the Naukluft Mountains attests to a considerably wetter climate during the recent past.

The Naukluft Mountains are of particular interest in the ancient geological history of this part of the country. The mountains are composed of three main geological formations – the Rehoboth–Sinclair basement complex, sedimentary formations of the Nama Group and "nappes" of the Naukluft Nappe Complex. The basement is found mainly on the west side of the mountain complex and consists of metasedimentary and volcanic rocks, gneisses and granites, varying in age from 1 000 to about 2 000 million years. The overlying Nama sediments, consisting mainly of dark (black) limestone, were deposited about 600 million years ago when the entire south-western part of the southern African subcontinent was covered by a shallow tropical sea.

The Naukluft "nappes" forming the top part of the mountains are very large, sheet-like units of sedimentary rocks, which were emplaced along low-angle fault- or fracture-planes known as thrusts. These movements occurred some 500 to 550 million years ago and were related to active earth forces associated with a period of crustal mobility and mountain building in the Damara Orogenic Belt, an ancient, deeply eroded chain which is known to have existed in the area of the Hakos and Auas mountains and the Khomas Hochland to the north.

The vegetation of the Naukluft complex has been classified by Giess as Semi-desert and Savanna Transition (Escarpment Zone) (Vegetation Type 4). On account of the variety of soil types, depths, slopes and water retention capabilities the vegetation is not only varied but also complex: a mosaic of five main plant communities has been identified. The most common plants are the *Commiphora*, *Acacia* and *Euphorbia* species.

The mountains are the habitat of a number of protected plants, such as *Lithops schwantesii* and *Trichocaulon* species. Two interesting *Aloe* species also occur in the complex. The small *A. sladeniana* is restricted to the mountains of the western escarpment, occurring mainly in the Naukluft and Zaris mountains. It grows in the mountain and plateau plant communities, where it forms dense groups in rock crevices. Pale pink flowers are produced in January and February. *A. karasbergensis* can be distinguished by its thornless, yellow-white leaves. The pale pink to red flowers can be seen in January and February. This species is restricted to the south of the country and reaches its northernmost limit of distribution here in the Naukluft Gorge.

The vegetation community most visitors are likely to encounter is the gorge community of the Naukluft. These communities are confined to gorges with springs, of which there are about ten in the complex. The gorge communities are rich in species and more than 150 have been recorded in the Naukluft River. A characteristic tree of the river banks is the common cluster fig (66) which attracts large numbers of birds when in fruit.

The other plant communities are those of the plateau, mountain, gravel plains surrounding the mountain complex, and the sandy plain transitional community before the start of the sand dunes.

The majority of the more than 50 mammal species recorded in the complex are either nocturnal or small and thus easily overlooked. Consequently the impression can easily be gained that the area is poor in mammal life. Nearly a third of the mammals are rodents, while the carnivores are represented by 13 species. A further 24 smaller mammal species are thought to occur, but have not been positively recorded.

The mammals you are most likely to spot are the kudu, Hartmann's mountain zebra, springbok, klipspringer, steenbok, chacma baboon, rock rabbit and dassie rat. Gemsbok are the most common inhabitants of the gravel plains and sand dunes west of the complex, although springbok and ostrich (1) also occur.

To date some 190 bird species have been recorded for the mountain complex. Several bird species which require specialised habitats such as krantzes for breeding occur in the park. Among these species are black eagle (131), augur buzzard (153), lanner falcon (172) and Bradfield's swift (413). Birding can be rewarding as the complex lies in an area which is the southernmost limit of several species typical of the north of Namibia, such as Rüppell's parrot (365), Monteiro's hornbill (462), Herero chat (618) and chestnut weaver (812). At the same time, it is the northernmost limit of distribution of a number of true Karoo species such as Karoo robin (614) and cinnamonbreasted warbler (660).

The birds of Naukluft can be broadly divided according to their habitat preferences into the following categories: (a) kloofs with perennial streams, (b) mountain slopes and cliffs, (c) the plateau, and (d) the gravel plains surrounding Naukluft.

Species you might spot in the kloofs with perennial streams include hamerkop (81), pied barbet (465), pririt batis (703), brubru (741) and common waxbill (846).

Be on the lookout for mountain chat (586), Layard's titbabbler (622) and dusky sunbird (788) on the slopes. Rockrunner (662) is restricted to the northern and eastern slopes.

The plateau is the habitat for species such as Ludwig's bustard (232), sabota lark (498) and bokmakierie (746), whose loud onomatopoeic call is often heard, as well as the uncommon longbilled lark (500).

Summer visitors to Naukluft include black cuckoo (378), European bee-eater (438) and lesser grey shrike (731). Klaas's cuckoo (385) and diederik cuckoo (386) also occur, but are more frequently heard than seen.

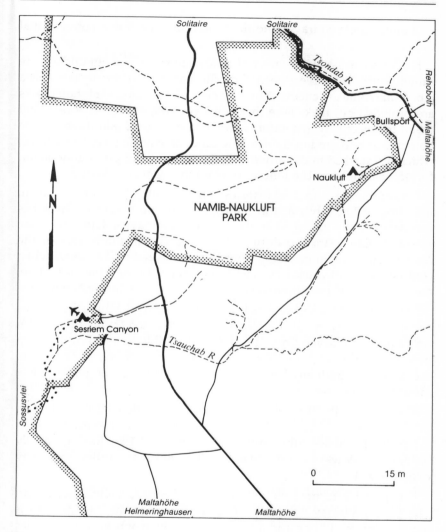

Sesriem and Sossusvlei

Sesriem is reached by taking the turnoff signposted about 69 km south of Solitaire on route 36 between Solitaire and Maltahöhe. The entrance gate to Sesriem is reached 12 km beyond the turnoff.

Sesriem is a delightful camping site on the edge of the vast sand dune sea of the Namib and the only place which affords visitors the rare opportunity to travel into the sand dune desert in a conventional car.

Facilities consist of a number of shady campsites laid out under huge camel thorn (168) trees. Each campsite has its own braaiplace and a tap, while some are encircled by a stone wall. Two small ablution blocks are provided but make sure that you have your shower before 22h00 when the electricity generator is switched off. Petrol and diesel can be obtained at Sesriem but there are no other amenities, except cooldrinks which are stocked in the office. A rest camp providing accommodation for 450 people is in the long-term planning stage.

One of the most amazing features of the Namib, the Sesriem Canyon, lies about 4 km south of the campsite. Here the Tsauchab River has carved a gorge – up to 30 m deep – into the gravels deposited some 15–18 million years ago during a wetter phase in the history of the Namib. The canyon probably dates back some 2–4 million years when continental uplift caused the incision of not only the Tsauchab River, but also most of the other westward-flowing rivers in the Namib.

From the parking area a track leads into the canyon, where the various conglomerate layers can be seen clearly. After good rains the canyon holds water for several months and it is possible to swim in the deep pool where the track reaches the canyon floor. As you walk up into the canyon it gradually becomes narrower until in some places it is a mere 2 m wide.

The name of the Sesriem Canyon is said to be derived from the fact that the early travellers had to join six ox thongs to lower a bucket to the pools. To the west the canyon, which is about 1 km long, gradually becomes shallower until the river broadens out into a valley on its way to Sossusvlei.

It is possible to travel to within 5 km of Sossusvlei in a sedan car. The 60 km journey from the office at Sesriem to the parking area is usually covered in one and a quarter hours. Four-wheel-drive vehicles can continue to the parking area at the vlei – but remember that the area is ecologically very sensitive and it is an offence to leave the track, which is demarcated with stakes. An early start is advisable as the sand dunes are seen at their best immediately after sunrise when the orange contrasts sharply with the dark shadow side. Confirm departure and return times at the tourist office at Sesriem, as these vary according to sunrise and sunset.

Twenty-four kilometres after leaving the camp you cross the Tsauchab River and from here the road continues along the broad river valley. Numerous dead camel thorn (168) trees indicate an old river course and provide evidence that the river once followed a more southerly course.

It is thought that the Tsauchab once flowed into the Atlantic Ocean, but that its course was blocked by the encroaching sand dunes. Archaeological, geomorphological and biological research into the Tsondab River further north, which also ends in a pan today, has revealed that decreasing water flow, coupled with obstruction by sand dunes, blocked the flow of the river some 70 km inland from the Atlantic coast about 60 000 years ago. Over thousands of years the Tsauchab River has, nevertheless, managed to keep open part of its course, ending at Sossusvlei – a clay pan 65 km south-west of Sesriem.

The sand dune desert occurs as widely dispersed patches north of the Orange River, becoming a vast sea of dunes north of Lüderitz until it is abruptly stopped by the Kuiseb River, which acts as a barrier. However, near the mouth of the river, the sand dunes march northwards across and out of the Kuiseb Delta until barred by the Swakop River. Except for a small, isolated patch north of the Huab River, east of Toscanini in the Skeleton Coast Park, the sand dunes are found again only in the vicinity of Torra Bay – 240 km beyond the Swakop River. South of Terrace Bay a tongue of the sand sea juts southwards towards Torra Bay. North of Terrace Bay, however, the sand dunes stretch discontinuously along the coast to the Kunene River, which also forms a significant barrier.

It is thought that vast quantities of sand were carried into the Atlantic Ocean by the Orange and Fish rivers during erosional phases. This material was subsequently moved northwards and deposited on the shore by the vigorous longshore drift under the influence of the strong coastal south-westerly wind regime.

The spectacularly crested dunes at Sossusvlei are known as star dunes. These dunes are normally formed where the wind regime is low energy and multi-directional. In the Sossusvlei area, these dunes can reach up to 325 m above the Tsauchab River, although free-standing examples may only be about 220 m high.

West of Sossusvlei is a 60 km wide belt of linear dunes – the largest area of the Central Namib sand sea. These north/south trending dunes lie diagonal to the prevailing south-westerly winds and reach lengths of up to 50 km. The linear dunes are lower than the dunes of Sossusvlei, being some 60–100 m high, and are separated by dune streets up to 1,5 km wide.

Closer to the coast lies a 10–20 km wide belt of crescentic dunes, including transverse and barchan types. These dunes lie roughly perpendicular to the path of the south-west wind which is dominant along the Namib coast.

One of the most fascinating aspects of the dunes of the Namib is the way in which the creatures that live here have adapted to survive in their inhospitable environment. In fact the Namib's almost entirely barren dune country is the only area of its kind in the world where a fauna has evolved. According to the founder of the Desert Ecological Research Unit at Gobabeb, Dr Charles Koch, the presence of animals with a high degree of adaptation implies a great age for the Namib Desert.

The dune grass, *Stipagrostis sabulicola*, forms small dunes in the sand dunes, and these are the centre of life for plant-dependent species. During the early morning hours the fog precipitates on the live and dead plants, thus supplying the only source of water for the greater part of the year.

The dunes are the habitat of several species of tenebrionid beetles, lizards, spiders and other animals which derive their water requirements from dew, light rain and especially fog which, for an average of 100 days a year, reaches up to 50 km into the desert.

Among the unusual animals are the nocturnal gecko *Palmatogecko rangei*, which has webbed feet, allowing it to move rapidly over the soft sand. It feeds on small insects and is, in turn, preyed upon by the "dancing white lady of the Namib", *Orchestrella longipes*, a spider which lives in tunnels constructed in the sand dunes. To prevent it from being covered with loose sand, *Orchestrella* lines its tunnel with a cobweb whilst digging. The dancing white lady hunts mainly at night, sometimes catching prey larger than itself. Another interesting inhabitant is the sand-diving lizard *Aporosaura anchietae*, which lives on the dune slip faces. Studies of the behaviour of this species have revealed that the males maintain a well-defined dominance hierarchy, defending their territory from lower-ranking subordinate males who also live in the same general area. In this way the dominant male increases the probability of breeding with the females which occur within its territory.

Also living in the sand dunes is the *Comicus* cricket, which lives in the cool, moist, deeper layers of sand during the day. Lobed feet allow this species, which feeds at night, to move with ease over the soft sand.

The largest reptile of the sand dunes is the side-winding adder (*Bitis peringueyi*), which has an average length of 20–25 cm. For the greater part of the day this species conceals itself in the sand with only its eyes and the tip of its tail exposed. This is not done only to protect itself from extremes of temperature, but also to lie in ambush for geckos and other small reptiles.

One of the few mammals inhabiting the dunes is Grant's golden mole (*Eremitalpa granti namibensis*) which was first recorded in 1837 by Captain James Alexander. The species was lost to science until in 1962 a scientist discovered a skull fitting its description in owl pellets at Sossusvlei. In 1963 the golden mole was "rediscovered" in the Kuiseb River – 126 years after it was first collected by Alexander. This species, which has neither ears nor eye-sockets, is dormant during the day, usually at the base of a grass tuft or hummock, emerging at night to feed on insects and their larvae.

Research into this unique ecosystem, which has attracted scientists from all over the world, is being carried out by the Desert Ecological Research Unit at Gobabeb, on the banks of the Kuiseb River. The Research Station is closed to the general public, but an open day is usually held once a year.

The Central Namib

The Central Namib can be approached along any of a number of routes. From Windhoek this section of the park can be approached via three passes, the Bosua, Us and Gamsberg passes (see pp 106–10), but the park can also be approached from Swakopmund or Walvis Bay. A highly recommended route is the one via the Kuiseb Canyon, which can be approached either from Windhoek along the Gamsberg Pass (route 49) (C26) or from Sesriem over Solitaire along route 36. This route is joined 73 km north of Solitaire by route 49 (C26) over Gamsberg Pass.

No permits are required for through traffic. However, should you wish to explore the park along any of the tourist roads (over 400 km, of which 100 km are negotiable by four-wheel-drive vehicles only) you

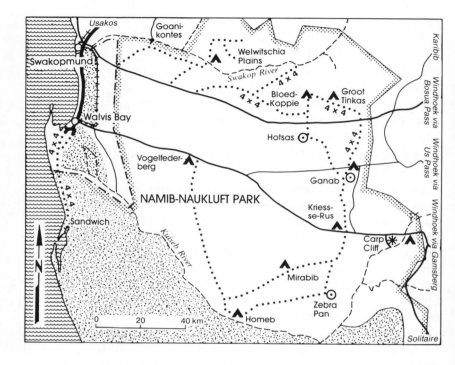

require a permit, obtainable from the tourist offices at Hardap and Sesriem, or the DNC offices in Swakopmund, Lüderitz and Windhoek, during the week. Over weekends permits can be obtained from Charly's Desert Tours and Hans Kriess Service Station in Swakopmund and from Troost Transport, Namib Ford and CWB service stations in Walvis Bay. Camping permits can also be obtained at the above-mentioned places.

Facilities in this section of the park are limited to campsites with braaiplaces, picnic tables, refuse bins and field toilets. There are camp-sites at Kuiseb Bridge, Kriess-se-Rus, Homeb, Mirabib, Vogelfederberg, Ganab, the Swakop River, Bloedkoppie and Groot Tinkas – the latter accessible by four-wheel-drive vehicle only.

Visitors approaching from Sesriem will notice that they re-enter and leave the park north of Sesriem. This narrow corridor forms a vital link between the Naukluft complex and the remainder of the Namib Park, allowing unimpeded movement of gemsbok.

Further north the road descends into the grammadoelas carved by the Gaub River, a tributary of the Kuiseb River. Some 73 km north of Solitaire the Gamsberg Pass road joins in from the right and after another few kilometres of travelling through the deeply scarred landscape the road descends to the Kuiseb River. Provided you have the necessary permit the campsite below the bridge is an ideal stop for a tea break.

Rising in the Khomas Hochland near Windhoek, the Kuiseb River plays an important role in preventing the northward encroachment of the dunes from the Namib sand sea. Owing to the relatively high rainfall in its catchment area it is one of the largest rivers to cross the Namib between the Orange and the Kunene rivers.

About 20 km west of the Kuiseb Canyon campsite is the turnoff to the Carp Cliff viewpoint, which provides magnificent views of the Kuiseb Valley and Gamsberg sector of the Great Escarpment. As you stand on the canyon rim at Carp Cliff, some 180 m above the present river, it is hard to believe that you are actually in an ancient bed of a former Kuiseb! Sections of the Kuiseb Canyon clearly illustrate that this river system represents a valley within a former valley. At the Carp Cliff viewpoint the well-rounded boulders and cobbles on the canyon rim were laid down on an enormous alluvial fan that stretched from about the Gamsberg area to south of Sandwich. At that time, some 15–18 million years ago, there was no deeply incised Kuiseb Canyon and the alluvial fan gravels were laid down in braided streams over an even earlier Kuiseb drainage system. This earlier system, probably dating back 20–40 million years, is represented by the greyish brown to whitish sandstone underlying the well-rounded gravels at Carp Cliff. During those earlier times, the Kuiseb Canyon did not reach the Atlantic Ocean but was blocked, as the Tsauchab River is today at Sossusvlei, by dunes of an ancient sand sea.

The deeply incised course of the Kuiseb is, therefore, geologically a youthful feature. The incision is attributed to a change in base level caused by uplift of the southern African subcontinent some 2–4 million years ago. About 1–1,5 million years ago, the Kuiseb bed was choked with some 30–40 m of its own sediments. Subsequently these deposits were cemented by lime-charged underground waters, and today can be seen as terrace deposits lining the Kuiseb course. Significantly, wedges of linear type dunes are also incorporated into these conglomeratic terrace deposits, providing the first evidence of an association between the Kuiseb River, as we know it today, and the main Namib sand sea.

This association also testifies to the antiquity of the barrier that the Kuiseb River has formed to the northward encroachment of dunes from the sand sea.

A short (15 minute) walk leads to a large overhanging cliff – Carp Cliff, where two German geologists who feared internment during World War II, Henno Martin and Hermann Korn, lived for more than two years. In an arid area such as the Kuiseb Canyon the name might seem somewhat misplaced, but during their stay here they found carp, probably washed downstream by floods, in one of the shallow pools of the Kuiseb River. Their classic story, *The Sheltering Desert*, relates how they and their dog, Otto, managed to survive against all odds in this inhospitable area.

The vegetation of the Namib between the Kuiseb and Huab rivers has been classified by Giess as Central Namib (Vegetation Type 2). A variety of plant species occurs in the Kuiseb and Swakop rivers, the most conspicuous being ana tree (159), camel thorn (168), ebony tree (598) and needle bush (622). The most important grasses are of the genera *Stipagrostis* and *Eragrostis*, which form dense stands on the eastern plains after rains. On the gravel plains the annual plants are largely restricted to the dry river courses. Tree and shrub species occurring here include ana tree (159), camel thorn (168) and buffalo-thorn (447). Further west the vegetation of the dry gravel Namib is desertic dwarf shrubland consisting of plants such as *Salsola* species and *Arthraerua leubnitziae*.

To date some 63 mammal species have been recorded in the Namib Desert, the most commonly seen larger mammals being Hartmann's mountain zebra, gemsbok and springbok. The mountain zebras occur mainly in the eastern part of the park, especially the Kuiseb and Swakop canyons. Gemsbok are fairly widely distributed after the summer rains, but concentrate in large numbers in the south-eastern plains and the Kuiseb River area during the dry season. Also widely distributed is the springbok. Klipspringer occur in suitable rocky habitats, especially the rocky canyons in the upper reaches of the Swakop, Khan and Kuiseb rivers, unlike most small cover-dependent antelope, which rely on silence and concealment to avoid predation. In their open habitats, klipspringer rely on spatial cohesiveness, by synchronising their activities and by persistent vigilance of the family group. In an area with limited resources, adaptation is often the key to survival and in the Kuiseb Canyon klipspringer have been observed feeding at heights of up to

5,4 m in ana trees (159), their principal food resource. This exceptional behaviour is attributed to the relative shortage of food within the home range of the klipspringers, which have to compete with domestic goats owned by the Topnaar Khoikhoi living at Homeb, along the Kuiseb River.

Among the predators the black-backed jackal is the most widely distributed, preferring riverine, coastal and grassveld habitat types. Leopard also occur, but are limited to the Kuiseb and Swakop canyons and the mountainous areas of the north-east.

Spotted hyaena occur in the eastern part of the park and research has shown that the species composition of their prey is directly related to availability. In two groups, gemsbok were the most important food item in their diet, while in a third group gemsbok and mountain zebra were almost equally represented. The research revealed that more male gemsbok were eaten, but that the female mountain zebra outnumbererd male mountain zebra. The difference in mortality between male and female gemsbok has been attributed to injuries inflicted by males on each other making the loser of the contest easy prey for hyaenas. The greater number of female mountain zebras taken has been attributed to the aggressiveness of stallions.

Although brown hyaena are more abundant along the coast, two definite records exist for the Kuiseb River. In contrast to the spotted hyaena, which move down the watercourses towards the coast, the brown hyaena appears to move up the two main watercourses before dispersing onto the gravel plains.

Welwitschia Drive

A most enjoyable excursion from Swakopmund is the Welwitschia Drive (remember to obtain your permit and a guide pamphlet from the DNC offices in Swakopmund). The guide gives the time for the drive as about three hours, but it is advisable to set aside half a day. By allowing extra time you can include Goanikontes, an old riverine farm in the Swakop River (a short detour off the drive) and enjoy a picnic lunch at the shady picnic sites in the Swakop River on your way back.

Several interesting features of the route have been marked and numbered and these numbers correspond with those in the pamphlet, which provides a short explanation of each point of interest. Among these are the lichen fields, relics of World War I, the giant *Welwitschia* of Husab and the old Von Stryk Mine. Your visit to this fascinating desert will be further enhanced if you take along a copy of *Namib Flora – Swakopmund to the Giant Welwitschia via Goanikontes*, by Patricia Craven and Christine Marais. Some 54 plant species found along the route are illustrated and described in the book, which makes interesting reading.

Most visitors travelling through the Namib are unaware of the fact that its lichen fields have attracted the attention of scientists from all over the world. To date some 60 Namib species have been identified, but it is estimated that more than 120 species occur in the Namib Desert. Lichens consists of two primitive forms of plant life – fungi and algae. The thread-like fungi can absorb moisture from the air, whereas the unicellular algae contain chlorophyll and can consequently produce sugar and starch. The algae are therefore dependent on the fungi and likewise the fungi depend on the algae for carbohydrates, a relationship known as symbiosis.

Most of the lichens obtain their moisture from the fog which penetrates the desert in places for up to 100 days a year. The lichen fields between Swakopmund and Terrace Bay are, consequently, among the largest of their kind in the world. The hue they give to the plains is best seen during the early morning, as they soon dry out in the heat of the day. Some species are eaten by springbok and gemsbok during periods of excessive droughts.

Equally interesting is the prehistoric-looking *Welwitschia mirabilis*, which is undoubtedly one of the most fascinating plants in the Namib Desert. The enormous specimen at Welwitschia Plains is estimated to be more than 1 500 years old.

Sandwich

Sandwich Lagoon is situated about 40 km south of Walvis Bay and can only be reached by four-wheel-drive vehicle. Permits are required and can be obtained at CWB Diensstasie, Suidwes Diensstasie and Troost Coach Hire in Walvis Bay or from the DNC office in Bismarck Street, Hans Kriess Motors or Charly's Desert Tours in Swakopmund. The lagoon is open throughout the year between 06h00 and 20h00 with overnight camping strictly prohibited. The collection of mussels and worms is forbidden, as is fishing in the lagoon, because it is thought to act as a nursery for young fish.

The route to Sandwich, signposted in Walvis Bay, leads past Meersig, where you leave the town, continuing in a southerly direction towards the salt works. Some 4 km after leaving Walvis Bay the road forks, with the right-hand road signposted to Paaltjies, 8 km on. You can either follow the road to Paaltjies and then continue along the beach to Sandwich or follow the recommended route further inland. For this route, take the left-hand road. The road is easily followed through the salt works and the Kuiseb Delta, but further along there are several tracks leading off to the right which should be ignored. About 16 km beyond the fork you reach the fence of the Namib-Naukluft Park, where a notice informs you that you are not allowed beyond this point without a permit. The fence also indicates the southern border of the Walvis Bay enclave. From here it is roughly 20 km of four-wheel-driving to the Sandwich Lagoon. You may not drive beyond the fence north of the lagoon, but are free to explore the area on foot. Visitors should remain on the shore – a closer approach to the salt marsh and tidal mudflats will disturb the birdlife and spoil the outing.

Covering about 20 km², the lagoon stretches for roughly 15 km in a north/south direction, with a maximum width of 3,3 km. On its eastern side the lagoon is flanked by 100 m high dunes along the base of which freshwater seepage pools are to be found.

The lagoon is a wetland of international importance for migratory shorebirds in Africa. To date more than 113 species have been recorded, including 18 Palaearctic waders, 20 seabirds, 34 waterbirds and 18 landbirds. Under optimal conditions the lagoon is used for overwintering by nearly 50 000 migrant birds.

Both greater (96) and lesser (97) flamingo occur, numbering up to 5 500 and 1 500 respectively in October. While the greater flamingo favours the fringes and sandbanks of the open lagoon, the lesser flamingo prefers the extensive mudflats in the south.

Among the uncommon species recorded here are ringed plover (245), Kittlitz's plover (248), turnstone (262), common (264) and marsh (269) sandpiper, Caspian (322), swift (324), whiskered (338) and whitewinged (339) tern. Dabchick (8), although uncommon, are resident, while South African shelduck (103) and moorhen (226) might also be spotted.

Mammals are not well represented here, but the coast is the habitat of small numbers of black-backed jackal and brown hyaena. Surprisingly there are also a few resident gemsbok.

Originally named Port D'Ilheo, the lagoon is also known as Sandwich

Harbour, which is said to be a corruption of the original Dutch name *zandvisch*. Sandwich was once a deep-water anchorage for sailing vessels and was used by early navigators in preference to Walvis Bay, where water could only be found some 5 km inland. In addition the bay was considered safer and did not suffer from fog to the same extent as Walvis Bay.

The changing shoreline of the bay is evidenced by the fact that the shoreline is indicated with dots rather than solid lines on most maps of Sandwich drawn before 1900. The northern end of the lagoon was an open bay with a depth of 5 fathoms (approximately 9 m) when the area was surveyed by Lieutenant C Oldham of HMS *Sylvia* in 1880. Some 12 years later, however, a sandbar of 3 m was reported at the mouth.

Over the past two centuries Sandwich has served various purposes. It is highly likely that early whalers used Sandwich for shelter during storms and in the mid-1800s a trading station was established here by De Pass, Spence and Company. Cured fish, shark liver oil, sealskins and guano were exported from Sandwich to Cape Town and Mauritius. Towards the last decade of the previous century the South West Africa Company established a meat canning factory at Sandwich, the cattle being obtained from pastoral Khoikhoi. This venture was short-lived, though, and was soon forced to close down. Between 1904 and 1906 the harbour found yet another use – as a backdoor for gun-running to the Herero and Nama who rose against the German authorities.

Large quantities of guano were collected from the natural sand islands in the lagoon by the Deutsche Kolonialgesellschaft and shipped to Germany between 1910 and World War I. The company sold its rights in 1923 and during the following 13 years various companies held the right to exploit the deposits. In 1937 the concession was taken over by Fisons Albatros Fertilizers. The company decided to raise the level of Long Island and to enlarge it by pumping sand from the bed of the lagoon. A diesel and a sand pumping machine and other equipment were imported from The Netherlands and after being transported overland from Walvis Bay mounted onto a barque. By the end of 1938 about 4 ha had been reclaimed, but in the following year the work was interrupted by the outbreak of World War II. Reclamation work recommenced in August 1942 and by December that year the island covered 8 ha. The company's operations were seriously jeopardised in 1943 because the mouth of the lagoon had silted up, causing the islands to form part of the northern sandspit. Jackal moved in, causing the birds to leave. In addition, the war resulted in spare parts being unobtainable for the trucks which transported the guano.

The mouth was washed open by the first spring tide in April 1944, the water level in the lagoon returned to normal and the birds returned. The same problem was experienced the following year and once again the spring tide of April 1946 opened the mouth. In 1947 large quantities of guano were collected, but the mouth once again silted up and no guano was removed after this date. As a result the concession was cancelled in 1956. In the following years the sea and the sand dunes reclaimed their rightful place, leaving only a few pieces of rusty machinery and the barque as evidence of man's activities here.

SWAKOPMUND

Swakopmund, situated about 35 km north of Walvis Bay, is SWA/Namibia's premier holiday town and can be reached either along the tarred road via Usakos (B2 route) or by taking one of the scenic drives through the Khomas Hochland and the Namib (refer to p 106).

The town's Nama name – Tsoakhaub – originates from the words *tsoa* and *xoub*, which are translated as "posterior" and "excrement". Although the name initially seems to have obscene connotations, it refers appropriately to the brown colour which the sea takes on when the river is in flood.

Swakopmund owes its existence to a decision by the German Reich to establish a port along the coast to provide access to and from the interior of the German protectorate of Deutsch-Südwestafrika, proclaimed in 1884. As the Walvis Bay enclave had already been proclaimed a British possession and other possible sites along the coast were unsuitable, the choice fell on Swakopmund. Two beacons to mark the landing spot were erected north of the Swakop River by the crew of the *Hyena* on 4 August 1892.

The first building – barracks for troops – was erected a month later, and according to records the settlement that year had seven inhabitants. On 23 August 1893, 120 *Schutztruppe* and 40 settlers disembarked from the *Marie Woermann* and by 1897 Swakopmund had 113 inhabitants. Initially, many of the buildings were prefabricated wooden houses, imported from Germany.

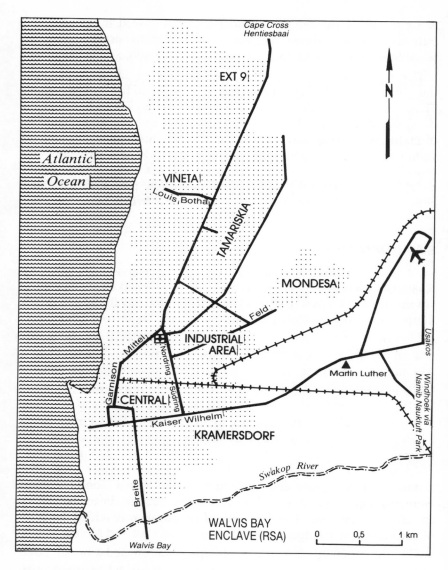

A walking tour

The town is a blend of stately German buildings dating from early this century and modern buildings, and your Swakopmund experience will not be complete without a walk to admire them, as well as visiting other places of interest. A suggested walk, requiring about two and a half hours, can be undertaken by consulting the Swakopmund town map. Numbers marked on the map correspond to the following text.

1 War Memorial Situated on the edge of the municipal gardens, the memorial was unveiled on 10 November 1963 and honours those killed in World War II.

2 Lighthouse Construction of the 11 m high lighthouse was completed in July 1902 and in 1910 a further 10 m in height was added.

3 Kaiserliches Bezirksgericht Originally built as a magistrate's court, this building has served as the summer residence of top government officials. Carl Schmidt was the architect and F W Ortloff, the chief state builder at the time, was in charge of the construction, which was completed in 1901–2. Various alterations have taken place – in 1905 five rooms were added and in 1945 the wooden tower was added.

4 Marine Memorial A Berlin sculptor, Mr A M Wolff, was responsible for the design of this memorial dedicated to the First Marine Expedition Corps, who took part in the suppression of the Herero Uprising of 1904–5. The Marine Infantry from Kiel commissioned the work and the unveiling ceremony took place in July 1908.

5 Trendhaus This house was restored to its former glory in 1974 by the architect Cooke and is another reminder of the beautiful colonial architecture, with the window boxes giving it an almost Bavarian appeal.

Carl Schmidt drew up the plans for Robert Stolz, but they were not followed too carefully – originally only the left half of the building appeared in the plans.

6 and 7 Altona House and Ludwig Schröder House The Woermann Shipping Line opened an office with living quarters in Swakopmund in 1900. Three years later an additional house was added onto the Woermann Line headquarters on the corner of Post and Moltke Streets. Today this building is known as Ludwig Schröder House.

In time it once again became necessary to provide additional accommodation and Altona House in Moltke Street, designed by Friedrich Höft, was built in 1904–5 as an extension to the Woermann Line headquarters. The extension incorporated a signal tower and an attic gable, to break what might otherwise have been a monotonous façade.

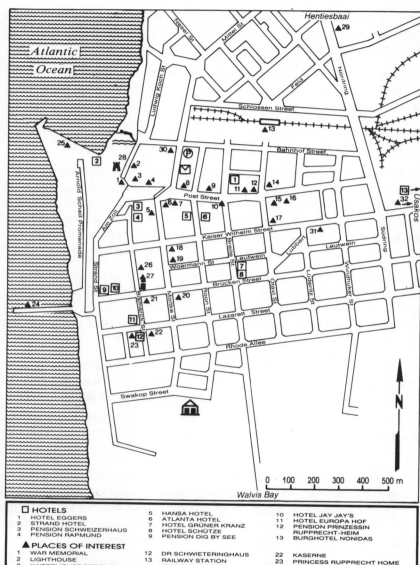

□ **HOTELS**

1	HOTEL EGGERS	5	HANSA HOTEL
2	STRAND HOTEL	6	ATLANTA HOTEL
3	PENSION SCHWEIZERHAUS	7	HOTEL GRÜNER KRANZ
4	PENSION RAPMUND	8	HOTEL SCHÜTZE
		9	PENSION DIG BY SEE

10	HOTEL JAY JAY'S	
11	HOTEL EUROPA HOF	
12	PENSION PRINZESSIN	
	RUPPRECHT-HEIM	
13	BURGHOTEL NONIDAS	

▲ **PLACES OF INTEREST**

1	WAR MEMORIAL	12	DR SCHWIETERINGHAUS	22	KASERNE
2	LIGHTHOUSE	13	RAILWAY STATION	23	PRINCESS RUPPRECHT HOME
3	KAISERLICHES BEZIRKS-		(BAHNHOF)	24	THE MOLE
	GERICHT	14	GERMAN SCHOOL	25	THE MOLE
4	MARINE MEMORIAL	15	DEUTSCHE EVANGELICAL	26	WOERMANN HOUSE
5	TRENDHAUS		LUTHERAN CHURCH	27	ART GALLERY
6	LUDWIG SCHRÖDER HOUSE	16	PARSONAGE	28	MUSEUM
7	ALTONA HOUSE	17	VILLA WILLE	29	PRISON
8	OLD POST OFFICE	18	KAISERHOF	30	OLD MAGISTRATE'S BUILDING
9	ST ANTONIUS HOSPITAL	19	DEUTSCHE-AFRIKA-BANK		(ALTES AMTSGERICHT)
10	ADVERTISING PILLAR	20	HOHENZOLLERN BUILDING	31	OMEG HOUSE
11	OLD GERMAN RESIDENCE	21	MC HUMAN FLATS	32	MARTIN LUTHER

8 Old Post Office The telephone exchange and post office as well as staff were housed in this beautifully symmetrical building, which opened its doors to the public on 1 April 1907. Initially there were 120 post-boxes. Public entrance was through the centre door, while side doors to the stairways gave access to the staff quarters on the first floor. Redecker was the architect and the Bause brothers were responsible for the construction. The building served as the post office for sixty years, until modern offices, just around the corner, came into use on 31 March 1967. Since then the municipality has occupied the building.

9 St Antonius Hospital Still serving the town as a hospital today, the building's foundation stone was laid in March 1907 and it was opened in March the following year. Otto Ertl was the architect. The hospital was staffed by sisters of the Franciscan order and continued to serve as a Catholic hospital until 1987.

10 Advertising Pillar In approximately 1905, when Swakopmund had 1 433 civilian residents, advertising pillars (or in German, *Litfass-Saulen*) became part of the town scenario. These pillars were named after the printer E Litfass, who introduced the idea in Berlin in 1855. Businesses, including shops and hotels, displayed notices on the pillars, on which official notices could also be read. This is the only original pillar remaining in the town.

11 and 12 Old German Residence and Dr Schwieteringhaus Although you will pass a fair number of old German-style houses on your tour, it is worth stopping here at these attractive buildings. The imposing corner house served as doctors' consulting rooms from 1910.

13 Railway Station (or Bahnhof) This is one of the finest station buildings in southern Africa and was declared a national monument in 1972. The ornate building was designed by C Schmidt and built in 1901, in a style locally termed "*Wilhelminischer Stil*".

14 German School In June 1912 a competition was announced by the town councillors for a building to house both the government and municipal secondary schools. Although separate entrances and classrooms were required, facilities such as the library would have to be shared. The building was designed by Emil Krause, an employee of Metje & Ziegler, who won the competition, and it was completed in October 1913. It harmonises beautifully with the baroque style of the Lutheran Church and parsonage across the road.

15 and 16 Deutsche Evangelical Lutheran Church and Parsonage In 1906 Dr Heinrich Vedder established a Lutheran congregation in Swakopmund and on 18 December 1910 the foundation stone of the church, designed by Otto Ertl, was laid. Ertl was undoubtedly influenced by the re-awakening of the baroque, during the Wilhelminische era (1884–94), which stems back to the Reichstag building in Berlin. F H Schmidt was the builder and the church was consecrated on 7 January 1912.

The three bells in the bell tower were imported from Apolda, Germany, where they were cast by Franz Schilling.

The parsonage, adjacent to the church, was completed in July 1911.

17 Villa Wille Karl Hermann Wille, a notable builder of the town, built this elegant house for himself. Although a single-storey house was originally planned, it was built as a double-storey, and its style is in keeping with the nearby church complex. Building was completed in 1911, but sadly Wille was killed in action in 1915. It is said to be one of the most beautiful buildings in Swakopmund and the decorated tower is particularly eye-catching.

18 Kaiserhof Situated on the corner of Kaiser and Moltke streets, the Hotel Kaiserhof was opened in May 1905. Sixteen rooms on the first floor could accommodate 26 guests, with additional accommodation available on the ground floor. Fire destroyed the hotel in 1914 but it was later rebuilt, without the first floor, and housed the Standard Bank for some time.

19 Deutsche-Afrika-Bank On 4 October 1909 the Swakopmund branch of the Deutsche-Afrika-Bank opened here for business. Constructed by the firm of F H Schmidt, the design incorporated several neo-classical tendencies – seen here in SWA/Namibia for the first time. The exterior of the building has not changed over the years and has been occupied by First National Bank (then the National Bank and later Barclays) since 1922.

20 Hohenzollern Building The Hohenzollern building, with its almost exotic decorations, is undoubtedly the finest example of Victorian baroque in Swakopmund. It was built in 1905/6 for Hermann Dietz as a hotel. Later it housed the municipal offices and at present (1988) the building is being renovated and converted into sectional title flats.

Originally a cement cast of Atlas adorned the building. As it was feared that Atlas would collapse, the cast was removed and was replaced with a fibreglass replica during the renovations.

21 M C Human Flats This building was erected by the Bause brothers, who built several smaller houses in Swakopmund from 1902 onwards. These buildings are mostly characterised by their interesting façades, which were decorated with a wide variety of embellishments.

As you continue down Bismarck Street, three old houses dating back to early this century create a quaint street scene.

22 Kaserne The Second Railway Company landed in Swakopmund in October 1904 to construct the wooden jetty and in 1906 completed the Kaserne, which served as barracks. Built in an L-shape, the Kaserne is similar in design to the Alte Feste in Windhoek and Fort Namutoni in Etosha and although the massive building has every appearance of a fort, the fact that it was built as a barracks is evidenced by the large windows.

The crests of the then German Federal States remain on the wall of the entrance hall, as well as a plaque commemorating those killed in action.

Today the Kaserne is a youth hostel, although it served as a school for nearly half of this century, from 1927 to 1975.

23 Princess Rupprecht Home Now a private hotel housing a maternity home in one wing, the original building dates back to 1901 when the German authorities erected a military hospital. It was built at the coast as the sea air was considered healthy for convalescents.

24 Jetty The original wooden jetty, which was completed by April 1905, was badly damaged by spring floods and the borer worm *Teredo navalis*, which found its way into the structure, necessitating the continuous replacement of pillars. The jetty was in service until 1914 and was dismantled in 1916 by the South African occupation forces. Construction on the solid iron pier commenced in 1911 but was brought to a standstill with the outbreak of World War I and, as the necessary harbour facilities were available at Walvis Bay, the South African government did not continue with its construction. Although it was originally planned to be 640 m long, the jetty stretches into the Atlantic Ocean for only 262 m. It was equipped with five cranes to assist with the unloading of ships, as well as a railway line.

Over the decades the pounding sea took its toll and by the mid-1980s it became necessary to close the jetty as the structure was becoming unsafe. However, some R220 000 was raised by the *Save the Jetty Fund*, which was established to raise funds to replace and repair the iron supports, and the jetty was officially re-opened on 13 December 1986. At the entrance to the jetty two drill bits used in the construction of the old pier have been mounted.

25 The Mole This was an attempt by the early settlers to construct an artificial harbour and the government architect, F W Ortloff, was responsible for planning the project. Construction began in September 1899 and five months later the 375 m pier was completed. Unfortunately, no consideration was given to the currents along the coast and by July 1904 a sandbank had formed at the entrance, restricting movement of vessels to high tide. By 1906 the harbour had silted up, creating a sheltered beach, but by then the wooden jetty was in use. Today pleasure boats are launched from the Mole.

Other places of interest

The following buildings have not been included in the walking tour as you would probably be in need of a rest before being able to appreciate them fully. However, during your Swakopmund visit do make an effort to visit them.

26 Woermann House Pride of Swakopmund is Woermann House, with its elegant, panelled walls and stucco ceilings. The building was designed by Friedrich Höft as headquarters for the Damara and Namaqua Trading Company. The building was completed in 1905 and the "Damara Tower" was incorporated as a look-out post for ships and ox-wagon trading "spans" from the interior. In 1909 the building was acquired by the trading firm of Woermann & Brock and became known as Woermann House. After World War I the building was used as a school hostel for 40 years and gradually fell into an almost derelict state, but it was restored in the mid-seventies and now houses the Public Library. The view from the top of the tower gives you a good perspective of the town. Woermann House is open Monday to Thursday from 9h00 to 12h00 and 15h00 to 19h00, and on Friday and Saturday from 9h00 to 12h00.

27 Art Gallery The art gallery, where an interesting collection of work by local artists can be seen, is also housed in Woermann House. Visiting hours from April to August are between 16h30 and 18h30 daily and from September to March between 17h00 and 19h00 daily.

28 Museum A visit to the Swakopmund Museum, housed where the original German customs house stood when Swakopmund was a port, should not be missed. The museum is open daily from 10h30 to 12h30 and 16h00 to 18h00. Exhibits include the flora and fauna of the Namib Desert, several marine dioramas, a historical section with items dating from the German period and an excellent ethnological collection. An 80 page book, *Swakopmund – A Chronicle of the Town's People, Places and Progress*, can be purchased at the museum and will give you an invaluable insight into the town.

29 Prison One could easily pass this building without realising that it is in fact a jail. This is perhaps because Otto Ertl designed it to provide staff accommodation in the main building, with the side buildings serving as the actual jail. Heinrich Bause was responsible for the construction, which was completed in 1909 at a cost of 121 500 Mark. You may not photograph this building as it still serves its original purpose.

30 Old Magistrate's Building (Altes Amtsgericht) You will notice that this building, with its gables and turrets, is very similar to the jail (29). They were both designed by Otto Ertl and built during the same period (1907–8), so this is hardly surprising. The building was intended as a school but lack of funds resulted in the state completing it and using it as a magistrate's court. It was later used as school hostel and in 1972 the municipality took over the building and restored it to provide additional office space.

31 OMEG House Early in the 1900s Swakopmund was connected to the interior by way of two separate railway lines – the Otavi Line to the Tsumeb copper mine and the State Line to Karibib and later Windhoek. Each line had its own terminal building, namely the state railway station (13) and OMEG House. OMEG House served as goods sheds for the Otavi Minen-und Eisenbahn-Gesellschaft until 1910, when the state took over the line (the State Line, running parallel to the Otavi Line for 145 km, had proved uneconomical so it was closed). However, as the Otavi Line's terminal buildings in Kaiser Wilhelm Street (OMEG House) proved inadequate the railway line was diverted and the state station was used as the ending point of the railway line.

You will be impressed by the simplicity of this building; note the roof, which is typical of the period.

32 Martin Luther Just outside Swakopmund, alongside the B2, the strange sight of a steam engine surrounded by a few palm trees may attract your attention. Stop and look at "Martin Luther", a steam tractor acquired from a Mrs Dehne in Halberstadt, Germany, and imported in 1896 to haul supplies from the port through the desert to the interior. Unfortunately it was not long before the tractor broke down and was abandoned because of high repair costs. It was subsequently given its odd name because of the famous statement made by Martin Luther: "Here I stand; God help me, I cannot do otherwise," which aptly described the position of the tractor. Martin Luther was restored and declared a national monument in 1975.

Hansa Brewery If you are interested in visiting the brewery, telephone Hansa Brauerei at (0641) 5021.

Excursions from Swakopmund

Welwitschia Drive
(see p 141)

Walvis Bay
(see p 157)

Sandwich
(see p 142)

Swakopmund salt works/oyster farm and Cape Cross

The salt works are situated about 7 km north of Swakopmund off route 76 (C34) to Terrace Bay. Production of the concentrated brine at the salt pan, known as Panther Beacon, began in 1933 but by 1952 the salt source was exhausted. Seawater has since been pumped into open evaporation and concentration ponds from which the crystallised salt is removed with mechanical scrapers. Impurities are removed in the washing and screening plant and the salt is graded to different grain sizes. It is used mainly in the plastic, chemical and paper industries. A visit can be arranged by telephoning (0641) 2611.

Situated on part of the salt works is the Richwater Oyster Company, which started cultivating oysters in 1985. About half a million seed oysters are imported every month from Guernsey in the English Channel. Initially the oysters are cultivated in a shallow, 35 ha seawater pond under ideal conditions – not only does the pond offer protection, but the water temperature is warmer. In addition, the seawater along the west coast is highly nutritious. The oysters are kept in the nursery pond until they reach about 25 mm in length, when they are transferred to open shelves in cement channels.

Continue for 113 km northwards to Cape Cross. Refer to p 164 for further information.

Rössing Uranium Mine tour

(see p 124)

Nonidas

About 12 km east of Swakopmund on the B2, on the Swakop River side of the road, is the unusual sight of a castle-like building. This is the Burg Hotel Nonidas, built around the ruins of a police station and customs post dating back to 1892.

If the history of the German occupation of the country interests you, do call in at the hotel. The bar forms part of the old building and photographs of the ruins before restoration are on display. Numerous museum pieces in the bar add to its authentic atmosphere and take you back to the turn of the century.

Camel rides

On a farm situated between Burg Hotel Nonidas and the Rössing Country Club, on the B2 east of Swakopmund, is a camel farm run by Mrs Elke Erb. Here you have the opportunity of riding a camel, a transport method which was fairly common at the turn of the century for police patrols.

The camels graze along the Swakop River during the morning and rides are conducted in the afternoon at an hourly rate. For the more adventurous, an overnight trip into the desert can be arranged. You are, however, responsible for your own meals and must take your sleeping bag along.

For more information contact Mrs Erb, Tel (0641)–363.

Fishing and pleasure boat cruises

Details can be obtained from the *Namib I* office in Woermann House (26).

Excursions offered by tour operators in Swakopmund

Various day and half-day tours of Swakopmund, the Namib Desert and places of interest close by are conducted by: DAS (Desert Adventure Safaris), Tel 4072, and Charly's Desert Tours, Tel 4341.

Where to eat in Swakopmund

- *Atlanta Hotel Restaurant*, à la carte,
  6 Roon Street, Tel 2360
- *Bacher's Braai*, steaks and traditional South African dishes,
  9 Moltke Street, Tel 4806
- *Bayern Stubchen*, German home cooking,
  13 Garnison Street, Tel 4793
- *Brücken Café*, breakfast, cakes, light meals (closed at night),
  Brücken Street, Tel 5328
- *Burg Hotel Nonidas Restaurant*, German traditional dishes,
  12 km out of Swakopmund on B2, Tel 4544
- *Café Anton*, breakfast, cakes, light meals (closed at night),
  corner of Bismarck and Post streets, Tel 2419
- *De Kelder*, à la carte,
  Moltke Street, Tel 2433
- *Erich's Restaurant*, fresh fish and steaks,
  21 Post Street, Tel 5141
- *Europahof Hotel Restaurant*, à la carte,
  Bismarck Street, Tel 5061
- *Grünen Kranz Hotel Restaurant*, à la carte,
  Breite Street, Tel 2039

- *Hansa Hotel Restaurant*, à la carte,
  Roon Street, Tel 311
- *Jay Jay's Restaurant*, traditional South African dishes,
  8 Brücken Street, Tel 2909
- *Kücki's Pub Restaurant*, steaks, seafood and pizzas,
  22 Moltke Street, Tel 2407
- *La Trattoria*, Italian dishes,
  Breite Street, Tel 2826
- *Putensen Café*, cake, light meals (closed at night),
  Kaiser Wilhelm Street, Tel 2034
- *Schutze Hotel Restaurant*, à la carte,
  Breite Street, Tel 2718
- *Strand Hotel Restaurant*, à la carte,
  The Mole, Tel 315
- *Western Saloon Restaurant*, steaks and seafood,
  Moltke Street, Tel 5395

WALVIS BAY

Walvis Bay, 35 km south of Swakopmund along route 2/1, is a haven for those seeking the outdoors and offers opportunities ranging from angling to a variety of watersports and bird-watching.

The town takes its name from the bay on which it is situated. Originally named Golfo de Santa Maria da Conceicao by Bartolomeu Dias on 8 December 1487, it was later renamed Golfo da Baleia, translated as "bay of the whales".

On account of the absence of fresh water near the coast, nearly three centuries passed before foreign powers began to show an interest in Walvis Bay. In 1784 American whalers began using the bay and when rumours of mineral deposits and large herds of livestock in the interior reached the Cape, the vessel *Meermin*, under the command of Captain F Duminy, was sent out to annex the bay. On 23 January 1793 the Dutch flag was raised in the bay, but two years later, when the Cape was occupied by the British, Captain Alexander was sent to Walvis Bay and established Britain's claim to the enclave.

Settlers from the Cape arrived in 1844 and in the following year Heinrich Scheppmann of the Rhenish Mission Society landed in the

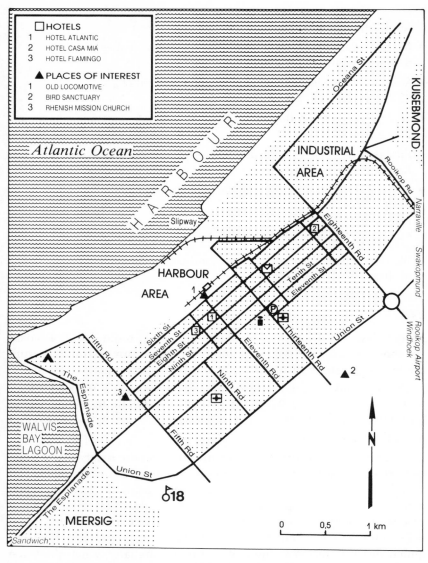

bay and established a mission station for the Topnaar Khoikhoi at Rooi-
bank on the Kuiseb River.

The British viewed the increasing involvement of the Germans in
Greater Namaqualand and Damaraland after 1840 as a threat to their

interests and the enclave was formally annexed on 12 March 1878 by Commodore Richard Dyer. In 1884 the administration of the enclave was transferred to the Cape Colony and in 1910 Walvis Bay became part of the Union of South Africa. Between 1922 and 1977 the enclave was administered as if it were part of the mandate of South West Africa, but since 1977 the 1 124 km² enclave has been administered as part of the Cape Province.

Watersports

The lagoon, reached by following Tenth Street into Dias Street and then turning into the Esplanade, is ideal for wind-surfing and boating. There is a slipway for launching pleasure craft near the angling club-house and visiting yachtsmen are welcome to call at the yacht club at the end of the Esplanade.

Angling/Crayfishing

Fishing regulations applicable to the Walvis Bay enclave differ in some respects from those applicable to the rest of the SWA/Namibia coast. Regulations do change from time to time and it is, therefore, advisable to obtain information about the latest regulations from the inspectors of the Directorate of Sea Fisheries at 204, 2nd Street, Walvis Bay, Tel (0642) 5968. Anglers will find the angling column in the Friday edition of the *Namib Times* useful.

Only four crayfish, with a minimum carapace length of 85 mm, may be caught per person per day in the Walvis Bay enclave. The open season stretches from 1 November to 30 June.

Angling and the collection of bait is not permitted in the lagoon.

Paaltjies, about 12 km south of Walvis Bay, is a popular angling spot in the enclave and is renowned for steenbras and cob catches, especially between December and April. It is reached by following a well-sign-posted hard-surface salt road from Meersig along the lagoon and through the salt works. Toilets have been provided here.

There are also several angling spots along the coast between Swakopmund and Walvis Bay – the rocky beaches are ideal for galjoen.

Picnicking

The Langstrand (Long Beach) resort, 16 km north of Walvis Bay, comprises several tidal pools, a jetty, shaded picnic places, ablution facilities and caravan sites. The Walvis Bay enclave is administered as part of South Africa and these amenities are reserved for whites.

Day camping facilities have also been provided at Dune Seven – the highest easily accessible dune in the enclave. As no water is available here, visitors must take their own supply along. The dune is reached by turning onto route 36 (C14) (signposted Rooikop and Windhoek via Gamsberg Pass) at the traffic circle as you enter the town. The turnoff to the dune is signposted to the left about 8 km on.

Bird-watching

The lagoon offers excellent opportunities for bird-watching – the Walvis Bay wetland is the most important coastal wetland for birds in southern Africa and the second most important in Africa. The wetland comprises three complementary sections – the lagoon, other intertidal areas and the saltworks, each of which supports at least a third of the birds at some stage in the tidal or annual cycle. The number of birds counted in 1977 and between 1983 and 1987 varied between 37 000 and 79 000.

The importance of the Walvis Bay wetland is underlined by the fact that it supports 50 per cent of the world population of chestnutbanded plover (247), as well as 3, 2 and 1 per cent of the world population of greater flamingo (96), lesser flamingo (97) and curlew sandpiper (272), respectively. In addition, the wetland supports 18 per cent of the southern African race of the blacknecked grebe (7).

Walvis Bay supports about 42 per cent of the total southern African population of greater flamingo and 60 per cent of the subcontinent's lesser flamingo population.

Of the resident species the kelp gull (312) is generally the most numerous, numbering up to nearly 3 000. Other residents include white pelican (49), greyheaded gull (315) Hartlaub's gull (316), Caspian tern (322), swift tern (324) and Damara tern (334).

It has been estimated that more than 120 000 wading birds which breed in northern Eurasia migrate to overwinter along the Namib Coast and, of this number, some 43 000 (37 per cent) could use the Walvis Bay wetland. Numbers of Palaearctic migrant waders during counts varied between 2 400 and 34 000, with curlew sandpiper (272) and sanderling (281) the most numerous species. Other fairly common species include grey plover (254), knot (271) and little stint (274).

Among the uncommon occurrences are Terek (263) and marsh (269) sandpipers and whimbrel (290). The most common resident wader is the whitefronted plover (246), while small numbers of blackwinged stilt (295) and African black oystercatcher (244) also occur.

Other species which are rare along the Namib Coast, but recorded at the wetland, are European oystercatcher (243), Mongolian (250) and sand (251) plovers, as well as common redshank (268).

The vast amount of information which has been collected over the past few years is the result of a project initiated in 1983 by the Walvis Bay Round Table Organisation. This project aimed to (a) determine the importance of the lagoon for purposes of conservation and recreation, (b) determine the effects of past development on the system, (c) draw the lagoon to the attention of the people of Walvis Bay, and educate them to appreciate and understand the importance of the system, and (d) monitor the system so that any changes might be quickly identified and investigated. The 1983 count was conducted by two researchers of the FitzPatrick Institute of the University of Cape Town, while subsequent counts were carried out by members of the SWA Bird Club in conjunction with two ornithologists of the DNC.

Those keen on bird-watching will also find the Bird Paradise at the municipal sewage disposal works alongside the Rooikop Road well worth a visit. It is reached by turning left into Thirteenth Street when entering the town from the Swakopmund side. The turnoff to the Bird Paradise is signposted 500 m further on. Some of the tracks in the sanctuary are unsuitable for sedan cars, so take care! Water is no longer pumped into the ponds closest to the road, but into those further inland. This was done in an attempt to reduce the problems experienced with mosquitoes by the residents on the outskirts of the town.

Old narrow-gauge railway and locomotive

About 5 km east of Walvis Bay, on route 36 (C14), an embankment on your left will attract your attention. Here the weathered remains of a section of the narrow-gauge line built during the previous century to transport goods to and from the harbour and the terminal at Plum, east of the dunes, can be seen. The railway line was built before the arrival of a locomotive and at first mules were used to cart the goods on the line. The terminus at Plum comprised a galvanised iron store, two-roomed cottage and stable. In 1899 a locomotive was landed in Walvis Bay and after it had been used in the harbour for some time, attempts were made to use it on the line between Plum and the harbour. Shifting sand, however, posed a constant threat and the line was eventually abandoned – in March 1905 the acting magistrate of Walvis Bay reported: "Some abandoned sections of the line are for more than half a mile buried under mountains of sand 30 feet high." The locomotive, named *Hope*, is a national monument and can be seen in front of the Walvis Bay railway station in Sixth Street.

Rhenish Mission Church in 5th Road

Dating back to 1880, the church was one of the first 12 buildings in Walvis Bay. It was originally prefabricated from timber in Hamburg in 1879 and erected in the harbour area the following year. Increased activity in the harbour resulted in the building being dismantled and moved to its present site. To prevent wood rot from setting in, it was decided to plaster the outside walls. The first service was held in 1881 and the church served its original purpose until 1966. It was subsequently saved from being demolished through the interest taken in the building by the Walvis Bay Lions Club.

Salt works

The 3 500 ha salt works south of Walvis Bay produces 95 per cent of the salt required by the chemical industry in South Africa – about 400 000 tons of salt are produced annually. Visits to the salt works can be arranged by telephoning Walvis Bay 2376.

The harbour

Permits to visit the commercial port (and the fishing harbour), which has a synchro-lift capable of lifting vessels of up to 2 000 tons, can be obtained at the offices of the former SA Railway Police station between the South African Transport Services office block and the Harbour Café off 13th Road. Remember to bring a passport or identity document along.

Excursions from Walvis Bay

Excursions from Walvis Bay are the same as those from Swakopmund. (See p 154.)

Day and half-day excursions offered by tour operators

Gloriosa Safaris (Tel 2455) conducts various day trips to the Namib.

NATIONAL WEST COAST TOURIST RECREATION AREA

The huge National West Coast Tourist Recreation Area stretches northwards for some 200 km from just outside Swakopmund to the Ugab River and inland for about 50 km. The area is managed as a tourist area and is especially popular with surf anglers.

Facilities for camping and caravanning are available at regular intervals along the coast. The Mile 4 caravan park, 7 km north of Swakopmund, comprises 480 camping and caravan sites and is said to be one of the biggest caravan parks in southern Africa. Amenities include communal kitchens with gas stoves and washing-up facilities, eating areas and ablutions. Camping sites managed by the DNC have been established at Mile 14, Jakkalsputz, Mile 72 and Mile 108. Amenities include communal facilities and ablutions. There are filling stations only at Mile 72 and Mile 108, which each have a kiosk open during the SWA/Namibian school holidays. Water must be purchased at a minimal fee and there is a small fee for hot showers.

There are only two holiday villages north of Swakopmund – Wlotzkas Baken and Hentiesbaai. Wlotzkas Baken, a small fishermen's village, is 32 km north of Swakopmund. Named after a local fisherman of that name and a survey beacon on the coast, this quaint fishermen's village began developing in 1936. There are no facilities here.

Hentiesbaai, 42 km on, is a popular summer resort. The town was named after a Kalkfeld businessman, Hentie van der Merwe, who first visited the freshwater spring on the beach in 1929. The abundance of game, game birds, good fishing and fresh water brought him back year after year and as the popularity of the bay grew it became known as Hentiesbaai. The first permanent inhabitants started settling here in the early 1950s and today the town comprises about 1 000 houses, several shops, garages, a hotel and a post office. Unless private accommodation is hired, you will have to stay in the hotel, as there is no caravan/ camping site.

Sport facilities include tennis courts, a squash court and a 14 hole golf course with grass greens and tees and sand fairways.

The West Coast Tourist Recreation Area is renowned for its excellent catches of galjoen and cob, as well as steenbras, geelbek and blacktail. Anglers unfamiliar with the coast are advised to consult the *Namib Times*, which publishes an angling column in the Friday edition, and should acquaint themselves with the size and bag limitations (obtainable from the Directorate of Sea Fisheries in Swakopmund).

The stretch of coast between the ocean and the main road between Swakopmund and Terrace Bay is the breeding ground of 70 per cent of the world population of the Damara tern (334). Their total breeding population worldwide is estimated at less than 2 000 pairs, 90 per cent of which breed along the Namib coast. The Damara tern is listed as rare in the *African Red Data Book – Birds* and in South Africa the number of breeding pairs is estimated at about 120.

These birds migrate from areas as far north as the Gulf of Guinea, arriving along the Namib Coast during September and October. To avoid predation of eggs and chicks by kelp gulls (312), crows, black-backed jackal and brown hyaena, nests are made on gravel plains and salt pans between 2 and 5 km away from the coast. Unfortunately their breeding season overlaps with the peak tourist season and their breeding habitat is being seriously threatened by irresponsible offroad driving.

Cape Cross Seal Reserve

The reserve, 70 km north of Hentiesbaai along the coastal road, is open daily from 16 December to the end of February, and from 1 March to 30 June only on Saturdays, Sundays, public holidays and during the Easter holidays, between 08h00 and 17h00. From 1 July to 15 December it is open between 12h00 and 16h00 on Wednesdays only. Permits are obtainable at the office in the reserve.

Cape Cross is the home of between 80 000 and 100 000 Cape fur seals – one of three species of fur seals occurring in southern Africa. The colony becomes a hive of activity when the bulls start arriving in mid-October to establish their territories which are vigorously defended against any would-be intruders.

About 90 per cent of the pups are born within a 34-day period beginning late November/early December, after a gestation period of nine months. The pups congregate in dense "pods" while their mothers are feeding out at sea and are vulnerable to predation by black-backed jackal and brown hyaena, which are responsible for a mortality rate of about 25 per cent. On her return from feeding at sea the cow locates her pup by a combination of scent and call.

Males have an average body mass of 187 kg, while the average female weighs 75 kg. Research has shown that they eat the equivalent of about 8 per cent of their body mass per day. Roughly half their diet consists of pilchards and maasbankers, while octupuses, squid and other cephalopods constitute about 37 per cent, and rock lobsters and crustaceans make up the remaining 13 per cent.

The seals at Cape Cross have been exploited for their skins and other products for almost a century. In 1895, the year in which the slaughtering of seals at Cape Cross began, 2 500 skins were exported and over the years the industry has experienced mixed fortunes. Today the seal population is controlled by culling.

Cape Cross was also of economic value for another reason – guano. Towards the closing years of the last century a start was made with guano collecting and in 1895 6 000 tons of guano were collected from the "islands" in the salt pans south of Cape Cross. The concession holders, the Damaraland Guano-Gesellschaft, faced numerous problems, however, and by 1902 guano production had decreased to only 500 tons and the operation closed down the following year.

Cape Cross is also of historic interest as it was here that the first European, Diogo Cão, set foot on the coast of SWA/Namibia in 1486. He erected a limestone cross or *padrão* with a height of just over 2 m and weighing about 360 kg here, and in time the site became known as Cape Cross.

For 407 years the *padrão* withstood the ravages of nature until, in January 1893, Captain Becker of the German cruiser *Falke* removed the cross and took it to Germany. A granite replica of the *padrão* was made in 1894 on instructions of Kaiser Wilhelm II and erected at Cape Cross on 23 January the following year. In addition to the original Portuguese and Latin inscriptions on the column and pedestal, a German coat of arms and an inscription in German were added on the column. The inscription reads: "Erected at the command of the German Kaiser and

King of Prussia Wilhelm II in 1894 on the site of the original which was weathered by the years."

Visitors to Cape Cross will be surprised to see two crosses. In 1974 the area around the site was landscaped and a number of paved circles and semi-circles were built on different levels, each of which depicts part of the history of Cape Cross. These circles and semi-circles represent the Southern Cross – symbolic of the direction in which Cão sailed.

Facing the terraces, the cross erected on the instructions of Kaiser Wilhelm II is to your left (on the highest level). The stones on the terrace have been laid out to form a star, symbolic of the importance of stars to early navigators. A second cross is to be seen on the second terrace to the right. This cross, an authentic replica of Cão's *padrão*, was commissioned by the National Monuments Council and unveiled in 1980 on the very spot where the original *padrão* stood. Based on a plaster cast of the original, the cross was cut from Namib dolerite – the same hard stone which forms the rocky outcrop at Cape Cross. The dolerite was obtained in the vicinity of Trekkopje, 77 km east of Swakopmund. The Cão family crest and the wording of the original *padrão* in Latin, Portuguese, English, Afrikaans and German can be seen on the other three levels.

SKELETON COAST PARK

The Skeleton Coast Park is renowned for its excellent fishing and the solitude it offers those seeking to escape everyday life.

The Ugab River is its southern boundary, and the Skeleton Coast Park stretches north to the Kunene River. The park, which covers over 1,6 million ha, is divided into two zones – the southern section, between the Ugab and Hoanib rivers, and the northern section, which lies between the Hoanib and Kunene rivers. The latter has been demarcated as a wilderness area and tourists can only enter the area by means of exclusive fly-in safaris conducted from Windhoek by the concessionnaire.

Terrace Bay can be reached either from Swakopmund along the main coastal road (44, D2301, D2302 [C34]), passing through the Ugab Mouth Gate (369 km), or via the Springbokwasser Gate (D3245 [C39]) when approaching from Khorixas (276 km).

The park was opened for through-travel in October 1988, but travellers must be in possession of the necessary permit, which must be obtained from the DNC reservation office in Windhoek or its information office in Swakopmund. This route is especially convenient for those travelling from Swakopmund to Etosha National Park and vice versa.

Tourist facilities in the southern section comprise only a caravan/ camping site at Torra Bay and fully inclusive accommodation at Terrace Bay. Torra Bay is open to the public only during the December/January school holidays, when basic commodities can be purchased at a kiosk. Petrol is obtainable at Torra Bay during this period only. At Terrace Bay, 51 km north, fully inclusive hotel-type accommodation, including three meals a day, freezer space and under-cover parking is available. There is also a filling station and a shop.

Visitors to the Skeleton Coast Park should note the following important points:

- Unless you have a reservation you will not be permitted to enter the park at Ugab River or Springbokwasser.

- You must cross the Ugab River before 15h00, while the checkpoint at Springbokwasser must be passed before 17h00.

- You may not leave the main road except in the demarcated angling area at Terrace Bay.

The coast is a fisherman's paradise and hundreds of anglers are attracted to its fishing waters year after year. Of the four species most eagerly sought, cob and galjoen account for more than half the annual catch, the balance being made up mainly by steenbras and blacktail. Mackerel, white stumpnose and strepie are caught occasionally. Although there are exceptions to the rule, galjoen and blacktail are caught in turbulent surf off rocky areas. Cob and steenbras, on the other hand, favour sandy or pebble beaches or are taken from rocks in deeper water.

The park is characterised by its level coastline, only occasionally broken by scattered rocky outcrops. The southern section consists of flat gravel plains, but north of Terrace Bay high dunes occur in the immediate vicinity of the coast.

The vegetation between the Ugab and Huab rivers falls within the Central Namib Type (Giess Vegetation Type 2), while that north of the Huab is classified as Northern Namib (Giess Vegetation Type 1). The vegetation is relatively sparse, the most common species being dollar-

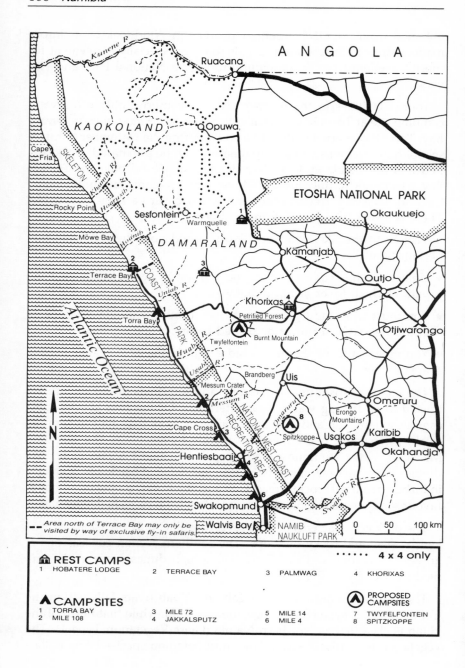

Area north of Terrace Bay may only be
visited by way of exclusive fly-in safaris.

🏛 REST CAMPS			••••• 4 x 4 only
1 HOBATERE LODGE	2 TERRACE BAY	3 PALMWAG	4 KHORIXAS

▲ CAMP SITES			ⒶPROPOSED CAMPSITES
1 TORRA BAY	3 MILE 72	5 MILE 14	7 TWYFELFONTEIN
2 MILE 108	4 JAKKALSPUTZ	6 MILE 4	8 SPITZKOPPE

bush (*Zygophillum stapfii*), brakspekbos (*Z. simplex*), and occasional stands of ganna (*Salsola* species).

Mammals are not represented in large numbers along the coast and are mainly limited to black-backed jackal, brown hyaena, and occasionally Cape fur seal. A rather unusual inhabitant is the "coastal" lion. Numbering possibly less than five individuals along the entire Skeleton Coast, these lions are uniquely adapted to utilise coastal resources and have been observed feeding on whitebreasted (55) and Cape (56) cormorants, seals and even beached whales. They do not inhabit the coast permanently, but use the river courses which cut through the Namib to move between the coast and the interior.

Far more prolific is the birdlife occurring along the coast. As a result of the nutrient-rich ocean off the Skeleton Coast Park, large numbers of sea- and shore birds are attracted and some 47 species of these habitats have been recorded. The coastline and wetlands attract at least 17 Palaearctic migrants and to date over 203 bird species, excluding 23 off-shore and 10 outside their normal limits, have been recorded in the park.

During a survey of the coast and adjacent wetlands between Cape Cross and the Kunene River in November/December 1981, a total of 44 000 birds of 64 species were counted. Waders made up 13 800 (30 per cent) of this number, 90 per cent of which were Palaearctic migrants.

The most common waders along the coast are whitefronted plover (246), grey plover (254), turnstone (262) and sanderling (281), while curlew sandpiper (272) and little stint (274) are abundant at wetlands.

Among the uncommon sightings are Terek (263), marsh (269), whiterumped (277) and broadbilled (283) sandpiper as well as whimbrel (290).

As a result of the sensitivity of the Namib coast substrate and the inaccessibility of the northern part of the Skeleton Coast Park, visitors are only allowed into this area under the guidance of a private concession holder. Enquiries can be made with Mr L Schoeman, Skeleton Coast Safaris, P O Box 2195, Windhoek 9000, Tel (061) 51269 (home). The safaris are fully inclusive of return flights, meals, drinks (including alcoholic beverages) and accommodation. Groups must consist of a minimum of 4 persons and preferably not more than 12. Persons who are unable to form their own groups can be integrated into groups, but need to be flexible so far as safari dates are concerned.

Fly-in safaris lasting five days depart from Windhoek throughout the year. After a lunch and refuelling stop in Swakopmund, the flight continues northwards along the coast to the base camp near Sarussas, halfway between Rocky Point and Cape Frio. The base camp is situated outside the wind- and fog-belt, about 20 km inland.

The base camp is centred around a huge *omumborumbonga* or leadwood (539) tree which serves as the camp's lounge-cum-dining room.

Guests are accommodated in small igloo tents equipped with stretchers, foam-rubber mattresses, sheets, pillows, sleeping bags and lamps and torches. Washbasins are also provided, while each tent is equipped with a chemical toilet.

Although animals such as springbok, gemsbok, black-backed jackal and ostrich are frequently encountered, the emphasis of the safari is on the singular beauty and strange solitude of the area. During the safari, trips by four-wheel-drive vehicle are undertaken to various places of interest such as the Hoarusib Canyon, the seal colony at Cape Frio, Rocky Point, the roaring sand dunes and various waterholes in the area.

This safari can be extended to include the Etosha National Park. Guests can either make use of Skeleton Coast Safaris or make their own arrangements for Etosha.

9 KAOKOVELD

DAMARALAND - background

Damaraland is a name that conjures up visions of indescribable beauty, rugged mountain scenery and uniquely adapted animal life. Stretching for about 600 km from north to south and about 200 km from east to west, this untamed landscape has something to offer all visitors, whatever their interests.

Well-known features such as the Spitzkoppe, Petrified Forest, Burnt Mountain and Twyfelfontein are managed by the DNC as conservation areas and are accessible by sedan cars along well-maintained roads.

However, with the exception of the above-mentioned tourist attractions, all of Damaraland, between the Hoanib River in the north, the Usakos/Swakopmund tarred road in the south, the Skeleton Coast Park in the west and the boundaries of the measured farms in the east, has been divided into five concession areas. To enter these areas it is necessary to obtain the required permit and to comply with whatever conditions are applicable in the area.

When exploring these areas it is necessary to be totally self-sufficient in respect of all your requirements. Punctures are a frequent occurrence, and in addition to two spare wheels and a pump (!) it is advisable to carry a tyre repair kit, tyre leavers, gaiters and spare tubes. Petrol is available at Uis Mine, Khorixas and Palmwag Lodge, but not at Sesfontein.

Parts of Damaraland are renowned for their wildlife, which has adapted to survive in arid conditions. However, during the late 1970s and early 1980s the elephant and black (hook-lipped) rhino populations in Damaraland and Kaokoland (together known as the Kaokoveld) came under severe pressure as a result of illegal hunting. It has been estimated that elephant numbers in the Kaokoveld decreased from 300–400 in 1970 to a mere 70 in 1982.

In mid-1983 a system of local game guards appointed by area headmen was started by conservationist Garth Owen-Smith, who headed the Namibia Wildlife Trust's Damaraland/Kaokoland Desert Project, in conjunction with the legendary nature conservator Chris Ayre. By the end of 1985 over 60 people had been convicted of illegal hunting and the system is considered one of the world's most successful anti-poaching operations.

In 1986 Garth-Owen Smith conducted a census to determine the numbers of black rhino north of the veterinary fence. A total of 34 adult rhino and 17 calves were counted, while the number of sub-adult rhino was estimated at between 10 and 17. Identity files based on sex, age, horn size and shape, ear marks and spoor size were compiled on each adult rhino that could be positively identified.

Studies on the feeding behaviour of the black rhino showed that they have the ability to eat plants such as _Euphorbia virosa_ which has strong chemical defences against herbivores, while welwitschia (21.1) are lightly browsed wherever they are available. Although there are numerous waterholes, the rhinos range so widely that they may travel up to 25 km at night, often over extremely rocky terrain, to reach water.

The area is also known for its elephant population, which numbered about 158 north of the veterinary fence during a DNC census in July/August 1986. These elephants are often referred to as desert or desert-dwelling elephants – a term which has given rise to much controversy. According to some scientists, these elephants do not constitute separate populations, but are simply Etosha elephants which seasonally follow their age-old migration patterns. Another viewpoint is that three distinct elephant populations can be identified. The eastern population, which lives in an area with a rainfall of 250–300 mm per year, migrates freely to and from the Etosha National Park, Owambo, and sometimes into the Outjo district. The transitional population moves seasonally in a mainly north-east/south-west direction and infrequently makes contact with the eastern and western populations. Their home range lies in the 150–200 mm rainfall zone. The western population, also referred to as the desert-dwelling elephants, lives in the westernmost part of the Kaokoveld in the northern Namib Desert, an area which receives less than 150 mm of rain per year. According to Mr Slang Viljoen, who did his Masters degree on the distribution of larger mammals in the Kaokoveld, these elephants inhabit this area permanently and there is no contemporary or historical record of a movement eastwards.

These elephants normally travel 25 km per day, but distances of up to 70 km per day between food and water sources are known. During the dry season they can go without water for up to four days and unlike elephants elsewhere in Africa do not uproot trees. Comparisons of aerial photographs taken in 1963 and 1983 of the Hoanib River, where the largest concentration of desert-dwelling elephants occurs, showed a negligible decline in the number of large trees, from 2,38 to 2,33 per ha. However, it has been found that *Acacia* seeds that have passed through the digestive tract of an elephant have a germination success rate of up to 57 per cent compared to natural germination of 12 per cent. Research in the Hoanib River revealed that this method of seed dispersal and germination exceeded the "destruction" of ana trees (159) by far. Other animals inhabiting the area also benefit in a number of ways. During periods of drought, seeds in elephant dung are an important source of food for birds such as guineafowl, francolin and rock pigeon. In addition, branches that are out of reach to other browsers are broken off by the elephants. Another interesting point is that the removal of branches and leaves reduces the transpiration surface of trees, which probably enables them to survive on less water during dry periods.

In order to obtain more information about the movement of the elephants, six in Damaraland and three in the Etosha National Park were fitted with radio collars, which are monitored by satellite, in August 1987. A bull marked in Etosha was plotted 30 km south of Ruacana Falls in February 1988, while an elephant was plotted east of the Grootberg within a week after being fitted with a radio collar south of Palmwag.

KHORIXAS

Khorixas, the administrative centre of Damaraland, is ideally situated for those wishing to explore well-known tourist attractions such as the Petrified Forest, Twyfelfontein and the Burnt Mountain. It can be reached along route 76 (C35) via Uis, from Outjo along route 65 (C39) or from Torra Bay via routes 3245 and 2620 (C39). Other possibilities are the direct route from Kamanjab (route 76 [C35]) or route 2620 from Kamanjab via Grootberg and Palmwag and route C39 (previously 2620).

The rest camp in Khorixas offers a variety of accommodation ranging from two-bed units to luxury bungalows, as well as a caravan/camping site. All bungalows are equipped with linen, towels and a fridge. Other facilities include a swimming pool, shop where basic foodstuffs can be purchased, restaurant and bar. The turnoff is signposted (Khorixas Ruskamp) about 2 km west of the town, the rest camp being reached about 1 km on.

Formerly known as Welwitschia, Khorixas now takes its name from the Khoekhoen name for a tree with edible berries resembling currants. It has been suggested that the name refers to the real mustard tree (622), locally also known as the *waterbos*.

The D2620 (C39) to Torra Bay follows the Aba-Huab River valley, passing through numerous river courses which should be approached with caution following rains as the road surface could be washed away.

PETRIFIED FOREST

The turnoff to the Petrified Forest, where dead and "living" fossils – petrified trees and the welwitschia (21.1) – can be seen, is signposted (Versteende Woud) 42 km west of Khorixas on route D2620 (C39).

Despite being declared a national monument in 1950, this unusual feature suffered badly at the hands of souvenir hunters over the years. Following negotiations between the DNC and the Damara Representative Authority the area was transferred to the Directorate in 1986. Plans are underway to provide picnicking facilities and a control post at the site to prevent its further destruction. It is prohibited to remove or damage even the smallest piece of petrified wood!

The "forest" lies on a small sandstone rise and covers an area of about 800 m by 300 m in the Aba-Huab River valley. The trees occur in sandstone of the Ecca Group, a subdivision of the Karoo Sequence, and are about 260 million years old. The name "Petrified Forest" is a misnomer as the trees did not grow where they are found. It has been suggested that they were carried here by floodwaters, following the onset of warmer climatic conditions after the Dwyka glaciation. Evidence for the assumption that the trees grew somewhere else is the fact that no roots or branches are present and only trunks are found. The trees were uprooted and transported by rivers to their present site where they were stranded on sandbanks or shoals. This is inferred from the position of many stems which are orientated parallel to each other. Subsequently they were embedded in sand also deposited by the rivers. Opal-filled cracks in the logs suggest that many of the trees dried out before being embedded in the sand.

The trees were deposited in an oxygen-depleted environment, preventing decay of the organic material and creating ideal conditions for petrification. Silica-rich water penetrated the logs, filling the cells, bark and other parts, where silica precipitated. This long process went together with the hardening of the sediments into sandstone. Nearly 200 million years later, after uplift of the whole area, erosion in a warm, often arid climate removed the overlying rocks and finally exposed the petrified trees. Remnants of at least 50 trees can be seen on the plateau – some only partly exposed, while others reveal their full length. A good indication of the size of these trees is a partially exposed trunk with a length of more than 30 m and an estimated circumference of 6 m. The growth rings and the texture of the bark are so well preserved that one can easily mistake the petrified trees for logs.

The trees belong to the Gymnospermae or cone-bearing plants (ie the seeds are not enclosed in an ovary, as is the case with Angiospermae or flowering plants). Gymnospermae are a group of plants which flourished between 300 and 200 million years ago. Present-day members include the cycad order and the yellowwood, pine, cypress and welwitschia families. Research has shown that the trees were not of a single species and at least four varieties have been identified.

WONDERGAT, TWYFELFONTEIN, ORGAN PIPES AND BURNT MOUNTAIN

Approaching from the Brandberg in the south along route 76 (C35), these well-known tourist attractions can be reached by turning onto the D2612, 21 km north of the Ugab River. There are, however, several farm gates along this route, which carries relatively little traffic. The usual approach is to take the turnoff, signposted Twyfelfontein/Verbrandeberg, 78 km west of Khorixas on the D2620 (C39).

Wondergat

Just less than 11 km along route D3254 you will notice a track (suitable for sedan cars) branching off to the right. It is worthwhile making a detour here to the Wondergat, about half a kilometre on. It is thought that this deep hole was created when a subterranean river swallowed a chunk of earth. On one side it is possible to scramble onto a ledge from where you have a better view into the hole – take care, however, of the loose gravel around the edges.

Twyfelfontein

Returning to the D3254 you turn right, continuing for 3 km before turning right onto route D3214 (signposted Twyfelfontein and Ver-brandeberg 13 km). A short distance on you cross the Aba-Huab River, where the DNC plans to establish a campsite for visitors to this fascinating area. The campsite is due to be completed in 1990–91. The turnoff to Twyfelfontein is signposted a few kilometres on, and after another 4 km the road ends at a parking area.

On account of the heat and the fact that the rock engravings are difficult to see in direct sunlight, it is advisable to explore the area either early in the morning or in the late afternoon.

The slopes above Twyfelfontein are littered with large rock slabs, with the largest known concentration of Stone Age petroglyphs in SWA/Namibia. The barren surroundings and rock-strewn slopes seem a most unlikely place for any human habitation, but there is a small spring near the base of the hill and this has been providing water to animals for thousands of years. The water and abundance of game also attracted Stone Age people and indications are that they inhabited the area for centuries. Crude stone tools, the remains of huts and pottery revealed that they were later followed by Damara people, who named the fountain *Ui-Ais* – The Spring. In 1947 the farm was acquired by Mr D Levin who named it Twyfelfontein (Doubtful Fountain), as he doubted whether the spring could have supported man and game for thousands of years.

Following the report of the Odendaal Commission in 1964, the farm was incorporated into Damaraland, but as no control was exercised (despite the site having been declared a national monument in 1952) some of the engravings were unfortunately damaged, defaced and in some instances even removed. Twyfelfontein is now managed by the DNC as a conservation area.

The area is criss-crossed by numerous paths and you will be well advised to allow at least two hours for your visit. Some rock slabs have as many as 70 engravings, while a rhino measuring 92 cm by 55 cm and an elephant measuring 57 cm by 73 cm are two of the larger individual engravings to be seen.

To date more than 2 500 engravings have been recorded. The engravings have not been dated, but occupation of the area has been dated at between 370 BP and 3450 BP. According to Willcox (1984, p.163) six time phases are represented. The earliest stage consists of signs and symbols which have been cut up to 19 mm deep into the rock. Among these are circles, circles with dots, circles with rays, and concentric circles. Antelope and their spoor were portrayed in the second stage by rubbing and polishing within the outline. Petroglyphs of the third stage were engraved by cutting the outline and then chiselling away the space within. This stage has the best naturalistic animals. A variety of animals such as rhino, antelope, giraffe and ostrich were depicted in the fourth stage, which continued to use the same technique as in the third stage. Naturalistic and semi-naturalistic animals were still represented, together with their spoor, but subjects also included cattle and sheep. An interesting petroglyph in this stage includes a lion with an unusually long, L-shaped tail with a paw-print at the end and spoor instead of paws. Also interesting about this engraving is that the lion appears to have been depicted with an antelope in his mouth. Closer inspection, though, will reveal that the lion is not actually eating the antelope but that the engravings have been superimposed. There are at least 30 other engravings on this slab, including snakes, giraffe, rhino and zebra. The final (sixth) stage is represented by caricature-like animals, including cattle, which have been scratched or pecked into the rock.

With the exception of the northern Cape, where engravings and paintings occur together, the rock art in South Africa is generally geographically separated, which has given rise to the belief that the two art forms were the work of different peoples. In SWA/Namibia, however, both forms of art often occur together, for example Twyfelfontein and the Grosse Dom Ravine in the Brandberg. Unlike the rock engravings, which were executed on exposed slabs, the paintings at Twyfelfontein were executed in a number of small rock shelters.

An analysis of over 16 400 rock engravings in SWA/Namibia by Scherz (1975, p. 290) has revealed that animals, animal spoor and abstract motifs (geometrics) are represented more or less equally, namely 32, 31, and 30 per cent, respectively. Human figures only comprise 2 per cent. By comparison, an analysis of 14 059 rock paintings shows that humans comprise nearly 66 per cent of the subjects portrayed and animals 32 per cent (Scherz, 1986, pp. 30, 56, 57).

Organ Pipes and Burnt Mountain

Returning to the D2354, you turn right, travelling along a wide valley, with the Burnt Mountain, better known as the Verbrandeberg, to the right. The Organ Pipes are reached 3 km beyond the turnoff. At present the formation is not signposted, but you will notice a small gorge on your left, soon followed by a parking area on a rise, also to your left. Leave your car here and descend along one of the paths leading to the Organ Pipes, a mass of perpendicular dolerite pillars.

The Organ Pipes are exposed in a gorge roughly 100 m long and reach a maximum height of 5 m. They were formed by the intrusion of a dolerite sheet, a plutonic rock, into the shales of the Karoo Sequence some 120 million years ago. Owing to shrinkage during cooling the dolerite split at joints in angular columns and was subsequently, after erosion of the overlying rocks, exposed to weathering.

From the parking area you have an excellent view of the Burnt Mountain, part of a 12 km long east/west trending mountain rising some 200 m above the surrounding landscape. During the heat of the day the mountain is stark and uninviting but in the early morning and late afternoon it presents a kaleidoscope of colour.

The Karoo shales and limestone which formed the mountain were deposited some 200 million years ago. About 120 million years ago, doleritic lava intruded these rocks, causing wide-ranging contact metamorphism. Hydroxides and oxides were released, giving the rocks their distinctive coloration. Closer examination of the rocks reveals an amazing variety of colours ranging from red to orange, black, grey, white and purple. A puzzling feature of the area is a slag-like heap of rock and coarse-grained sand about 1 km east of the Organ Pipes. Also to be seen here amongst the rocks are a few small, straggly welwitschia (21.1) plants.

SPITZKOPPE

The imposing Spitzkoppe, also known as the Matterhorn of South West, can be reached from Usakos, Hentiesbaai or Uis. If you are travelling along route B2 between Usakos and Swakopmund, take the turnoff signposted Henties Bay/Uis, 23 km west of Usakos. The road forks 1 km on – take the road signposted Hentiesbaai (route 1918) and continue for 17 km before turning onto route 3716. The turnoff to the Spitzkoppe

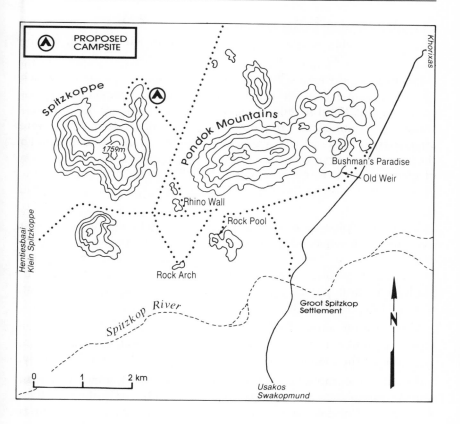

is reached after another 10 km. From Hentiesbaai, travel west along route 1918 for about 103 km before turning onto route 3716. To get to Spitzkoppe from Uis, turn onto route 1930 (signposted Usakos) 1 km east of Uis. Continue along this road for 75 km before turning onto route 3716.

Rising some 700 m above the flat surrounding plains, the Gross Spitzkoppe have a height of 1 829 m. Immediately to the east lies the dome-shaped Pondok Mountain and about 10 km south-west the 1 572 m high Klein Spitzkoppe.

The Spitzkoppe area is managed as a conservation area by the DNC. No facilities are provided at present and if you decide to camp here you will have to be totally self-sufficient. The DNC, however, plans to provide campsites at Spitzkoppe in 1989–90, in which case it will be necessary to obtain a permit, so do make enquiries before setting off.

Geologically the area is correlated with the Damara Sequence, which dates back some 750–500 million years, and the younger Karoo Sequence, about 350–150 million years. During the break-up of the Gondwana supercontinent in Karoo times, large parts of southern Africa were affected by volcanic activity. Vast amounts of lava were extruded through the Spitzkoppe, Brandberg and Erongo volcanoes. Subsequent intrusion of granitic magma formed the Spitzkoppe, Brandberg and Erongo complexes, while erosion has exposed the granitic cores to form typical *inselbergs*.

The Gross Spitzkoppe was first ascended in 1946, up the north-west face, and then remained inviolate for 10 years before the second successful ascent. In 1960 a three-man party pioneered a route up the precipitous west face. The mountain, parts of which are graded as E-grade, remains popular with local as well as overseas mountaineers and is a good day's climbing.

There are numerous fascinating rock formations in the area – one which resembles a shark's mouth, a natural rock arch and many more – so consult the map and do take time to explore the area thoroughly.

As with other mountains in the arid areas of the country, early man found a refuge here and rock paintings can be seen at Bushman's Paradise in the Pondok Mountain, east of the Spitzkoppe. The paintings are reached by following the road which leads along the base of the Pondok Mountain. On your way to Bushman's Paradise you will notice a small stone dam which is filled by runoff from the smooth boulders when the area occasionally gets its meagre rainfall. This dam was built near the turn of the century when the Deutsche Kolonialgesellschaft für Südwestafrika established a farming operation on the farm Spitzkoppe in 1896. Further along you reach the ascent to Bushman's Paradise. A chain handhold helps you to scale the steep, smooth slope and from the top you have a good view of the surrounding, usually barren, plains. After a short scramble up to the right at the end of the chain handhold you will find yourself looking down into a surprisingly vegetated amphitheatre, a botanist's dream, and can now make your way to the large overhang at the head of the amphitheatre. Despite the fact that the paintings under the overhang were declared a national monument as long ago as 1954, they have been defaced extensively by vandals and there is not much left to see. However, it is still worth visiting the site just to view the area, which you are sure to agree has been aptly named "Bushman's Paradise".

If you have sufficient time there is an alternative descent which requires about three-quarters of an hour. Continue down the valley, following a fairly well-worn path which leads to a narrow cleft on your right. Care should be exercised here, although this short section is not difficult or dangerous. After a short while you reach the base of the Pondok Mountain, from where you turn right and continue to the starting point, about 10 minutes on.

UIS

Uis is usually by-passed when travelling via Omaruru along route 64 (C36) to the Brandberg and beyond. The mining village, which has retained the Khoekhoen name meaning "place of brackish water", is reached 125 km after leaving Omaruru.

All of the town's amenities, including the shop and petrol station, are controlled by the mining company IMCOR. Petrol can be obtained between 07h00 and 19h00 Monday to Saturday and between 10h30 and 16h30 on Sunday. A small supermarket/bakery is open between 08h30 and 14h00 and between 17h00 and 19h30 Monday to Saturday and from 11h00 to 14h00 and 17h00 to 19h30 on Sunday.

As early as 1911 the presence of tin in the area was confirmed by a Dr Paul and in 1922 Mr Etemba Schmidt erected a mining plant in the Kartoffel River. But it was only in 1951, with the establishment of the Uis Tin Mining Company (SWA) Ltd, that mining was carried out on a large scale. However, ISCOR (the South African iron and steel giant) acquired the mining rights in 1958 and their subsidiary, IMEX, took over the mine. IMEX became known as IMCOR in 1966.

Visits to the mine, on weekdays between 09h00 and 15h00, can be arranged by telephoning the mine office at (062262) 22.

BRANDBERG

The Brandberg, in central Damaraland, offers a number of tracks to be explored by four-wheel-drive vehicle (see p 185) but the most popular

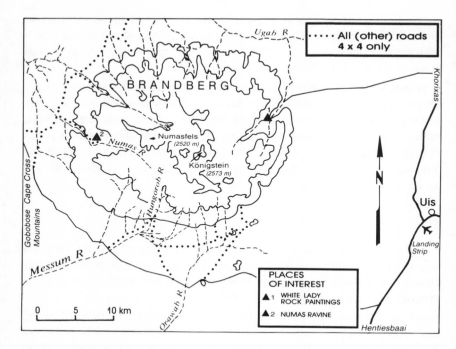

tourist attraction, the White Lady in the Tsisab Ravine, is accessible to sedan cars, provided you are prepared for a fairly strenuous walk of about three hours there and back.

As with other tourist areas in Damaraland, the Brandberg forms part of a concession area. Although no permits are required at present (1988), plans are underway to build a rest camp near the entrance to the Tsisab Valley, which will also control access to the Brandberg concession area. Other than the planned rest camp there are no accommodation facilities in the Brandberg.

A visit to the White Lady or any other ramble in the Brandberg is best accomplished either in the early morning or late afternoon, to avoid the mid-day heat, which can become unbearable. Also remember a sunhat, sunscreen lotion, and at least two litres of water per person.

The White Lady

From Uis, the White Lady is reached by following the Kamanjab road (route 76 [C35]) for 14 km, after which you turn left onto the road signposted Witvrou (Afrikaans for White Lady). The road ends 28 km on and from here a well-worn path marked with ochre-coloured antelope spoor leads you to the Maack Shelter – about 60–90 minutes' walk.

Following their climb of Königstein in January 1918 – the first successful ascent – Reinard Maack, a surveyor, Professor A Griess, a Windhoek high school principal, and Lieutenant George Schultze of Keetmanshoop "discovered" the paintings while resting on their descent.

Maack, who saw the paintings first, was convinced that they had definite Mediterranean characteristics. This interpretation was shared by the world authority on rock art, the Abbé Henri Breuil, who attended a joint British–South African Congress for the Advancement of Science at the University of the Witwatersrand in 1929. It was here that the Abbé was shown a watercolour copy of the painting made by Maack. Breuil believed the central figure to be that of a white woman. Thirteen years later, Breuil examined photographs of the paintings and, on showing them to a colleague, was told that the central figure was reminiscent of a young woman athlete of Cretan origin. Over the next few years the White Lady of the Brandberg became internationally known and for a considerable time the Mediterranean origins of the paintings were accepted, although not without criticism by some archaeologists. The acceptance of this theory has been attributed to the fact that archaeology during Breuil's time was centred in Europe. Africa was shrouded in a veil of darkness and southern Africa was regarded as an unlikely region for any innovations – hence any unusual discovery was immediately attributed to an external or foreign source.

Detailed research has led modern archaeologists to believe that the paintings represent indigenous people. Several interpretations on the local origin of the art and the sex of the figures have been advanced. According to these interpretations the absence of breasts and the presence of a bow are sufficient evidence to prove the White "Lady" to be male! Furthermore, the white colouring is thought to represent body paint, commonly used by medicine men.

Within a 1,5 km radius of the White Lady there are ten major and seven minor sites with rock paintings – including Jochmann Shelter, which takes its name from *Oberleutnant* Hugo Jochmann, who recorded the first rock paintings in the Brandberg here in 1909. Among the animals depicted are a snake with ears, a lion (a species seldom depicted in paintings in SWA/Namibia) and a 2 m long unidentified animal. Nearby is a cave with several excellent paintings of ostriches, while several of the shelters have good paintings of giraffes.

Several hundred other sites have been located on the massif, many of which were painstakingly traced by the rock art authority, Harald Pager, who spent nearly eight years in the Brandberg. Unfortunately, he died before he could complete his work here.

The mountain not only attracted Stone Age people, but also pastoralists. One of the most dense concentrations known of stone-walled sites associated with pastoral people in the central Namib is situated on the southern side of the mountain. There is clear evidence that these people retreated to the mountain plateau as the plains grasses began to wither. It has been estimated that while a herd of 100 sheep would need 500 ha of grazing to survive on the plains for six months, the same herd could in principle be maintained on 10 ha of the grassy plateau at the 2 000 m contour for a similar period.

The Brandberg massif consists of a granite core rimmed by Karoo sediments. The original volcano was active during Karoo times (about 180 million years ago) and following the volcanic activity large amounts of granitic magma intruded. Over many millions of years the sediments were eroded, laying bare the hard granitic core and carving a number of deep valleys into the massif, the most dramatic being the Tsisab Ravine in the north-east and the Numas Ravine in the west. Rain, extremes of temperatures and wind combined to weather the granite into large boulders, some of which fill the valleys.

On first impressions, you are likely to imagine that it would be impossible for animals to live in such a harsh environment. However, steenbok, restricted to suitable cover, gemsbok and springbok inhabit the plains surrounding the Brandberg, while the more rocky areas attract klipspringer and Hartmann's mountain zebra. These animals are dependent on a few perennial springs that rise in the lower reaches of some of the valleys. Leopard, black-backed jackal and aardwolf occur but are seldom seen because of their nocturnal behaviour. Dassie rats and elephant shrews can usually be seen scurrying amongst the rocks.

Two colourful birds occurring in the area are the rosyfaced lovebird (367) and Rüppell's parrot (365), which fly noisily between trees. Other species you are likely to spot include scimitarbilled woodhoopoe (454), redeyed bulbul (567), mountain chat (586), pririt batis (703) and dusky sunbird (788). Look out for the Herero chat (618), which only occurs in a narrow belt from the Naukluft Mountains to south-western Angola. Rock pigeon (349) and palewinged starling (770) are abundant.

THE NUMAS RAVINE

Those interested in rock paintings, as well as rambling, will find the Numas Ravine rewarding. Unfortunately, however, the final section of the road to Numas is not suitable for sedan cars.

From Uis, continue along the Henties Bay road (R76 [C35]) for 10 km before turning onto the road signposted Brandberg West (D2342). About 40 km further on you pass through the usually dry riverbed of the Messum, and after roughly 14 km be on the lookout for a fairly indistinct track turning off to the right. After another 2 km a track from the right joins up and 6,5 km further on the track splits, with the route to Numas continuing to your right for 4 km to the head of the valley.

From the end of the track it is a good 20 minutes' walk to the first paintings – a 1,5 m long python with a head of a large-eared buck, and a 0,9 m high giraffe. This site is situated on the north-facing wall of a granite koppie which forms an "island" between the river proper and the old sandy river terrace to the south.

Continuing up the valley, you soon pass a well-vegetated area in the riverbed, which holds water after good rains. A few large fig trees (*Ficus* species), rushes and an African star-chestnut (474) mark the spot. From here, keep to the right-hand side of the ravine and after another 20 minutes' walking you will come across a permanent spring which is surprisingly well concealed by vegetation.

It seems likely that this area was popular with the Stone Age inhabitants, who left numerous rock paintings on the boulders and in the overhangs here. Take your time exploring the area and your efforts will be well rewarded, as many of the finely executed paintings are still well preserved.

MESSUM CRATER

This geologically interesting formation is reached by following the track along the left-hand bank of the Messum (south of the D2342) which is crossed about 40 km after turning onto the D2342 from Hentiesbaai (route 76 [C35]) and is accessible with four-wheel drive only.

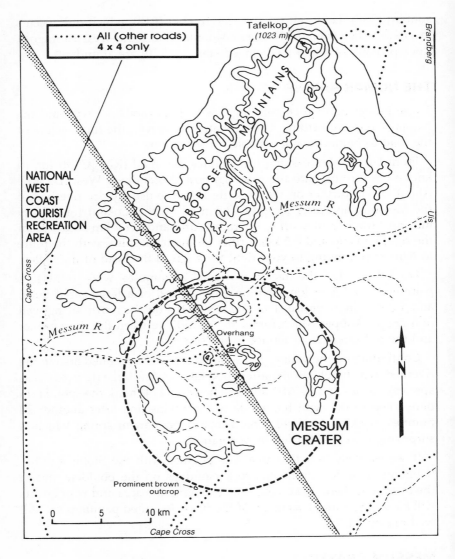

After following the river course for about 11 km the Messum takes a wide loop and here you leave the river, continuing in a south-westerly direction to reach the crater edge after about 8 km. Turn right and follow the course of a tributary of the Messum River, which is rejoined about 9 km on.

You now continue westwards along the Messum River and after 3 km you will notice a break in the crater rim with a track leading up into the crater. Once inside the crater you head south for about 7 km before the road veers right, heading towards a rocky outcrop. Here there are a number of well-protected sleeping places and an excellent view of the surrounding crater rim. The row of poles just west of the outcrop marks the eastern boundary of the National West Coast Tourist Recreation Area.

To continue your journey, take the track leading westwards and turn south just beyond the boundary poles. The track leads to an opening at the southern end of the crater. On leaving the crater you continue south for a short distance before heading for a prominent brown outcrop to the south-west. Stop here and tap the large round boulders which are surprisingly musical!

From here a well-defined track which crosses several river courses, slowing down progress, is followed for 32 km. Do not leave the track as it leads through lichen fields. These are particularly outstanding lichen fields and it is worth while stopping here to have a closer look at these incredible plants. You will be amazed by the way the plants unfold and change their colours when water is sprinkled onto them. (For more information about lichens, refer to p 142.)

The track joins the coastal route (C34) between Swakopmund and Terrace Bay just north of Cape Cross.

DOROS CRATER CONCESSION AREA

This area can be explored only by four-wheel-drive vehicle and is approached either via the Brandberg West Mine or the Goantagab Mine south-west of Khorixas. However, it is essential to obtain the necessary permit by writing to Mr Louw Schoeman, P O Box 2195, Windhoek 9000, Tel (061) 51269 (home).

The concession area covers the central-western part of Damaraland. Wildlife is not as abundant as in the Palmwag concession area (see overleaf), the main attraction being its fascinating scenery and interesting geology, which includes the Doros Crater, the Krone Canyon and a petrified forest. In the vicinity of Gai-ais fountain stones packed in circles provide evidence of an early settlement, while structures dating back to the German pioneering days are also to be seen.

Owing to the rugged nature of the terrain a two-vehicle party is advisable when exploring this area. In the past, indiscriminate off-road driving has disturbed the sensitive substrate and to prevent this from continuing unchecked, plans are afoot to restrict entry into the area. Inhabitants of SWA/Namibia will be allowed to explore the area in their own vehicles, but will be accompanied by a guide provided by the concessionnaire. Visitors from outside SWA/Namibia will, however, have to join a fully inclusive safari. A six-day safari which includes the highlights of the concession area as well as the Skeleton Coast Park is conducted by Louw Schoeman. The starting/ending point of the safari is Palmwag Lodge.

PALMWAG CONCESSION AREA

Palmwag Lodge, the base of the Desert Adventure Safaris (DAS) concession area in Damaraland, can be approached from Torra Bay along route 3245 (C39), from Khorixas along routes D2660 (C39) and D2620 and from Kamanjab via Grootberg along route D2620. The lodge is reached by turning off the D2620 onto route D3706, signposted Sesfontein, 37 km north of the Torra Bay junction. After about 5 km you pass through an animal disease checkpoint, the so-called Red Line, and less than 1 km on you reach the turnoff to the lodge.

Palmwag is a delightful rest camp situated amongst real fan palms (24) alongside a perennial spring in the Uniab River. Guests are accommodated in a number of three- and four-bedded reed huts. Cooking is not permitted inside the huts because of the fire hazard, but braaiplaces are provided, while breakfasts and à la carte lunches and dinners are served in the rustic restaurant where there is also a bar.

There are two swimming pools where guests can cool off during the heat of the day. For those who prefer to rough it, a campsite served by ablutions is available.

Although Palmwag can be reached in a sedan car, the numerous tracks that criss-cross the area are negotiable by four-wheel-drive vehicle only. Details about the concession area – including suitable roads and places worth visiting – can be obtained from the reception office at Palmwag. Remember to obtain the necessary permit before setting off into the concession area – failure to do so could result in a fine of R100 per person, a regulation which is strictly enforced.

Those who do not have the use of a four-wheel-drive vehicle may undertake a guided safari tailored to suit the party. The safari leader is well acquainted with the area and the service is very reasonably priced – especially if the costs can be shared amongst a number of visitors.

Among the sites well worth visiting is Van Zylsgat, a deep pool where the Uniab River has carved its way through the solid rock bed. Even months after the summer rains the pool is up to 6 m deep.

Animals you might spot are giraffe, springbok, Hartmann's mountain zebra, gemsbok, kudu and steenbok. The area is also renowned for its elephant and black (hook-lipped) rhinoceros, which are uniquely adapted to survive in an extremely arid environment.

Reservations can be made with Desert Adventure Safaris, P O Box 339, Swakopmund 9000, Tel (0641) 4072.

HOBATERE GAME PARK

Bordering on the north-western edge of Etosha National Park, Hobatere Game Park is best approached by taking the Ruacana road (route 67) (C35) from Kamanjab, the turnoff to the park being signposted about 70 km beyond Kamanjab.

Hobatere, one of five concession areas in Damaraland, caters for up-market visitors. The park is geared towards photographic safaris, but consideration is also being given to the possibility of hunting safaris in the near future. The emphasis is on personalised service and visitors can explore the park only with a professional guide. Animals to be seen include elephant, gemsbok, giraffe, kudu, springbok, black-faced impala, Hartmann's mountain zebra and lion, as well as several smaller mammal species.

Accommodation comprises a few rustic reed cottages and a maximum of about 30 guests can be accommodated. Reservations can be made with Mount Etjo Safari Lodge, P O Box 81, Kalkfeld 9000, Tel (06532) 1602.

WARMQUELLE

Approaching from the south along route D3706, the Hoanib River which forms the southern border of Kaokoland, is crossed 70 km out of Palmwag. After another 9 km you reach Warmquelle. Originally known as Warmbad, the settlement derives its name from the hot springs which rise here.

Turn right at the signpost indicating the turnoff to the school and follow the road, which bears to the left after about 100 m, for about half a kilometre to the springs, surrounded by large, shady fig trees. The temperature of the springs which surface here is considerably lower than that of other artesian springs in the country and the water is best described as lukewarm.

The first gardens were laid out below the springs by Dr C A Schlettwein, who purchased the farm Warmbad from a Mr Lambert at the turn of the century. Lambert originally bought the 4 000 ha farm from the Topnaar Khokhoi tribe of Captain Jan Uichanab for 2 000 Mark. Of this price 810 Mark was deducted to redeem the tribe's debt to Lambert while half the balance was paid directly to the tribe. The remainder of the purchase price was paid over to the magistrate in Outjo, who was authorised to use the money in the best interests of the tribe. The agreement between Lambert and Jan Uichanab was concluded in Outjo in October 1899 and approved in December the same year. In December the following year the resale of the farm to Schlettwein was approved.

Schlettwein bought the farm on the assumption that the young German colony would eventually build its own harbour, as Walvis Bay was a British possession. He was convinced that the harbour could only be built in the north of the country, but was unaware that his plans would eventually be thwarted by the cost of a connecting railway line and World War I. Schlettwein set about cultivating vegetables, tobacco, maize and lucerne, which were sold to the German *Schutztruppe* stationed at Sesfontein. The area under cultivation was gradually extended, making it necessary to use a better method of irrigation, and around 1910–11 an Italian named Oldani designed and built an aqueduct, the remains of which can still be seen.

After World War I the Warmquelle property was acquired by the government, in exchange for a farm in the Kamanjab district, in order to enlarge the reserve created for the Topnaar Khoikhoi.

Also worth visiting in Warmquelle is the Ongongo Waterfall, where you can have a much-appreciated swim, particularly after a long day's drive! From the aqueduct the fall is reached by following the track which continues past the school. After 3,7 km you reach a track branching off to the left – leave your car here if you do not have a four-wheel-drive vehicle and walk upstream for about 800 m. If you have a four-wheel-drive vehicle turn left, ignoring a turnoff to the right a short distance on, and cross the river. Follow the track on the western bank of the river upstream for about 1 km before turning right to the parking area in the riverbed. The waterfall and its interesting tufa formation are reached after a walk of about 200 m upstream. The area around the waterfall is part of a concession area controlled by Desert Adventure Safaris (DAS) and plans are afoot to develop day camping facilities and later also a campsite in the vicinity. Visitor numbers could therefore be restricted and before visiting the area enquiries should be made with DAS or with the Herero Administration, Private Bag 13180, Windhoek 9000, Tel (061) 38510.

SESFONTEIN

A few kilometres west of Warmquelle you pass into the Sesfontein enclave, which forms part of Damaraland. Sesfontein, which owes its name to six springs surfacing in the area, is reached about 31 km beyond the Hoanib River along route 3706.

The historic German military barracks in the settlement are a few hundred metres off the road and can be reached by taking the turnoff opposite the Elias amXab Primary School. Following the outbreak of rinderpest (cattle plague) in 1896 the German authorities established a number of control posts in the north of the country, Sesfontein being the most westerly. Later the post was also used to combat poachers and gun-runners operating from Angola. The construction of a road between Outjo and Sesfontein in 1901 made it possible to transport building material to Sesfontein for the building of a military station. During the years 1905–6 the station was converted into a fort which accommodated 40 soldiers and 25 horses. A 5 ha garden where wheat and dates were cultivated was laid out and some of the palm trees can still be seen today. The gardens were irrigated by an extensive system of furrows leading from a spring a few hundred metres west of the fort.

In 1909 Sesfontein ceased to be used as a military post, but continued to be occupied by three police officials until it was abandoned in 1914, without ever having seen military action.

Over the years the fort fell into disrepair until in 1987 the Damara Representative Authority started a restoration project, with a view to using the building as a museum and offices for the local tribal leaders. They also plan to encourage the traditional lifestyle of the people by giving demonstrations of tobacco rolling and local crafts at the complex.

KAOKOLAND

Covering some 48 982 km², Kaokoland is a mountainous tract of largely unspoilt wilderness, uniquely adapted wildlife and the home of the Himba, a tribe which has been little affected by civilisation. In recent years the area has become increasingly popular with tourists wanting to get off the beaten track.

After consulting the Department of Transport road map you might get the impression that Kaokoland is easily accessible along a network of district roads. However, be warned, none of these "roads" are signposted and as most are merely tracks which are hardly maintained, a four-wheel-drive vehicle is a must. A two-vehicle party is recommended on account of the rugged terrain and absence of any facilities.

Uncontrolled tourism in the area has given rise to concern and negotiations are currently under way to proclaim a nature reserve stretching from the Hoarusib River in the south to the Kunene River. The proposed reserve will adjoin the Skeleton Coast Park in the west and continue eastwards for 30–40 km.

Entry into the reserve will be controlled by the DNC, while tourism will be controlled by a private concessionnaire. Details of entry into the reserve and concession area had not been finalised at the time of going to press.

It is possible that the area between the Hoarusib and Hoanib rivers might also be controlled by a concessionnaire.

Should you plan a visit to these areas it is, therefore, advisable to make enquiries about entry conditions with The Secretary, Herero Administration, Private Bag 13180, Windhoek 9000, Tel (061) 38510.

There are three main routes to the area: from the north-east along the B1 and route 92 (C46) via Oshakati and Ruacana, from the south along route 67 (C35) via Kamanjab and Opuwo, or via the D3706 through Sesfontein. At present the route via Oshakati is not recommended because of the security situation in Owambo.

Once in the area there are numerous possibilities – the 1:500 000 topographical map 1711 (Opuwo) shows most of the major tracks, springs and settlements and is useful when planning your trip. Do not count on covering too great a distance in a day as progress is often very slow, with an average of 25 km per hour on a fairly good track. Remember that petrol is only available at Opuwo in the east and Palmwag in the south and you must, therefore, ensure that you have sufficient fuel.

Opuwo is the administrative seat of Kaokoland and the only town in the entire region. Here you can stock up with "luxuries" such as cooldrinks and fresh bread obtainable from the bakery next to the garage. Petrol is available from Monday to Saturday between 07h00 and 18h00 and on Sundays between 09h00 and 17h00. You must be totally self-sufficient in respect of all other supplies, including water. Although there are numerous springs marked on the topographical map, the water is often brackish. Also remember to take emergency spares as there are no garages other than at Opuwo.

Be aware of the dangers of camping in the wild, as lions are sometimes present in the area. If travelling up to the Kunene River, remember that there are crocodiles in the river. A mosquito repellent, as well as precautions against malaria, are essential in the summer.

District roads in eastern Kaokoland are excluded from the proposed game reserve/concession areas and remain accessible to tourists. This part of Kaokoland is extremely rugged and mountainous with challenging passes such as Robbie's Pass, between Sesfontein and Kaoko Otavi on the D3705, where it is often necessary for the motorist to repair stretches of the track.

Until as recently as two decades ago Kaokoland was a wildlife paradise. Large-scale poaching has, however, decimated animal numbers in the area, especially those of elephant and black (hook-lipped) rhinoceros.

Herds of elephant still roam in the Hoanib and Hoarusib rivers, but their existence is also threatened by tourists. Camps are often made at springs in the riverbeds, thereby preventing the animals from obtaining much-needed water, often at the end of a long journey. The animals are then forced to find another waterhole, which could be 30–40 km distant. When elephants are spotted tourists invariably attempt to get as close as possible to take photographs, and as the elephants often have no way of escaping from the narrow river valleys they are put under severe stress.

Giraffe are frequently seen along the river courses, which also offer food and shelter to kudu. Springbok, gemsbok and ostrich inhabit the plains, while the more mountainous areas are the habitat of herds of Hartmann's mountain zebra.

The entire region is the home of some 16 000 people, most of whom live in eastern Kaokoland. The Himba number about 6 000 people and small Himba settlements are passed fairly frequently when travelling through the area. Their beehive huts are made from saplings, usually mopane, which are covered with a mixture of mud and cattle dung. The settlements are often deserted as the pastoral Himba are continuously moving with their herds of cattle and goats in search of grazing. You might be fortunate enough to pass a family on the move – it is difficult to conceive that all their worldly possessions are wrapped in the animal skins carried with them.

The Himba women, with their bodies covered in butterfat to which powdered oxides have been added to protect their skin against the harsh climate, are physically striking. Married women can be distinguished by their leather headdresses and other adornments including necklaces, belts and wide copper bracelets. If you intend photographing these people take along supplies of sugar, maize meal and tobacco, which is much appreciated as payment – as there are no shops in the area money is of little use.

During their epic journey from the Transvaal to Angola between 1874 and 1881 the Dorsland Trekkers travelled through Kaokoland and settled for a short while at Kaoko Otavi and at Otjitundua, which is also known as Rusplaas. The ruins of a two-roomed house built at the Otjitundua fountain was declared a national monument in 1951. Several houses and a church were built at Kaoko Otavi, but after 18 months the trekkers moved further north. These structures have all since disintegrated.

10 NORTH

WATERBERG PLATEAU PARK

The turnoff to the Waterberg Plateau Park is signposted 27 km south of Otjiwarongo on route B1 (1/7). Here you turn onto route 101 (C22) and continue for 41 km before turning left onto route D2512, which is followed for 27 km to the entrance gate of the park.

The reddish brown buildings of the DNC rest camp have been designed to blend with the natural surroundings and can house 220 people in accommodation ranging from luxury bungalows to tourisettes (bus quarters). A number of caravan and campsites are also available. Other facilities include a licensed restaurant in the old German police station, a shop, swimming pool and a filling station.

The Waterberg Plateau Park is not geared towards "open" tourism and tourists are not permitted to drive freely in the park. Although there are several reasons for this, the main one is the management's concern to protect the country's rare and endangered species. Tourist roads will, understandably, interfere with this objective and visitors are, therefore, only allowed onto the plateau by way of tours in open, four-wheel-drive vehicles. However, to compensate for the restriction on travelling in the park, special hides built of stone and split poles and viewpoints from which animals can be observed have been constructed. In this way, the wilderness atmosphere of the park is preserved and visitors can enjoy their natural surroundings more fully.

One of the best ways of exploring this unique park is to undertake a wilderness trail. These trails are conducted on the second, third and fourth weekend of every month between April and November. The trails begin at 15h00 on Thursdays, ending early Sunday afternoon. No set routes are followed and the distances covered each day vary, but generally do not exceed 15 km.

Hutted accommodation, camp beds with mattresses, backpacks, all cooking and eating utensils, water-bottles and basic first aid equipment are supplied, which means that trailists only need to provide their own food and sleeping bags.

Only one group, which must consist of at least six people and a maximum of eight, is accommodated on the trail at a time. Advance reservations are essential and can only be made at the DNC office in Windhoek.

The Waterberg plateau rises about 200 m above the surrounding plains and reaches its highest altitudes on the western and southern sides. On the western edge is the Okarukuwisa Mountain. For the remainder, the plateau comprises an undulating landscape with deep sand and scattered granite koppies. Several fountains are found in the south and east of the park at the base of the perpendicular cliffs.

The vegetation on the plateau is a mosaic of tree and shrub savanna. The dominant species, with an average height of 10 m, are wild seringa (197), silver cluster-leaf (551) and several *Combretum* species. The grass cover comprises mainly tough sourveld grasses such as *Eragrostis* species and giant stick grass (*Aristida meridionalis*), which grows up to 1 m high.

The reserve was established primarily with a view to resettling and breeding rare and endangered species. To date roan, sable, tsessebe, buffalo and white (square-lipped) rhinoceros have been introduced. Also resident are blue wildebeest, common duiker, red hartebeest and eland. Other mammals found in the park include steenbok, klipspringer, wild dog, leopard, cheetah, black-backed jackal, side-striped jackal, caracal, lesser bushbaby and rock dassie. The DNC is considering the introduction of reedbuck, waterbuck and black (hook-lipped) rhinoceros in the near future.

Experienced bird-watchers can count on spotting anything up to 115 bird species in a two-day period covering all habitat types – plateau top, scree slopes, cliffs and the *Acacia* woodlands at the base of the plateau.

The only breeding colony of the Cape vulture (122) in SWA/Namibia is located on the cliffs of the Okarukuwisa Mountain and you might have the opportunity to see these birds gliding effortlessly over the surrounding plains in search of carrion. In the late 1950s the colony numbered about 500 birds, but as a result of the indiscriminate use of poisons by farmers and bush encroachment their numbers declined to less than 20 by 1980. In an attempt to save these birds from extinction

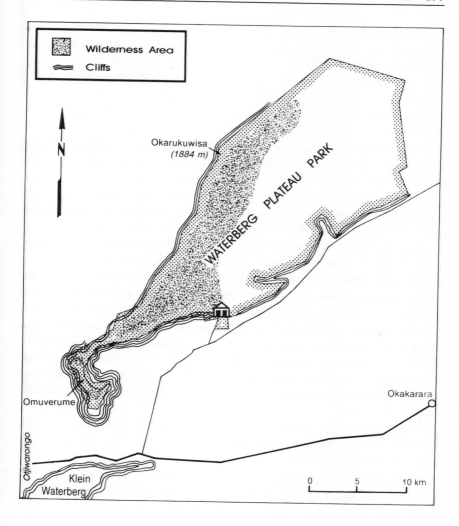

in SWA/Namibia the DNC has started a programme of controlled
burning to transform bush-encroached land under its control into the
grassland and parkland of the past and has also launched an extensive
education programme, especially among the farmers. In addition a
"vulture restaurant" has been established where carcasses of common
species such as gemsbok and kudu are placed on a weekly basis, enabling the birds to supplement their diet.

The park is also the of habitat of several bird species which are near endemic to SWA/Namibia, with 75 per cent or more of their world population occurring in this country. Among these you might spot Hartlaub's francolin (197), Rüppell's parrot (365), Bradfield's hornbill (461), Monteiro's hornbill (462) and rockrunner (662).

Prehistoric animals which roamed the area millions of years ago – the dinosaurs – left evidence in the form of their tracks in the rocks of the Waterberg. However, not only the dinosaurs left impressions here. The Stone Age people who lived at the foot of the mountain engraved animal spoor on rocks in the wilderness area.

Another fascinating aspect of the mountain is its geology. It is an erosional remnant of sedimentary rock deposited during the Upper Karoo Sequence some 200 million years ago. The foot of the mountain consists of mudstone and conglomeratic sandstone of the Omingonde Formation, overlain by fluvial and aeolian sandstones of the Etjo Formation, forming the plateau and the steep cliffs underneath the plateau.

The Karoo sediments of the Waterberg area are tilted towards the north-east and bounded in the north-west by a fault. The mountain was formed by a combination of this tectonic setting and the resistance of the Etjo sandstone against weathering. Rainwater seeps away into the Etjo sandstone on the plateau in joints and fractures until its further downward movement is hampered by the underlying impermeable Omingonde mudstone and it reappears in springs along the southern slope.

A Rhenish mission station was established at the Waterberg in 1873, but was destroyed seven years later during the Khoikhoi/Herero war and only rebuilt in 1891.

During the Herero Uprising of 1904 the deciding battle between the German Colonial Forces and the Herero took place at the Waterberg. Communication between the five German forces, with a combined strength of 96 officers, 1 488 men, 30 cannons and 12 machine guns, was severely hampered by the dense vegetation and it has been said that the victory of the Germans was largely due to the heliograph station which was erected on the plateau above Otjozonjupa. Reminders of this conflict can be seen in the graveyard near the resort office. The battle is still commemorated every year on the weekend either before or after 11 August by the Alte Kameraden, MOTHS, Pfadfinder, Boy Scouts and the Herero.

OTJIWARONGO

Otjiwarongo lies 174 km north of Okahandja on the main road to the north (B1). Originally known as *Kanubes* to the Herero, the name Otjiwarongo is said to mean "pretty place" or "place of the fat cattle" – an apt description, for the area is well known for its cattle ranches.

A Rhenish mission station was established here in 1891 after an agreement was signed between the Rhenish Mission and the Herero chief Kambazembi. In 1904 a military post was established at Okanjande, a few kilometres south of the present town.

To facilitate export of copper from Tsumeb, a railway line was built from Swakopmund to Tsumeb and the first train steamed into the newly completed station at Kilometre 378 on 2 April 1906 – recognised as the date on which Otjiwarongo was established. One of the three Henschel heavy-duty locomotives – No 40, built in 1912 and used until the 600 mm track was replaced by a 1,067 m track in 1960 – can be seen in front of the railway station in the town (also see p 122–3).

A tent was used for the first *Kaiserliche Postampt* (post office), which was taken into use on 20 April 1906, and a few months later, in September, the first shop was opened. The post office was replaced by a permanent building in 1907 and in the same year a police station was opened. The town received municipal status in 1939.

Visitors might be surprised to see a signpost on the town's main road indicating the turnoff to a crocodile ranch. This was, in fact, the first crocodile ranch to be established in the country. It is open daily between 09h00 and 18h00.

FOSSIL FOOTPRINTS – OTJIHAENAMAPARERO

On the farm Otjihaenamaparero, south-east of Kalkfeld, several dinosaur footprints can be seen. The turnoff to the site, which was declared a national monument in 1951, is signposted 29 km out of Kalkfeld on route 62 (D2414).

Several fossil tracks occur at Otjihaenamaparero, the most striking being those of a two-legged, three-toed dinosaur which can be followed over a distance of some 25 m. The age of these footprints in the red Etjo sandstone is estimated at between 150 and 185 million years.

Although there are no impressions of a tail, the dinosaur probably resembled a kangaroo, with powerful hind legs and comparatively short forelimbs. Unlike the kangaroo, however, these reptiles did not leap, but ran like an ostrich, and for a considerable time their footprints were mistaken for those of birds.

MOUNT ETJO SAFARI LODGE

Kalkfeld, 67 km north of Omaruru and 68 km south of Otjiwarongo, is usually approached along route 2/4 (C33). The village developed around the railway station established here in 1905 and was named by the Germans after the limestone deposits in the surrounding area.

Mount Etjo Safari Lodge can be reached either by turning off the B1 onto route 62 (D2414) (signposted Kalkfeld), 45 km north of Okahandja or by following route 62 (D2414) from Kalkfeld. The turnoff to the lodge is well signposted.

This private nature reserve offers highly personalised service aimed at upmarket visitors. Here guests have the opportunity to view game either from the comfort of an open safari vehicle under the guidance of an experienced ranger or on foot. Alternatively you can while the time away at one of the waterholes, where hides have been constructed. Special facilities are available for professional photographers.

Large mammals you might spot include elephant, white rhino, giraffe and several antelope species such as roan, eland, gemsbok, red hartebeest, blue wildebeest, kudu, nyala and the dainty Damara dik-dik. Predators include lion, cheetah and leopard. Not only is there the chance of spotting game, but bird-watchers will have a rewarding time at the waterholes.

The undoubted highlight of a visit to Mount Etjo is the close-up view you are afforded of lions feeding – an antelope carcass is used as bait and from a hide you have an excellent view of the lions feeding under floodlights.

Accommodation at Mount Etjo comprises hotel-type rooms situated close to a large dam. However, guests preferring to spend a night close to nature can sleep in a comfortable tree-top hide. Dinner is usually served in a large boma. For those in need of relaxation, an ideal place is the swimming pool, with its tranquil surroundings.

OTAVI

Otavi can be reached either from Otjiwarongo (181 km) or from Tsumeb (63 km) along the B1, or alternatively from Grootfontein (87 km) along the B8.

It has been suggested that the Herero named the spring around which the town grew *Otavi* as a metaphor linking the flow of the spring with a calf pushing against a cow's udder.

Just north of the town alongside the B1 an unobtrusive monument marks the spot where the capitulation conditions were signed on 9 July 1915 by General Louis Botha, Commander of the Union Forces, Dr Seits, Governor of South West Africa, and Colonel Victor Franke, Commander of the German forces in South West Africa. Although reference is often made to the Khorab Treaty and the Khorab Memorial, the treaty was in fact signed here, at Kilometre 500, and not at Khorab some 30 km north, where most of the German forces had gathered. The monument was erected in 1920 at the request of the then Governor-General of the Union of South Africa, Lord Buxton.

HOBA METEORITE

From Otavi the B8, leading to Grootfontein, traverses a valley between the Otavi Mountains and the Kupferberg, passing Gross Otavi, where Damara miners are known to have smelted copper during the 1800s and possibly even earlier. Kombat, formerly known as Asis, is reached some 40 km beyond Otavi.

Copper, lead and silver are produced at the Kombat Mine, which was operated between 1911 and 1925 by the Otavi Minen- und Eisenbahn-Gesellschaft. The mine was reopened in 1960 by Tsumeb Corporation Limited.

The turnoff to the Hoba Meteorite is signposted 54 km east of Otavi along route B8. Here you turn left onto route D2860, which is followed for 19 km before you turn onto route D2859. The turnoff to the meteorite is signposted a few kilometres on. It is also possible to approach the meteorite from Grootfontein along route D2860, the turnoff being signposted just west of Grootfontein on the B8.

Not only is the meteorite, which has a mass of 50 tons, the largest in the world, but its cuboid shape makes it unique amongst meteorites.

It was discovered in 1920 by one Jacobus Brits while he was hunting in the area. According to the statement he made soon afterwards, he "... spotted an unusual rock and sat on it. Only the upper portion was visible. The rock was black and was surrounded by limestone. I scratched it with my knife and saw it glistening. I chiseled a piece off and brought it to the South West Africa Company at Grootfontein. The director established that it was a meteorite." The statement can be seen in the museum at Grootfontein today.

It has been estimated that the meteorite struck the earth some 80 000 years ago. It consists of 82,4 per cent iron, 16,4 per cent nickel and 0,76 per cent cobalt. As a result of its relatively high nickel content, the meteorite is referred to as a nickel-rich ataxite. Other trace elements include carbon, zinc, copper, sulphur, chromium, iridium, germanium and gallium. The top surface of the meteorite is 295 cm x 295 cm, while its thickness varies from 55 cm to 122 cm.

It has been suggested that the meteorite broke up into several fragments during its journey through the atmosphere. Evidence for this is the two smooth side faces, which could be fracture planes. The possibility, therefore, exists that other fragments of the same meteorite could also have struck the earth and in the event of the break-up having taken place close to earth, they could well be in the close vicinity.

In 1921 the General Manager of the South West Africa Company, Mr T Tonnesen, sent a photograph and a letter giving details of the meteorite to the company's head office in London. According to the letter, the nickel content of the meteorite was estimated at about 10 kg. Mr Tonnesen informed his head office that the nickel would be "mined" using a saw and oxy-acetylene flame, but fortunately this idea was abandoned.

Despite being declared a national monument in March 1955, the meteorite suffered badly at the hands of the souvenir hunters over the years. During the first half of 1985, Rössing Uranium Limited made funds available and a project was launched in conjunction with the National Monuments Council to protect the meteorite against vandalism. The project included a demonstration wall where visitors can learn more about the origin of the meteorite, toilet facilities and a house for a full-time caretaker.

At the same time the surrounding area was made more attractive to visitors and a number of fireplaces were provided. Trees and shrubs in the vicinity of the meteorite have been numbered and can be identified from a list which is available at the information area. There is also a list of 13 bird species which are commonly seen in the area. The complex was officially opened in July 1987.

From Hoba West you can continue along route D2860 to Grootfontein, a more direct approach than retracing your original route.

GROOTFONTEIN

Grootfontein, situated 207 km north-east of Otjiwarongo, can be reached along route 1/8 (B1) to Otavi, from where route 8/1 (B8) is followed, or, alternatively, from Tsumeb along route 72 (C42).

Several stone and limestone buildings dating back to the German period and tall, shady trees give the town a distinctive character. A variety of flowering trees line the streets of the town, which is especially attractive during September and October when the blue-purple jacarandas and the red flamboyants create a blaze of colour.

Grootfontein takes its name from the fountain which for thousands of years attracted large numbers of game as well as people. The Herero referred to the area as *Otjivandatjongue* or "hill of the leopard", while the Nama named it *Geiaus, Geious* or *Kaiaus*, meaning large fountain. The fountain, on the northern perimeter of the town, can still be seen today and the popular Tree Park planted here by the South West Africa Company is a delight to the eye.

The fountain was used as a base by two elephant hunters, Green and Eriksson, as early as 1860. White settlers began arriving in the area around 1880 and in the mid-1880s a group of Dorsland Trekkers established the capital of the Republic of Upingtonia here after settling on land purchased from the Owambo chief, Kambonde. However, because of numerous problems the republic only lasted two years before it was abandoned.

The head office of the South West Africa Company was established at Grootfontein in 1893, the concession to prospect for minerals in the north of the country having been granted to the company the previous year. The population of the area increased further in 1896 when a number of Afrikaner farming families from the Transvaal settled here.

In 1896 the *Schutztruppe*, assisted by local labour, built a fort and administrative post at Grootfontein, which at the time was part of the Outjo district. Between 1900 and 1905 the fort was enlarged several times and after 1915 it was occupied by the military magistrate. The limestone extension was made in 1922, after which the building was used as a boarding school until the late sixties. The fort subsequently fell into disuse and was threatened by demolition. In the early 1970s, however, a public appeal was launched to save the historic building and a decision to demolish it was repealed at the last minute. The fort, between Upingtonia and Eriksson Streets, was restored in 1974, with funds provided by the National Monuments Council and the public, and today serves as a museum. Exhibits are centred around the early history of the area and include displays on the Republic of Upingtonia, the Dorsland Trek and the German colonial period. Contact Mr G Menge, Tel (06731) 2061, during office hours, to have the building opened as it is kept locked and does not have regular opening times.

Other reminders of the German era are the graves of several *Schutz-truppe* in the cemetery just past the turnoff to the showgrounds on the Grootfontein/Rundu road.

In 1908, the year after the town was established, the Otavi Minen-und Eisenbahn-Gesellschaft (OMEG) built a 91 km narrow-gauge railway line between Grootfontein and Otavi. Grootfontein attained municipal status in 1947 and today it is the centre of the country's cattle farming area.

TSUMEB

Tsumeb, 181 km north-east of Otjiwarongo on the B1, is the last town before the Etosha National Park. The history of the town is closely linked to the minerals and metals which have been mined here, first by the indigenous people of the area and later by mining companies.

Places of interest in Tsumeb, therefore, reflect the early mining days of the town. Of particular interest to visitors are the museum (formerly the German Private School), OMEG *Minenburo*, the Second Directors' Residence and the Roman Catholic Church.

Old German Private School (museum) Originally built as a school, this stone building in Main Street still serves an educational purpose, namely that of a museum. It is open between 09h00 and 12h00 and 15h00 and 18h00 (Monday to Friday) and on Saturday between 15h00 and 18h00. Of particular interest is the Khorab Room, where armaments recovered from the Otjikoto Lake are on display, as well as an interesting collection of rocks and minerals from the Tsumeb area.

The school was built in 1915, three years after the missionary Ferdinand Lang started teaching in a skittle alley barn behind the mine hotel. The building had hardly been taken into use when it had to be evacuated to serve as a hospital for German troops. Between 1920 and 1950 the building once again served as a school.

OMEG Minenburo Situated in Main Street, this is one of the most attractive buildings in Tsumeb – owing to its unusual design it is easily mistaken for a church. Built in 1907 by Joseph Olbrich, the *Minenburo* dominates all other buildings in the vicinity and the tower symbolises the importance and economic power of the OMEG company at the time.

Second Directors' Residence This building, on the corner of 3rd Street and 8th Road, dates back to 1912 and is characterised by the turrets used for ventilation. The house was built in 1912 as a second residence for directors of the OMEG company.

Roman Catholic Church The simple design of this church, which was consecrated in 1914, gives it an almost homely atmosphere. Named St Barbara, after the patron saint of mineworkers, it served as the only church in Tsumeb for 13 years. Particularly eye-catching is the unusual tower above the main entrance. The church is situated on the corner of Main and 3rd Streets.

Numerous Iron Age smelting sites at Gross Otavi, Otjikoto and Tsumeb provide evidence of the exploitation of the copper resources of the area for hundreds of years. During the second half of the last century the ownership of the Tsumeb/Otavi areas was much in dispute, with various tribes laying claim to the mineral-rich area and several white traders securing concessions.

Towards the end of the 1800s overseas investors began showing an interest in exploiting the mineral deposits in the country. A mining concession was granted to the South West Africa Company on 12 September 1892 and on 12 January the following year an expedition, under Matthew Rogers, visited Tsumeb to ascertain the occurrence of ore.

A new company, the Otavi Minen- und Eisenbahn-Gesellschaft, was founded in April 1900 to obtain more capital for the exploitation of the ore deposits. In August that year the chief engineer, Christopher James, and 33 miners arrived in Tsumeb. They set about building a road to the existing shafts, sank two new shafts and on 28 December 1900 a consignment of 181 bags of copper ore weighing nine tons left for Swakopmund by ox-wagon.

In May 1903, OMEG signed an agreement with the South West Africa Company in which it undertook to build a railway line to facilitate the export of ore. At first, a railway line from Port Alexander in Angola to Otavi and from there to the Witwatersrand goldfields was considered, but the Anglo-Boer War thwarted this plan, as the railway line would have been uneconomical for transporting ore only from Tsumeb. It was then decided to build a railway line between Swakopmund and Tsumeb. Work started in November 1903, but was disrupted when the Herero rebellion broke out two months later. The line was completed on 24 August 1906.

Rehabilitation of the old workings of James commenced in 1905, while a pipeline between the Otjikoto Lake and Tsumeb was completed in 1907. During its first full year of operation – April 1907 to March 1908 – the company showed a net profit of nearly 1,3 million marks.

Mining operations were adversely affected with the outbreak of World War I, which brought production nearly to a standstill. Full production was once again reached in 1921, when 85 000 tons of ore were mined. In August 1932 the mine was forced to close down as a result of the depression. The normal production rate was achieved in 1938, only to be disrupted once more by World War II. Today it is a major producer of copper, lead, silver, cadmium and arsenic trioxide.

OTJIKOTO LAKE

Some 24 km north-west of Tsumeb, alongside route B1, lies another natural wonder of SWA/Namibia – the well-known Otjikoto Lake. The name given to the lake by the Herero is translated as "deep hole" and is said to mean "the place which is too deep for cattle to drink water".

The first whites to cast their eyes on this natural phenomenon were the explorers Charles Andersson and Francis Galton, who camped on the edge of Otjikoto in May 1851. Andersson (1987, p. 181) described the lake as follows: "Otjikoto, one of the most wonderful of Nature's freaks, is situated at the northern extremity of those broken hills which take their rise in the neighbourhood of Okamabuti, and in the midst of a dense coppice. So effectually is it hidden from view, that a person might pass within fifty paces of it without being aware of its existence. Owing to its steep and rugged sides, cattle have no access to the water; and even a man can only approach this enormous well by means of a steep and slippery footpath."

Situated in an area of porous limestone formations, the lake was probably an underground cavern in the distant past. At some stage the roof collapsed, creating an elliptical sinkhole of some 100 m by 150 m. Despite the fact that Galton plumbed the depth of Otjikoto at 55 m, a figure still considered today as an acceptable average, rumours have persisted over the years about the "bottomless" lake.

The lake is the habitat of the Otjikoto cichlid – a fish species endemic to Otjikoto and the nearby Guinas sinkhole. Growing up to 14 cm in length, this cichlid occurs in a variety of colours. While some are a uniform greenish black colour, others have yellow, blue, white, grey or black stripes. These bright colours are thought to have developed because of the initial absence of predators, making camouflage unnecessary.

The absence of predators resulted in a population explosion of the Otjikoto cichlids, forcing the original inhabitants, the southern mouth-breeder (*Pseudocrenilabrus philander*) which is usually a shallow-water species, to the bottom of the lake.

Adaptations to the breeding habits of the Otjikoto cichlids, thought to be the result of the population boom, have also been observed. This species normally constructs its nests in the muddy bottoms of water bodies, but at Otjikoto the depth of the lake makes this impossible. As a result, nests are made in cracks in the lake walls. Because of their large numbers, suitable nesting sites are at a premium and those fortunate enough to secure one are forced to protect it vigorously from those seeking a nesting site.

In 1980 a larger fish, the large-mouthed kurper (*Oreochromis mossambicus*) was introduced into the lake and the Otjikoto cichlid population appears to have declined.

Although very little research has been carried out, it is thought that the Otjikoto cichlid is derived from the common vleikurper (*Tilapia sparrmanii*), which was carried into Lake Guinas by floods in earlier times and became an isolated population. It has been suggested that the Otjikoto cichlid was introduced into Otjikoto from Lake Guinas, but its true origin is uncertain.

Otjikoto is also of historical interest. In 1915, the retreating German force under Günter Wallbaum dumped part of its weaponry and ammunition into the lake to prevent it from falling in the hands of the pursuing Union force. Rumours circulated that the Germans had dumped between 300 and 400 wagon loads of ammunition as well as 24 cannons in the lake and a Department of Works team under Sergeant G Crofton was sent to the lake in 1916 to recover the weaponry. With the assistance of J de Villiers of the Special Intelligence Unit of the Union forces and a SA Railways and Harbours diver 5 cannons, 10 cannon chassis and three machine guns as well as 85 725 Mauser and 4 684 cannon rounds were recovered. The armaments were salvaged from an underwater reef and 54 years were to pass before three divers from Windhoek came across the wheels of what was taken to be a cannon at a depth of 41 m. A joint salvage operation was carried out by the South African Army, Tsumeb Corporation and the Windhoek State Museum and a Krupp ammunition wagon was uncovered. Despite its watery grave, the wagon was in almost perfect condition and can today be seen at the Alte Feste Museum in Windhoek.

Seven years later, in 1977, an ammunition carrier was recovered and at Easter 1983 another carrier was discovered and later brought to the surface.

Since May 1983 six more pieces have been recovered by three amateur divers from Tsumeb. Among these were a Sandfontein cannon which was captured from the Union forces during a battle in the German/SWA Campaign. These armaments were restored with great care by two employees of Tsumeb Corporation and can be seen in the Khorab Room at the Tsumeb Museum.

OUTJO

Outjo, 73 km north-west of Otjiwarongo, is on the main route (2/5, routes 67/68 [C38]) to the Okaukuejo rest camp in the Etosha National Park.

The first white to settle permanently at the spring was the trader Tom Lambert, who established himself here in 1880. In 1895 a German military force was stationed at Outjo and in the following year *Hauptmann* Ludwig von Estdorff had a number of erwen surveyed.

Places of interest dating back to the early German period include the old windmill tower, the Naulila monument and Franke House.

Work on the windmill tower began towards the end of 1900 and the structure was taken into use on 1 March 1902. The 9,4 m high tower was built from stone and clay and the power was generated by a wooden windpump mounted on the tower. Water was pumped into a 8 m³ cement dam from where it was taken by way of a 620 m pipeline to the barracks, hospital and stables.

The Naulila monument in the old German cemetery was erected in 1933 in memory of the German officials and soldiers murdered on 19 October 1914 by Portuguese soldiers at the fort of Naulila near the Kunene River in Angola. The monument also remembers the soldiers who died or went missing during the punitive expedition led by Major Victor Franke against Naulila in December 1914.

Also to be seen in Outjo is the old *Kliphuis* (stone house). Dating back to around 1899, it was one of the first houses erected in the town. The house, sometimes also referred to as the Franke House, was built on the instructions of Major Von Estdorff for the commander of the German troops at Outjo.

VINGERKLIP

The turnoff to the Vingerklip is signposted 27 km west of Outjo on route 65 (C39) to Khorixas, the formation being reached some 65 km on. The Vingerklip can also be approached from Khorixas, in which case you are advised to travel along route 65 (C39) for roughly 54 km and then turn right onto the D2743 for about 22 km. Although the formation can also be reached by turning onto the D2743 1 km west of Khorixas, this route is not recommended as it crosses several river courses which, though usually dry, can be difficult to negotiate.

The turnoff to the formation is opposite the homestead of the farm Bertram. A farm worker will collect a small entry fee once you have passed through the gate. From here it is about 1 km to the Vingerklip, where a covered picnic table provides welcome shade. The approach to the base of the formation is steep, with loose gravel, so do make sure you have sturdy shoes.

Also known as the *Kalk Kegel* (limestone skittle), the column of lime-stone conglomerate is situated atop a small hill. It has a circumference of roughly 44 m at its base and points skywards for some 35 m, seem-ingly keeping guard over the area. It is estimated that the conglomerate of which the formation is composed was laid down some 15 million years ago, making it the same age as the Sesriem and Kuiseb canyon conglomerates.

Situated on the floodplain north of the Ugab River, the Vingerklip is an erosional relic of the plateau which stretches for some 80 km in an east/west direction. During the Lower Tertiary, the Ugab River carved out a wide valley. However, in the course of a drier period, about 30 million years ago, with decreasing transport capacity, the river filled its valley with detritus ranging from fine sand to conglomerate. Towards the end of the Tertiary, uplift of the area and a more humid climate revitalised the erosion, resulting in a new incision of the river into its terraces. The Vingerklip was preserved as an erosional remnant (outlier) of the river deposits.

The first recorded ascent was in 1970 by an American climber, Tom Choate. This was possibly one of the earliest climbs in this country with mechanical aids. The first free climb was made three years later when a party led by Udo Kleyenstuber ascended the eastern face.

ETOSHA NATIONAL PARK

Etosha needs little introduction to wildlife enthusiasts. The park can be entered either through the Andersson Gate in the south via Outjo (route 68 [C38]) or the Von Lindequist Gate in the east via Tsumeb (route B1 and route 84 [C38]).

Etosha lies within an endemic malaria area and precautions are es-sential when visiting the park.

Accommodation is available in three rest camps, while a fourth rest camp is being planned for Otjovasandu in the extreme west of the park.

Accommodation in Namutoni and Okaukuejo rest camps is air-conditioned and these camps are, therefore, open to tourists throughout the year. Halali rest camp does not have air-conditioned accommo-dation as yet and is closed from 1 November to the second Thursday in March. (It will also be open throughout the year once air-conditioning

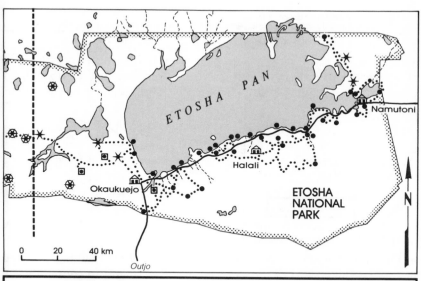

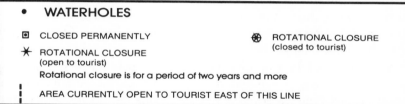

has been installed, but in the meantime the shop, restaurant and filling station are open to visitors passing by.)

Namutoni, in the east of the park, offers a choice of accommodation ranging from the picturesque fort to tourisettes (bus quarters), mobile homes, four-bedded tents (to be phased out) and caravan/camping sites.

Halali takes its name from a German tune traditionally sounded by the foresters on their horns to mark the end of a successful hunt. The camp was given the name after a long search to find the ideal site for Etosha's third camp ended at the foot of the small dolomite hill, 75 km west of Namutoni. Opened in 1967, the rest camp offers accommodation in bungalows, bus quarters, four-bedded tents (to be phased out) and caravan/camping sites.

Towards the end of the last century a control post was established

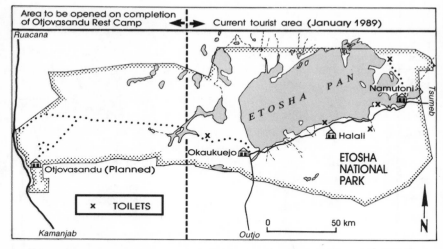

at Okaukuejo – one of four posts in the north of the country designed to combat the spread of foot-and-mouth disease and to contain illegal hunting and gun-running. The others posts were at Sesfontein, Namutoni and Karakuwisa. Unfortunately, the fort built at Okaukuejo in 1901 has long disappeared.

A special attraction of Okaukuejo, which was the first rest camp opened to tourists, is the waterhole just outside the perimeter of the camp. At night the waterhole is floodlit, giving visitors the opportunity to spot animals not often seen during the daytime. Accommodation varies from bungalows to bus quarters, four-bedded tents (to be phased out) and caravan/camping sites.

The camp today serves as the administrative headquarters of the park and is also the centre of the Etosha Ecological Institute, which was founded in 1974 to conduct research on various aspects of the park's ecology. If you are unfamiliar with animal spoor, walk past the entrance of the Institute where the cement walkway has been decorated with impressions of spoor. The Institute is not open to the general public, but visitors are welcome at the information centre next to the post office and at the exhibits in the tourist centre.

All three rest camps also offer the following amenities: a licensed restaurant; shop where basic foodstuffs, liquor, firewood and curios can be bought; swimming pool, petrol and diesel. Post offices operate at Namutoni and Okaukuejo. A network of gravel roads covering over

700 km traverses the park, leading to waterholes, the edge of the pan and various places of interest.

Stretching 120 km at its longest and a maximum of 55 km from north to south, the saline pan covers almost a quarter of the park. The pan is usually seasonally inundated with water from the Ekuma and Oshigambo rivers to the north – the extent of the flooding is determined by the summer rainfall in the catchment area. Most animals are unable to drink the water in the pan as the salt content can become twice as high as seawater. However, animals are attracted to the waterholes on the edge of the pan, which are supplemented annually with rainwater and fed by subterranean springs.

The vegetation of the park can, broadly speaking, be classified into two subtypes, namely a tree savanna in the east (Namutoni) and a shrub and thorn tree savanna in the west (Otjovasandu area). Several *Acacia* species, such as the water thorn (177.1), red umbrella thorn (181) and the umbrella thorn (188) and hairy umbrella thorn (188.1), as well as mopane (198) and a number of *Combretum* species, varying from shrubs to trees, are the most characteristic vegetation. The dominant grasses are *Anthephora, Enneapogon, Aristida* and *Stipagrostis*.

A species which arouses the curiosity of most visitors is the phantom tree (137), which can be seen in the appropriately named Sprokieswoud (Haunted Forest), 30 km west of Okaukuejo. This population is unique because phantom trees usually occur on hillsides. The number of these unusually shaped trees in the Sprokieswoud is estimated at about 900. The tender ends of their branches are browsed by elephant, gemsbok and giraffe. Waterholes in the vicinity were closed a number of years ago in an attempt to prevent destruction of the forest by elephant.

Those interested in the flora of the park will find the guide *Trees and Shrubs of the Etosha National Park* useful. The book, which can be purchased in the shops in the rest camps, contains descriptions of the nine major vegetation communities in the tourist area, illustrations and descriptions of 48 tree and shrub species, lists of plants occurring commonly in the three rest camps, indexes of botanical names, as well as common names in Afrikaans, English and German and a list of presently known plant species in the Etosha National Park.

The animals occurring in the park are typical of the southern savanna plains of Africa. The park is the habitat of five rare or endangered species, namely black (hook-lipped) rhinoceros, black-faced impala, roan, Hartmann's mountain zebra and the diminutive Damara dik-dik.

The most commonly seen species are Burchell's or plains zebra, springbok, gemsbok and elephant. Kudu, blue wildebeest and giraffe are fairly common, while red hartebeest, eland and steenbok are less frequently seen.

Carnivores include lion, cheetah, leopard, spotted hyaena and brown hyaena. Black-backed jackal are frequently seen during the late afternoons and early mornings.

The distribution of animals is related largely to the availability of food and water. Some species, however, prefer certain areas where you can normally expect to spot them. Large numbers of kudu are frequently seen in the Namutoni area, while common duiker occur in grassland with shrub cover north of Namutoni. The Klein Namutoni area is one of the best places to spot the Damara dik-dik, while red hartebeest favour the area between Halali and Okaukuejo.

Research on the drinking times of animals at waterholes in Etosha has shown that blue wildebeest and springbok are daylight drinkers, while red hartebeest, kudu and eland are morning drinkers. Zebra, gemsbok and warthog drink predominantly in the afternoon, while black rhinoceros, elephant, lion and jackal drink mainly between 18h00 and 24h00. About 66 per cent of hyaenas observed during the study drank between midnight and 06h00, while giraffe showed no clear preference.

The western part of the park is one of the few places in the country where both Burchell's zebra and Hartmann's mountain zebra occur. The latter prefers the mountainous areas around Otjovasandu which are to be opened to tourists on completion of the Otjovasandu rest camp, planned for 1991. Another species occurring primarily in the west is the eland, which favours the north-western part of the park, while gemsbok, although occurring throughout the park, also show a preference for the drier western part. Blue wildebeest, Burchell's zebra and springbok follow annual migration routes in search of grazing and rainwater, and following the first good summer rains large herds congregate on the plains north and west of Okaukuejo, where they remain until about April. As the field water diminishes and the grazing decreases, the animals move closer to the waterholes near Okaukuejo before moving to the Gemsbokvlakte plains, east of Okaukuejo. The cycle is completed when the animals return to the plains north and west of Okaukuejo a few days after the first heavy rains of the following rainy season.

Up to 1 500 elephants migrate seasonally from Etosha to Kavango, Damaraland and Kaokoland during the wet season. After an absence of nearly half a century, elephants reappeared in Etosha in the early 1950s. A large number of waterholes were subsequently created to attract the animals from surrounding farmlands. This, combined with an influx of elephants during the 1980–83 drought, resulted in such an increase in the population that culling became necessary and in 1983 and 1985, 220 and 315 elephants were culled. In addition, 35 elephant calves were captured and sold locally and abroad. Extensive research has been carried out on the population dynamics and movements of elephants in Etosha and in 1987 radio collars which are monitored by satellite were fitted to three (as well as a number of Damaraland elephants) in an effort to track their movements.

One of the problems which has been researched extensively by the Etosha Ecological Institute is the dramatic decline in the numbers of blue wildebeest since 1955. In that year the numbers of this species were estimated at about 25 000, but by 1978 they had decreased to only 2 200. An investigation conducted between 1974 and 1978 showed that the three major factors contributing to the population crash were all man-made. Possibly the most important factor was the erection of boundary fences in 1973, preventing the animals from migrating, especially during dry years. A second contributing factor was the numerous gravel pits opened during road building. These pits create ideal conditions for the spread of anthrax, a fatal bacterial disease, and an analysis of carcasses showed that 62 per cent of all blue wildebeest deaths resulted from anthrax. Thirdly, it was found that anthrax-infested carcasses, combined with the availability of water throughout the year at artificial water-points, provided a ready source of food for predators such as lion and hyaena. As a result these predators no longer needed to hunt or follow animal migrations, which in turn increased the survival rate of cubs. This created an abnormal predator/prey relationship and it was found that Etosha had more predators in relation to the available prey animals than any other African conservation area.

To reverse the downward trend, four recommendations were made, namely, the modification of the park's boundaries to include the seasonally well-watered grasslands north of the Etosha Pan, the control of anthrax, and indirect control of predators by the closure of water-points in areas where water was not naturally present throughout the year and caution with the creation of future artificial water-points.

The abnormal predator to prey ratio resulted in a unique birth control project whereby synthetic pregnancy hormone capsules were implanted into the neck muscles of ten lionesses. A constant flow of pregnancy-simulating hormones is released by the capsules, preventing ovulation for up to five years. Once the contraceptive wears off the lioness returns to fertility. However, by simply recapturing the lioness and removing the capsule it is possible to terminate contraception.

The project has been conducted over a number of years and treated lionesses were carefully studied to ensure that no behavioural abnor-malities occurred. All activities, such as resting, walking, hunting, fight-ing and mating, were monitored and timed to the nearest second. Monitoring took place during the day and at night, when lions are most active.

The alternative to this method of population control would have been culling, which not only destroys genetic material but could also give rise to other conservation problems.

The two researchers of the project, Dr Jock Orford from Windhoek, and a former Head of the Etosha Ecological Institute, Dr Hu Berry, received international recognition for their work when the project was described in the book *Rolex Awards for 1987*. Subsequently they were invited to present their findings at an international conference in America.

To date more than 320 bird species have been recorded in the park, which is the most important breeding area of the southern African populations of lesser (97) and greater (96) flamingo.

The largest numbers of species occur between October and April, when the summer migrants are present. The variety of species and their numbers also depend on the extent of the flooding.

During exceptionally good rainy seasons up to a million flamingoes congregate on the pans. In June 1969 the pan dried up earlier than usual and the lack of water forced the adult birds to leave, abandoning the chicks to their own devices. In the ensuing flamingo rescue op-eration 20 000 chicks were hand-caught and released at Fischer's Pan near Namutoni. Two years later the pan once again dried up earlier than usual and an estimated 30 000 young birds marched 30 km northwest to the nearest water at Poacher's Point. The marching chicks were fed by the adult birds, flying to and from the water, during their trek. In August the chicks started on the second leg of their trek to the last remaining water in the Ekuma River delta area. During the early stages of their march the adult birds feeding them had to make a round trip of 100 km. By the end of August the majority of the 100 000 chicks hatched between May and August had reached the safety of the water in the Ekuma River.

Another fascinating aspect of these birds is their ability to conserve energy. The secret of the flamingoes lies in their diet of nutritious, energy-rich algae. These organisms absorb energy directly from the sun and are eaten by the flamingoes without any loss of energy through intermediaries in the food chain. In addition, when flying at night, the cool, dense air gives greater impetus to their wing thrusts, reducing energy expenditure. According to calculations a flock of flamingoes leaving Etosha in the evening will arrive at Walvis Bay at dawn the following morning – a journey of about 500 km.

Among the less common species you might spot at Etosha are Wahlberg's eagle (135), Montagu's harrier (166), an uncommon Palaearctic migrant, gymnogene (169), Klaas's cuckoo (385), greyhooded kingfisher (436) and whitebellied sunbird (787).

Those interested in bird-watching will find the fieldguide *Birds of the Etosha National Park* useful. In addition to details of the identification, distribution, status and habits of 58 species, illustrated with colour photographs, the book also contains information on the five bird habitats in the park, as well as a checklist of birds recorded.

The first recorded descriptions of Etosha were by the travellers Francis Galton and Charles Andersson, who camped near what is now Namutoni in 1851. Andersson described the pan as "... covered with saline incrustations, and having wooded and well-defined borders. The surface consisted of a soft, greenish-yellow, clay soil, strewed with fragments of small sand-stone, of a purple tint."

The abundance of game attracted hunters and traders and steps to protect it were taken as early as 1892, when hunting regulations were promulgated. The outbreak of rinderpest in 1896/97 resulted in the extermination of large numbers of game and to prevent stock movement veterinary control posts were established at Namutoni, Okaukuejo and Rietfontein. These posts were later converted to permanent police posts. An unfired claybrick fort was built at Namutoni (completed in 1903), while a limestone fort was built at Okaukuejo.

On 28 January 1904 the fort at Namutoni was attacked by 500 Owambo. The garrison of four soldiers, later joined by three ex-servicemen, successfully held back the attackers until late in the afternoon when the Owambo retreated. Under cover of darkness they managed to escape and the fort was completely destroyed the next day when the Owambo discovered the building had been deserted.

Following the Herero Uprising of 1904 it was decided to rebuild Fort Namutoni in an asymmetrical quadrangle, approximately 60 m by 68 m, with a large watch-tower at the north-eastern corner. Namutoni lost its usefulness after the proclamation of Game Reserves 1, 2 and 3, and became delapidated. In 1910 the South African Police took over the fort and stationed five men there, but on 1 April 1912 the fort was closed. At the outbreak of World War I a brigade of South African troops under General Coen Brits was detailed to seal off the possible escape route of the German troops. The brigade travelled across Okaukuejo and Rietfontein and 190 German officers and troops surrendered at Fort Namutoni without a single shot being fired.

In the following years, the fort was used periodically by the South African Police, but its condition continued to deteriorate. Interest was renewed and a campaign launched to restore the building after one of its towers was destroyed by lightning in 1938. Twelve years later it was declared a national monument and in 1951 the South West African Administration made funds available for its restoration. The third Fort Namutoni, providing tourist accommodation, was officially opened in 1958. However, modernisation and renovations once again became urgently necessary and in 1983 work began on a modern restaurant and shop complex as well as 24 accommodation units east of the fort. At the same time the fort was extensively renovated and the fourth Fort Namutoni was officially opened on 10 August 1984.

Etosha was the first park to be proclaimed in SWA/Namibia and unbeknown to many visitors the park boundaries have undergone several changes. In 1907 Governor Friedrich Von Lindequist of the German Colonial Government proclaimed Game Reserves 1, 2 and 3. The

93 240 km^2 Game Reserve 2 comprised the Etosha Pan and the Kaoko-veld from the Kunene River in the north to the Hoarusib River in the south. In 1947 the Kaokoland portion of Game Reserve No 2 was demarcated for occupation by the Herero, while the Etosha portion was reduced by 3 406 km^2, divided into farms – an area known today as the Gagarus block.

Following the recommendations of the Elephant Commission of 1956, the size of the park was almost doubled to 99 526 km^2. Game reserve No 1, north-east of Grootfontein, was deproclaimed and in exchange the park was extended westwards by adding unoccupied state land between the Hoanib and Ugab rivers.

The recommendations of the Odendaal Commission of 1963, how-ever, resulted in the park being reduced drastically. No consideration was given to ecological boundaries or traditional game migration routes and game reserves had to be created elsewhere for the relocation of scarce and endangered species. Land was, however, added to the much-reduced Etosha by purchasing three farms in the Otjovasandu area, and two areas originally intended for deproclamation, the bergveld in the west and the sandveld north of Namutoni, were fortunately re-tained. Today the park covers an area of 22 270 km^2 – 77 per cent less than before the Odendaal Commission.

11 KAVANGO, CAPRIVI AND BUSHMANLAND

RUNDU

Rundu, on the banks of the Kavango River, is 248 km north-east of Grootfontein, along the B8. It does not offer many possibilities for holiday-makers, but if you are keen on fishing or bird-watching, many fruitful hours can be enjoyed on the banks of the Kavango River.

For more than 400 km the Kavango River forms the boundary between SWA/Namibia and Angola. The river, which rises in the central highlands of Angola, reaches its peak at Rundu around February/March, inundating the wide floodplains alongside the river. By far the greatest proportion of the Kavango's 110 000 people (1986 estimate) live in this narrow belt, and once the water has subsided, sorghum, millet (*mahango*) and maize are cultivated on the fertile ground.

The Kavango River is also an important source of protein to the Kavango people. Fish are caught by a variety of methods, with the women using funnel-shaped fishing baskets which you might notice at huts when passing by. Fishing traps and nets are also used and the men sometimes spear fish when travelling in a *watu* (dugout canoe), as well as trying their luck with a hook and line. The Kavango people are well known for their attractive woodwork, which is displayed alongside the road – often without a soul in sight, until you pull up.

KAUDOM GAME RESERVE

Situated north of Bushmanland, this 384 000 ha reserve in east Kavango was opened to the public in March 1986. Approaching from the north, the turnoff is signposted on the B8 at Katere, from where it is about 50 km to the reserve. This section is characterised by long stretches of

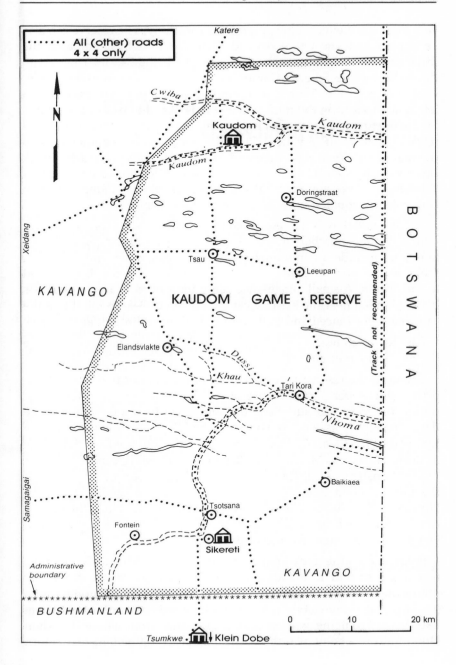

very loose sand which slow progress considerably. The reserve can also be approached via Tsumkwe and Klein Döbe in Bushmanland, the distance from Tsumkwe to the entrance gate being 74 km. To get onto the right track to Sikereti Camp you turn left at the four-way inter-section as you enter Tsumkwe. Using the school as a marker, you turn left again, following the track which winds past the back of the school. Ignore the first turnoff to your right, continuing until you reach a second track branching off to your right as the track begins to double back to the main road. Turn right here and head north until you reach a track signposted to Klein Döbe. Here you turn right again, continuing to a T-junction where you turn left and head for Sikereti Camp, which is conveniently situated only 24 km from the entrance gate.

Accommodation in the reserve comprises two rustic overnight camps with a limited number of wooden bungalows and campsites. Other amenities include a communal braai area, fresh water and ablutions. Only one group, consisting of a maximum of 12 people, is permitted at each camp. A small, lodge-style camp for groups of 12–16 people is being planned near the existing camp at Sikereti. Bear in mind that the camps are not fenced and that animals may pass through at any time.

East Kavango lies in an endemic malaria area, so remember to take the necessary precautions.

Travel in the reserve is restricted to a minimum of two four-wheel-drive vehicles per party because of its inaccessibility and often rough tracks. You must take sufficient food and water for a minimum of three days' travelling, as well as your own bedding and firewood. Ensure that you have at least 80 litres of petrol for the journey from Tsumkwe in Bushmanland to Mukwe near Bagani, as the sandy conditions often require constant use of four-wheel-drive. Begin your journey through the park in good time as travel is slow owing to sandy conditions. However, after the rainy season, which extends until March, the reserve can be quite wet, especially along the *omurambas* (river courses) and you should be geared for mud-driving.

From Sikereti the track follows the course of the Nhoma Omuramba, reaching a turnoff to Elandsvlakte after 24 km. Here you can either follow the route via Elandsvlakte and Tsau waterhole to Kaudom Camp (97 km) or continue along the Nhoma Omuramba to the waterhole at Tari Kora. From the waterhole a 14 km track follows the Chadum Omuramba to a point near the Botswana border, but you have to return along the same route. From Tara Kori a track heads in a northerly direction, reaching the Leeupan waterhole after 24 km. Here you have a choice of either travelling to Tsau (12 km) and then to Kaudom Camp (20 km) or continuing further north to the Kaudom Omuramba (29 km) and then following the Omuramba westwards for 11 km to the Kaudom Camp.

The vegetation of the reserve has been classified as Tree Savanna and Woodland (Northern Kalahari) (Giess Vegetation Type 11) comprising species such as wild seringa (197), Zambezi (206) and wild (236) teak and manketti tree (337). Copalwood (199), sometimes referred to as bastard or false mopane, also occurs and from a distance is easily confused with the mopane (198). Extensive reedbeds and grassland occur in the omuramba system of the Nhoma and Kaudom omurambas, while *Acacia* belts are found in the sand dune valleys and along the omuramba margins.

Good summer rains will result in luxuriant, tall grass, making game spotting difficult. In addition, game is more widely dispersed following the summer rains, on account of the availability of ground water.

Predators recorded in the reserve are lion, wild dog, leopard, spotted hyaena and black-backed and side-striped jackal. Game numbers can vary considerably depending on the season as well as the year. However, kudu, roan and gemsbok are usually abundant in the reserve, as well as blue wildebeest which can number anything between less than 100 to over 450. Small numbers of tsessebe, eland, red hartebeest and reedbuck also occur, as well as two smaller species, steenbok and common duiker.

Your chances of spotting elephant are usually good. Between 1985 and 1987 the numbers of elephant and giraffe increased sharply and these two species are at present the most abundant in the reserve, with numbers estimated at 528 and 665 respectively. Giraffe, however, are extremely difficult to spot as they blend in well with the wooded vegetation and will probably only reveal themselves to you at waterholes.

POPA FALLS REST CAMP

From Rundu, travel east for about 215 km along the B8 until reaching the turnoff (signposted Popa Falls, Botswana) and continue for about 5 km to the Popa Falls rest camp, which is well signposted.

The Popa Falls rest camp, on the southern bank of the Kavango River, is a welcome stop over for weary travellers in the often trying terrain of the area. Rustic cabins constructed from wild teak (locally known as dolfhout) planks with grass roofs are unobtrusive amongst the riverine vegetation, which has been disturbed as little as possible. Field kitchens, shady riverine campsites with braaiplaces and ablution facilities are also available to visitors. There is a small kiosk but you are well advised to be self-sufficient. Petrol is not available in the camp, but can be obtained at Divundu near Bagani Bridge.

From the camp it is a short walk to the Popa Falls – a wooden bridge has been constructed to assist one over the first rocky section. *Popa* means "it is here" and with a little scrambling and rock hopping you will find yourself surrounded by rushing channels of water and close to the main "falls", which are about 1 km wide. At this point the river divides into several courses and only part of the "falls" is evident. Do not expect to see a waterfall in the true sense of the word – rapids would be a more fitting term. Here the Kavango River cascades over a rocky section, losing about 2,5 m in height. However, the total fall of the river, including the rapids, over a distance of 22 km is 19,5 m.

If you remain on the main bank and make your way upstream you will have an impressive view over the river before it splits up over the rapids.

Facilities offered by the private lodge downstream from Popa include a licensed restaurant, game viewing and photo safaris to Mahango and Kaudom, and transfers from the nearby airstrip. Equipment such as boats, fishing rods and tackle can be hired. Enquiries can be made with Suclabo Lodge or at the tourist office at Popa Falls.

As with other areas at East Kavango, do remember anti-malaria precautions.

MAHANGO GAME RESERVE

The Mahango Game Reserve is reached about 25 km beyond the Popa Falls rest camp, which is used as a base to explore the reserve.

This 24 462 ha area, squeezed between the Botswana border and the Kavango River, was opened to the public in 1986. You are encouraged to explore the reserve on foot to admire the fascinating birdlife of the area, but no facilities for overnight or day visitors are provided. Swim-

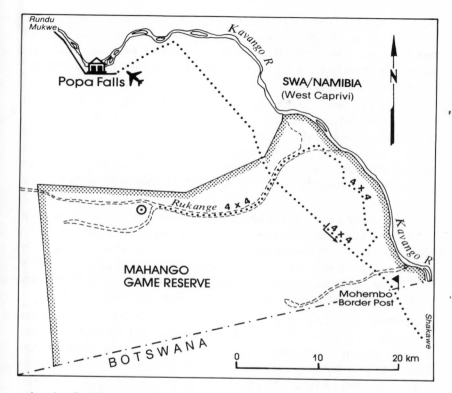

ming in the Kavango River is discouraged because of the presence of crocodiles and hippos, while some sections are contaminated with bilharzia.

The main road through the park links Bagani (SWA/Namibia) with Shakawe (Botswana) and those travelling to Botswana along this route do not require a permit for the park. Should you wish to deviate from the main road, however, a permit is obtainable at the entrance to the park (on the Popa Falls side). Once in the reserve you have two options. You can either turn right shortly after passing through the entrance gate and follow a track along the Rukange Omuramba for a few kilometres to a small waterhole, following the same return route, or you can take a longer, interesting circular drive leading down to and then along the Kavango River.

Five major habitat types occur in the reserve, with the deciduous woodland, which is dominated by copalwood (199), wild teak (236), wild seringa (197) and Zambezi teak (206), covering the largest area. The area along the Kavango River comprises floodplain made up of reedbeds, swamps, open flooded grasslands and papyrus. Wild date palm (22) are noticeable on the edge of the floodplain as well as a few large baobabs (467).

Birdlife is prolific – to date more than 300 species have been recorded – and keen birdwatchers may be well rewarded. Species seldom recorded elsewhere in the country include western banded snake eagle (145), finfoot (229), rock pratincole (306), coppertailed coucal (389), African skimmer (343), Pel's fishing owl (403), whiterumped babbler (562), chirping cisticola (676), swamp boubou (738) and brownthroated weaver (818).

Keep a wary eye open for herds of elephant making their way to or from the water. You will be surprised that an animal as large as an elephant blends so well with the vegetation and often you are only aware of them when they are almost next to you. The elephants move into Mahango from Angola, Zambia and western Caprivi during dry periods and consequently their numbers fluctuate considerably.

Animals associated with the river and the riverine vegetation are crocodile, hippopotamus, red lechwe, sitatunga and reedbuck. The reserve is an important habitat for roan and sable, both of which are limited to East Kavango, West Caprivi, Waterberg Plateau Park and a limited number of suitable farms. Both species prefer open woodland and are dependent on water. The greyish brown roan is slightly larger than the black sable, which has long, sweeping horns, curved backwards. Smaller antelope occurring in the reserve include steenbok and common duiker.

Other animals you may spot include blue wildebeest, buffalo, kudu, gemsbok, tsessebe, bushbuck, impala, warthog, baboon, vervet monkey and ostrich. Predators recorded in the reserve are lion (only occasionally), leopard and wild dog.

CAPRIVI GAME RESERVE

At Bagani, 206 km east of Rundu, you cross the Kavango River and pass through a military control point, entering West Caprivi. The next 191 km along the B8 takes you through the Caprivi Game Reserve to Kongola on the Kwando River. The game reserve falls within the operational area because of its strategic situation – travellers must complete the journey between the two control points within a specified time and may not deviate from the main road. It has been safe to travel in the region, however, for several years.

When travelling through the Caprivi Game Reserve from west to east the necessary military permit can be obtained at the military check point at Bagani Bridge. When travelling from east to west, the permit must be obtained at the Katima Mulilo military base.

On the stretch between Rundu and Katima Mulilo petrol is available only at Mukwe and Divundu (near Bagani Bridge and Popa Falls), more than 300 km west of Katima Mulilo.

The Caprivi lies within an endemic malaria area, so remember to take the necessary precautions when visiting the area.

The vegetation is fairly dense but on this often bumpy and dusty road (which should be travelled with caution), keep an eye open for game. While species such as roan, kudu and elephant occur throughout the reserve, most species tend to concentrate mainly along the Kwando River and the Malombe and Ndwasa pans in the east, owing to the absence of permanent surface water in the central areas. Species occurring here include blue wildebeest, Chobe bushbuck, giraffe, lechwe, reedbuck, impala, hippopotamus, sitatunga, waterbuck and Burchell's zebra.

The total length of Caprivi, which is 80 km at its widest, is 482 km. Katima Mulilo, in the east, on the Zambezi River, is the administrative centre of East Caprivi. The Caprivi, named after General Count Georg Leo von Caprivi di Caprara di Montecuccoli, who in 1890 succeeded Bismarck as German Imperial Chancellor, has an interesting international history. In 1893 Britain ceded the territory, which abuts on Zambia, Zimbabwe and Botswana, to Germany, which resulted in its incorporation into German South West Africa. After World War I the Caprivi Strip was incorporated into Bechuanaland (now Botswana), but in August 1939 South Africa took over the administration of the area.

EAST CAPRIVI AND KATIMA MULILO

After travelling through the Caprivi Game Reserve, you enter East Caprivi at Kongola, where you join tarred road (sheer bliss) which is followed for the next 117 km to Katima Mulilo. This area is a forestry reserve which, unfortunately, has been adversely affected by uncontrolled exploitation and human settlement. Patches of forest are being cleared by the inhabitants for subsistence farming, while indiscriminate burning is also degrading the forests.

Despite its remoteness, East Caprivi has become increasingly popular as a tourist destination in recent years. Except for the major route (B8) via Grootfontein and Rundu to Ngoma Gate on the Botswana border, driving in East Caprivi is mainly limited to four-wheel-drive vehicles. Places worth visiting are generally not signposted and, in addition, the floodplains in the triangle formed by the Zambezi and Chobe rivers east of Katima Mulilo are inundated and inaccessible after the summer rains.

Katima Mulilo, the administrative centre of East Caprivi, has been developing steadily in recent years. Here you can replenish supplies at the well-stocked supermarket. There is a bottlestore and butchery opposite the supermarket. Visit the daily market in the central business area of the town, where anything from dried and fresh fish to scones and sarongs are on offer by local traders. Ask for directions to the Caprivi Art Centre, where locally crafted soapstone and wood carvings are sold. Bank Windhoek is the only bank represented here but should be avoided over month ends unless you are prepared to queue for some time.

The Zambezi Lodge in Katima Mulilo comprises chalets, some of which overlook the Zambezi River, as well as a campsite for those who prefer less sophisticated accommodation. Amenities at the lodge include a thatched area where breakfast and lunch are served, a steakhouse, swimming pool and nine-hole golf course (equipment can be hired). The floating bar on the Zambezi River is an unusual attraction, while visitors wishing to explore the river can arrange boat trips (a maximum of 3 people is allowed for small craft and a maximum of 15 people for the cruise boat).

Sedan cars, microbuses and double cab four-wheel-drive vehicles can be hired at the Avis franchise operated in Katima Mulilo by Zambezi Lodge. Tariffs are calculated on daily rates plus kilometres.

For those wanting to dine out, there are licensed restaurants at the Zambezi Lodge, the military base and at the Katima Mulilo Yacht Club which overlooks the Zambezi River. Enquiries can also be made here about boat trips on the Zambezi River.

Well over 70 fish species have been recorded in East Caprivi and the Zambezi, which is easily accessible, offers excellent fishing opportunities. Tiger fish, western bottlenose, sharptooth catfish, banded tilapia (bream) and brownspot largemouth are amongst the most common species landed.

The bomb shelters in many gardens in Katima and along the Zambezi River might create some doubts as to your safety. These shelters were hurriedly constructed after an attack from across the Zambezi River in 1978 and have not been used since. For several years now there has been no cross-border conflict in the area.

Situated on the southern bank of the Zambezi River, Katima Mulilo is probably one of the few towns in SWA/Namibia where elephants are regular visitors. The elephants drink almost daily at the Zambezi River, making it essential to be on your guard when walking or driving along the river. The river provides ample opportunity for picnicking, fishing, boating and bird-watching. However, do not become complacent – in September 1987 the postmaster of Katima Mulilo fell victim to a crocodile. The river is also home to hippos and if you do not spot these usually submerged animals during the day, you will probably hear them in the evening as they leave the water to graze on the banks.

The vegetation of the river fringe comprises mixed woodland where copalwood (199), Zambezi teak (206), Kalahari apple-leaf (239), leadwood (539) and silver cluster leaf (551) are the most dominant species.

Birdlife in the Caprivi is prolific and you might spot several species which in SWA/Namibia generally occur only in East and West Caprivi. Among these are honey buzzard (130), blackcheeked lovebird (369), rackettailed roller (448), bearded robin (617) and broadtailed paradise whydah (863).

Along the Zambezi River you could see African fish eagle (148), whitecrowned plover (259), halfcollared kingfisher (430), whitefronted bee-eater (443) and little bee-eater (444). Keep an eye open for African finfoot (229), which favour the quiet reaches of the river.

Birds associated with the mixed woodland along the river fringe include greenspotted dove (358), pied barbet (465), forktailed drongo (541), whitebrowed robin (613), threestreaked tchagra (743), white helmetshrike (753) and blue waxbill (844).

Katima Mulilo to Chobe via Ngoma

Chobe National Park in Botswana and Victoria Falls in Zimbabwe are easily accessible from Katima Mulilo. Do remember, though, the necessary valid travel documents.

A 60 km journey from Katima Mulilo along the B8 (four-wheel-drive vehicle not essential) brings you to the Ngoma border post, which is open daily between 08h00 and 16h00. About 4 km on you reach Ngoma Bridge, where you cross into Botswana. As there is no border post on the Botswana side, you have to report at the police station in Kasane, 64 km on, before continuing your journey.

THE LINYANTI: NKASA AND LUPALA

Few people realise that SWA/Namibia has its own region of reed-lined waterways and wildlife-filled islands similar to the Okavango Delta in Botswana. After winding south-east for about 100 km, the Kwando River, also known as the Linyanti River, abruptly swings in a north-easterly direction, breaking up into a series of narrow channels in the Linyanti area. Still further downstream, the river is known as the Chobe. In good flood years, large areas of land become inundated and are accessible only by boat. However, in drier years the large islands of Nkasa and Lupala can be reached by four-wheel-drive vehicle.

Access to the region is along the D3511, either from the Kongola military control post in the west or from Katima Mulilo in the east (both on the B8). Approaching from the west, turn south off the B8 onto the well-signposted road to Sangwali. Once at Sangwali, remain on the track skirting the village and ignore the branch to the post office. Just south of the village is the first channel of the Linyanti River, which can usually be crossed in a four-wheel-drive vehicle. From here the track wends its way south to the island of Lupala, and the distance that can be travelled will depend on the level of the flood. The track to Lupala passes clumps of palm trees and riverine woodland, with reeds and rushes lining the water channels. The southern bank of the Kwando/Linyanti River is the common border between Botswana and SWA/Namibia and you should take care not to inadvertently cross the border – Botswana's game guards are constantly on the look-out for cross-border poachers.

At present (1988), you do not require a permit to enter the area, but as there is a possibility that it might be proclaimed a conservation area, it is advisable to make enquiries with the DNC. The area is unfenced and there are no facilities. Visitors to the Linyanti therefore need to take precautions against wild animals at night and while walking. Swimmers are warned to watch out for crocodiles! Precautions against malaria are also essential as this is a malaria endemic area. All supplies, including sufficient petrol, need to be taken along. The closest petrol points are at Katima Mulilo and Divundu, close to Bagani Bridge.

Although access is sometimes difficult, the area can be rewarding for the wildlife enthusiast and the bird lover, as well as anyone wanting to experience the wilderness. Large mammals include elephant, buffalo, hippopotamus, lion, leopard and sitatunga. Red lechwe also occur but their numbers have declined drastically because of poaching. Poaching is rife in the area so do not expect to get too close to animals, as they are wary of vehicles.

Birdlife is prolific and species recorded here include the African fish eagle (148), African (240) and lesser (241) jacanas, coppertailed (389), Senegal (390) and Burchell's (391) coucals, as well as several kingfishers and bee-eaters. One of the five species classified as endangered in the *South African Red Data Book – Birds*, the wattled crane (207), can also be seen here.

Should you be in need of a more comfortable stay in the wilds you can stay at the Lianshulu camp, north-west of Sangwali. Enquiries can be made with Desert Adventure Safaris, P O Box 339, Swakopmund 9000, Tel (0641) 4072.

LAKE LIAMBEZI

Continuing from Sangwali along the D3511 to Katima Mulilo, you will travel through several villages, reaching Linyandi after about 48 km. About 29 km beyond Linyandi, passing Situwe and Kanona, you reach Signu.

This is one of the best access points for those wishing to explore Lake Liambezi (provided it has water in it). Here you can get fairly close to the lake without having to fight your way through the extensive reedbeds which occur along the river further upstream.

Lake Liambezi dried up in 1985 – a phenomenon which is known to have taken place in the last century – after it received no inflow through the Bukalo channel. When full, the lake, which is bordered by a 20 000 ha swamp, covers an area of about 10 000 ha and has an average depth of 3–5 m. Should you wish to do some boating on the lake it is advisable to approach the local people to provide a guide and hire you a *mokoro* (dugout canoe). Watch out for crocodiles and hippo!

Liambezi is fed by both the Kwando/Linyanti River and the Zambezi River, which spills over onto the eastern floodplains when the river reaches a height of more than 6,8 m at Katima Mulilo. Water is also fed into the lake by way of the Bukalo and Kalengwe channels. Between 1955 and 1975 Liambezi received an inflow in this way every 2,3 years on average. The inflow of water via the Kwando/Linyanti is generally sufficient to counteract the evaporation of water, estimated at about 2 m of the surface area a year.

When full, Liambezi is an important source of protein to the local population and about a ton of fish is harvested daily. Before the lake dried up in 1985, a study was conducted to determine the effect of commercial exploitation on the fish population. It was found that the variety of species, their sizes and total numbers had hardly been affected when the results were compared with those of a similar study undertaken ten years previously.

From Signu you continue along the D3511 to Katima Mulilo, about 50 km on.

BUSHMANLAND

Since the opening of the Kaudom Reserve, Bushmanland has become increasingly popular with tourists. Route 74 (C44), which leads to the administrative centre of Bushmanland, Tsumkwe, is well maintained, but other roads in the area are generally suitable only for four-wheel-drive vehicles.

When planning a visit, do bear in mind that the panveld area south of Tsumkwe is generally water-logged and impassable after good summer rains. Visitors to Bushmanland must be totally self-sufficient for the duration of their stay. A two-vehicle party is recommended, but if you are travelling in one vehicle only it is advisable to inform the police in Tsumkwe before you leave and on your return.

Tourist attractions and settlements are either not signposted or badly signposted and you will need to rely on your sense of direction and plain common sense in getting around the area.

Petrol can be obtained in Tsumkwe, where you can also stock up with basic foodstuffs. There are no accommodation facilities there and as visitors are not required to obtain permits to camp, you may camp wherever you wish. Visitors must, however, choose campsites with the greatest circumspection, particularly near settlements.

Visitors are requested to respect the traditions and property of the inhabitants and to treat them courteously at all times. Ill manners, unfair bargaining and disrespect will result in mistrust and spoil the experience of other tourists.

For some visitors the main appeal of the area is its wilderness atmosphere, which varies from the dry sandveld in the west to the panveld, which at certain times of the year attracts large numbers of game. Bear in mind that your chances of spotting game depend on local conditions.

Other visitors are drawn to the area by a desire to see the San (Bushmen) who inhabit the area. Do not expect to encounter San in loincloths and with bows and arrows, though, as, contrary to the popular belief that these people still exist as hunter-gatherers, their way of life has changed dramatically in the past 20 years.

Bushmanland is the "home" of the Ju!Wasi San, whose traditional area once stretched from Rundu southwards to the Eiseb Omuramba in what is today Hereroland East, eastwards across the Aha Mountains to Botswana, beyond Tsau Kuri, to Lake Ngami, and from there in a north-westerly direction to Kavango. The Ju!Wasi is one of four subgroups of the !Khū-San who originally inhabited the central and eastern regions of SWA/Namibia. The other main groups are the Nama-San of the northern districts and Caprivi and the Cape-San of the southeastern parts of the country.

According to an investigation carried out in 1984 into the San population group in SWA/Namibia, no San group which lived exclusively from hunting and gathering could be traced, although according to reports a few hunting bands in south-east Kavango were said to be following their nomadic lifestyle. "Otherwise all San groups are characterised by one or the other form of acculturation. Western dress is common and rather the norm than the exception; the traditional beadwork and make-up no longer exist or are adapted to that of other cultures; eating and drinking habits have changed drastically, also the behavioural relationship between members of social groups; and their special observation abilities, which were vital in the struggle for survival, are disappearing amongst the younger generations." (Directorate: Co-ordination Development, 1984.) Two developments which have had a profound effect on the Ju!Wasi have been the development of Tsumkwe and the recruitment of San by the SA Defence Force (and subsequently the SWA Territory Force) since 1978.

Since 1960 there have been various attempts to introduce field and animal husbandry to the Ju!Wasi. In 1981 the Ju!Wasi Bushman Development Foundation was established with a view to establishing a viable subsistence economy, and small herds of cattle were made available to farmers. At present there are 13 settlements with a total population of about 500 and 400 cattle in East Bushmanland.

The vegetation of Bushmanland forms part of the Tree Savanna and Woodland (Northern Kalahari) (Giess Vegetation Type 11) and can be subdivided into several communities, namely the Sandveld, *Acacia* veld, Sandveld-*Acacia* veld communities and Calcrete communities.

The Sandveld in western Bushmanland is dominated by species such as wild seringa (197), wild teak (236), Kalahari apple-leaf (239), Rhodesian bushwillow (541), savanna bushwillow (543) and silver cluster-leaf (551).

Acacia veld occurs mainly in the *omurambas*, either as a tree and grass landscape or as a medium to open forest landscape. The most common species are shepherd's tree (122), camel thorn (168), black thorn (176) and red umbrella thorn (181).

In the transitional Sandveld-*Acacia* veld community the camel thorn is the dominant species.

The Calcrete veld in the east is a low to medium density forest landscape of *Acacia* and Lowveld cluster-leaf (550). Other species include red bushwillow (532) russet bushwillow (538) and leadwood (539). Also occurring in this community is the baobab (467).

Among the larger game are giraffe, kudu, blue wildebeest, eland, gemsbok, elephant and red hartebeest. Roan, buffalo and tsessebe also occur, but in smaller numbers. Predators include lion, leopard, cheetah, brown hyaena and spotted hyaena, as well as most of the smaller predators. With the exception of eland, gemsbok and giraffe, which occur in reasonably large numbers in the western sandveld, most of the game in Bushmanland occurs in the east of the region.

Although the migration patterns of the various species differ considerably, the central panveld south and north of Tsumkwe fulfils an important role in the ecology of the area. During the rainy season animals migrate from the panveld area, which becomes inundated with water, to the more sandy areas west of Nya-Nya Pan and a belt to the north of Tsumkwe. On account of the absence of permanent surface water in these areas, the animals migrate back to the panveld during the dry winter months.

The large pans such as Nya-Nya, /Autscha, Klein Döbe, Döbe and Makuri fulfil another important role in that they are rich in phosphate, thereby supplementing the phosphate-deficient natural grazing.

The natural appeal of eastern Bushmanland as a wilderness area and the absence of similar conservation areas in the rest of the country provided the motivation for calls to establish a nature conservation area as early as the mid-1970s. However, despite assurances that the San will be allowed to keep a limited number of stock, to engage in gardening, to gather *veldkos* in a traditional manner and to hunt, plans to create a game reserve have been opposed vigorously. In October 1987 the Cabinet of the Transitional Government announced that it had decided to allow trophy hunting in Bushmanland, but emphasised that a game reserve would not be proclaimed. A concession to hunt in the north-eastern part of the area was granted to a hunting outfitter and the Klein Döbe camp was set aside as a base camp.

12 SUGGESTED ITINERARIES

The following itineraries can be consulted when planning your tour and will, we hope, help you to avoid the mistake that many first-time visitors to the country make of trying to see too much in too short a time. These itineraries can be adapted to suit personal preference. Distances given are approximate only and allow for detours mentioned in the Regional Notes. Travelling to and from SWA/Namibia is not taken into account.

A triangle (▲) indicates where only camping is available.

21-DAY SEE SWA/NAMIBIA TOUR (arriving from Republic of South Africa)

	DAY	DESTINATION	DISTANCE
	Day 1	Ai-Ais	
	Day 2	Lüderitz	520 km
	Day 3	Lüderitz	50 km
	Day 4	Lüderitz	50 km
▲	Day 5	Sesriem via Duwisib	510 km
▲	Day 6	Sesriem	140 km
	Day 7	Naukluft	135 km
▲	Day 8	Naukluft	–
▲	Day 9	Namib	250 km
	Day 10	Swakopmund	170 km
	Day 11	Swakopmund (including Welwitschia Drive)	160 km
	Day 12	Khorixas via Cape Cross	430 km
	Day 13	Khorixas excursions	230 km
	Day 14	Etosha: Okaukuejo	290 km
	Day 15	Etosha: Halali	120 km
	Day 16	Etosha: Namutoni	160 km
	Day 17	Etosha: Namutoni	50 km

Day 18	Gross Barmen via Grootfontein	580 km
Day 19	Windhoek	110 km
Day 20	Hardap	270 km
Day 21	Kalahari Gemsbok: Mata Mata	330 km

14-DAY CENTRAL TOUR (commencing from Windhoek)

DAY	DESTINATION	DISTANCE
▲ Day 1	Naukluft	260 km
▲ Day 2	Naukluft	
▲ Day 3	Sesriem	135 km
▲ Day 4	Sesriem	140 km
▲ Day 5	Namib	250 km
Day 6	Swakopmund	170 km
Day 7	Swakopmund (including Welwitschia Drive)	160 km
▲ Day 8	Spitzkoppe	190 km
Day 9	Brandberg (once rest camp completed)	140 km
Day 10	Omaruru (guest farm)	230 km
Day 11	Omaruru (excursions)	100 km
Day 12	Gross Barmen	210 km
Day 13	Daan Viljoen via Otjimbingwe and Khomas Hochland	300 km
Day 14	Windhoek	20 km

14-DAY NORTHERN TOUR (arriving from Republic of South Africa)

DAY	DESTINATION	DISTANCE
Day 1	Ai-Ais	
Day 2	Hardap	560 km
Day 3	Windhoek	270 km
Day 4	Omaruru (guest farm)	300 km
Day 5	Khorixas via White Lady	320 km
Day 6	Khorixas excursions	230 km
Day 7	Etosha: Okaukuejo	290 km
Day 8	Etosha: Okaukuejo	100 km
Day 9	Etosha: Halali	120 km
Day 10	Etosha: Namutoni	160 km
Day 11	Waterberg	390 km

Day 12	Waterberg	
Day 13	Gross Barmen	250 km
Day 14	Hardap	360 km

14-DAY SOUTHERN TOUR (approaching from Republic of South Africa)

DAY	DESTINATION	DISTANCE
Day 1	Ai-Ais	
Day 2	Ai-Ais	
Day 3	Lüderitz	520 km
Day 4	Lüderitz	50 km
Day 5	Lüderitz	50 km
▲ Day 6	Sesriem via Duwisib	510 km
▲ Day 7	Sesriem	140 km
▲ Day 8	Naukluft	135 km
▲ Day 9	Namib	250 km
Day 10	Swakopmund	170 km
Day 11	Swakopmund (including Welwitschia Drive)	160 km
Day 12	Windhoek	360 km
Day 13	Hardap	270 km
Day 14	Kalahari Gemsbok: Mata Mata	330 km

30-DAY OFF-THE-BEATEN-TRACK TOUR (four-wheel-drive, approaching from north-western Botswana)

DAY	DESTINATION	DISTANCE
Day 1	Katima Mulilo	
Day 2	Katima Mulilo	20 km
▲ Day 3	Lake Liambezi	60 km
▲ Day 4	Lake Liambezi	20 km
▲ Day 5	Linyanti area	100 km
▲ Day 6	Linyanti area	30 km
Day 7	Popa Falls	300 km
Day 8	Popa Falls – visit Mahango	100 km
Day 9	Kaudom: Kaudom Camp	210 km
Day 10	Kaudom: Kaudom Camp	70 km
Day 11	Kaudom: Sikereti Camp	120 km

	Day 12	Grootfontein	370 km
	Day 13	Khorixas	420 km
▲	Day 14	Twyfelfontein	140 km
▲	Day 15	Damaraland Concession Area	160 km
▲	Day 16	Damaraland Concession Area	100 km
▲	Day 17	Damaraland Concession Area	100 km
▲	Day 18	Damaraland Concession Area	100 km
	Day 19	Brandberg (once rest camp completed)	260 km
▲	Day 20	Messum Crater	140 km
	Day 21	Swakopmund	170 km
	Day 22	Swakopmund	
		(including Welwitschia Drive)	160 km
▲	Day 23	Namib	130 km
▲	Day 24	Namib	60 km
▲	Day 25	Naukluft	200 km
▲	Day 26	Naukluft	
▲	Day 27	Sesriem	135 km
▲	Day 28	Sesriem	140 km
	Day 29	Hardap	310 km
	Day 30	Kalahari Gemsbok: Mata Mata	330 km
		or Ai-Ais	580 km

BIBLIOGRAPHY

The following sources have been consulted and will prove useful should you wish to obtain more detailed information. Books marked with an asterisk (*) are recommended as useful guide books.

Andersson, C J, 1987. *Lake Ngami.* (Facsimile reprint.) Cape Town: C Struik.

*Berruti, A and Sinclair, J C, 1983. *Where to Watch Birds in Southern Africa.* Cape Town: C Struik.

*Berry, C (undated). *Trees and Shrubs of the Etosha National Park.* Windhoek: SWA Directorate of Nature Conservation.

Berry, H H, 1972. "The great flamingo trek". *African Wildlife* 26 (2), 58–60.

Berry, H H, 1972. "Pelicans air-freight their fish 100 kilometres". *African Wildlife* 26 (3), 120–124.

Berry, H H and Berry, C U, 1975. "A check list and notes on the birds of Sandvis, South West Africa". *Madoqua* 10 (2), 5–18.

Berry, H H, 1980. "The energy-saving flamingo". *SWA Annual,* 101–102.

Berry, H H, 1983. "First catch your lion". *Rössing* (April 1983), 1–7.

Berry, H H, 1983. "The blue wildebeest problem at Etosha National Park". *African Wildlife* 37 (5), 192–197.

Bornman, C H, 1978. *Welwitschia – Paradox of a Parched Paradise.* Cape Town: C Struik.

Breslauer, J, 1965. "Saga of the narrow gauge railway". *SWA Annual,* 170–172.

Breuil, H, 1957. *Phillip Cave.* London: Abbé Breuil Publications.

Bridgeford, P A, 1985. "Unusual diet of the lion *Panthera leo* in the Skeleton Coast Park". *Madoqua* 14 (2), 187–188.

Brittan, M, 1979. *Discover Namibia*. Cape Town: C Struik.

*Bruwer, J J, 1985. *Aus 1915–1919: Vestiging, Bestaan en Sluiting van die Aus-Krygsgevangenekamp*. Windhoek: National Monuments Council.

Clement, A J, 1975. "Gross Spitzkoppe – Matterhorn of SWA". *SWA Annual*, 73–80.

*Clinning, C F and Jensen, R A C, 1973. *The Birds of the Daan Viljoen Park*. Windhoek: Nature Conservation and Tourism Division of SWA Administration.

Cooke, B V, 1975. "Insignia in the desert – Relics of the 1914–1915 military campaign in SWA". *SWA Annual*, 25–31.

Cooke, B V, 1982. "The battle of Gibeon". *SWA Annual*, 153–156.

*Craven, P and Marais, C, 1986. *Namib Flora – Swakopmund to the Giant Welwitschia via Goanikontes*. Windhoek: Gamsberg.

Directorate: Co-ordination Development, 1984. *Ondersoek na die Boesmanbevolkingsgroep in SWA*. Windhoek: Directorate: Co-ordination Development.

Directorate of Nature Conservation, SWA, 1982. *Etosha 75 – 1907–1982*. Windhoek: Directorate of Nature Conservation.

Duggan, A (ed), 1983. *Reader's Digest Illustrated Guide to the Game Parks and Nature Reserves of Southern Africa*. Cape Town: Reader's Digest Association of South Africa.

*Du Preez, J (undated). *Animals of Etosha*. Windhoek: Shell Oil SWA Ltd.

Du Preez, J and Grobler, I D, 1977. "Drinking times and behaviour at waterholes of some game species in the Etosha National Park". *Madoqua* 10 (1), 61–69.

Gaerdes, F, 1971. *Geskiedenis en Ontwikkeling van die Stad Okahandja*. Windhoek: SWA Scientific Society.

Gebhardt, L, 1973. "Sandwich Harbour – a sanctuary in the dunes". *SWA Annual*, 97–103.

*Giess, W, 1971. "A Preliminary Vegetation Map of South West Africa". *Dinteria* 4.

Ginsberg, L and Von Ludwiger, K, 1973. "Rock Climbing". *SWA Annual*, 107–111.

Hockey, P A R, 1982. "Waders (Charadrii) and other coastal birds in the Lüderitz region of South West Africa". *Madoqua* 13 (1), 27–33.

Iwanowski, M, 1986. *Travel Guide Southwest Africa/Namibia*. Dormagen, West Germany: V & S Verlag.

Jacobson, L, 1980. "The White Lady of the Brandberg – a re-interpretation". *Namibiana* II (1), 21–29.

*Jankowitz, W J, 1975. *Aloes of South West Africa*. Windhoek: Division of Nature Conservation and Tourism, Administration of South West Africa.

*Jensen, R A C and Clinning, C F, 1983. *Birds of the Etosha National Park*. Windhoek: Directorate of Nature Conservation and Recreation Resorts.

Jerling, H C, 1972. Uis. *SWA Annual*, 47–53.

Joubert, E, *Meesterplan: Namib-Naukluftpark – 'n Verslag met Beleid ten Opsigte van Doelstellings, Sonering en Benutting van die Naukluft-bergkompleks en Aangrensende Gruisvlaktes, insluitende Sesriem en Sossusvlei*. Windhoek: Suidwes-Afrika Administrasie, Afdeling Natuurbewaring en Toerisme.

Kinahan, J, 1986. "The Archaeological Structure of Pastoral Production in the Central Namib". *South African Archaeological Society Goodwin Series 5*.

*Kinahan, J, 1988. *The Pillar in the Mist: a History of the Dias Padrão at Lüderitz*. Windhoek: National Monuments Council.

Koch, C, 1970. "Living Sands". *SWA Annual*, 190–199.

Kok, O B and Van Wyk, A J, 1982. "Boomklimmende klipspringers in die Namibwoestyn". *Madoqua* 13 (1), 89–90.

Krynauw, D W, 1964. "The story of Namutoni". *Historical Monuments Commission of South West Africa, Publication No. 1*. Windhoek: Historical Mounuments Commission of South West Africa.

Krynauw, D W, 1969. "Twyfelfontein". *Historical Monuments Commission of South West Africa, Publication No. 3*. Windhoek: Historical Monuments Commission of South West Africa.

Krynauw, D W, 1969. "Kaap Kruis". *Historical Monuments Commission of South West Africa, Publication No. 4*. Windhoek: Historical Monuments Commission of South West Africa.

Lambrechts, H A, 1985. *Namibia – A Thirstland Wilderness*. Cape Town: C Struik.

Levinson, O, 1977. "Grootfontein and its colourful past". *SWA Annual*, 128–131.

Levinson, O, 1983. *Diamonds in the desert – The Story of August Stauch and his times*. Cape Town: Tafelberg.

Loutit, B D, Louw, G N and Seely, M K, 1987. "First approximation of food preferences and chemical composition of the diet of the desert-dwelling black rhinoceros". *Madoqua* 15 (1), 35–54.

*Louw, G N and Seely, M K, 1982. *Ecology of Desert Organisms*. London: Longman.

Marais, C, 1980. *Swakopmund – Our Heritage*. Windhoek: Gamsberg.

Marais, C, 1981. *Lüderitz – Our Heritage*. Windhoek: Gamsberg.

Marais, C, 1986. *Windhoek – Our Heritage*. Windhoek: Gamsberg.

Massmann, U, 1983. *Swakopmund – A Chronicle of the Town's People, Places and Progress*. Swakopmund: Society for Scientific Development and Museum.

Minie, J H, 1979. "Cape Cross". *National Monuments Council, Publication 4A*.

Mossolow, N, 1955. "Otjimbingwe". *SWA Annual*, 97–119.

Mossolow, N (undated). *Otjikango or Gross Barmen – The History of the First Herero Mission Station in South West Africa, 1844–1904*. Windhoek: Mossolow.

*Muller, M A N, 1984. *Grasses of South West Africa/Namibia*. Windhoek: Directorate of Agriculture and Forestry.

Olivier, W A and Olivier, S W (in prep). *The Guide to Backpacking and Wilderness Trails*. Johannesburg: Southern Book Publishers.

Owen-Smith, G, 1986. "The Kaokoveld, South West Africa/Namibia's threatened wilderness". *African Wildlife* 40 (3), 104–115.

Owen-Smith, G, 1986. "Censusing black rhino in north-western Damaraland by individual identification". Unpublished report.

Penrith, M J, 1979. "Otjikoto Lake". *SWA Annual*, 138–139.

Peters, W, 1981. *Baukunst in Südwestafrika – 1844–1914*. Windhoek: SWA Scientific Society.

Raper, P E, 1987. *Dictionary of Southern African Place Names*. Johannesburg: Lowry Publishers.

Robinson, M D, 1977. "Social status and energy expenditure of male Namib Desert sand-diving lizards". *Namib Bulletin*. Supplement *Transvaal Museum Bulletin* (2), 11–12.

Rössing Uranium Limited, 1985. *The Rössing Fact Book*. Windhoek: Rössing Uranium Limited.

Ryan, P G, Cooper, J and Stutterheim, C J, 1984. "Waders (Charadrii) and other coastal birds of the Skeleton Coast, South West Africa". *Madoqua* 14 (1), 71–78.

Ryan, P G, Cooper, J, Stutterheim, C J and Loutit, R, 1984. "An annotated list of the birds of the Skeleton Coast Park". *Madoqua* 14 (1), 79–90.

Scherz, E R, 1975. *Felsbilder in Südwest-Afrika* (vol 2). Köln, Wien: Böhlau Verlag.

Scherz, E R, 1986. *Felsbilder in Südwest-Afrika* (vol 3). Köln, Wien: Böhlau Verlag.

Schoeman, A, 1981. "Dunes of the Namib". *SWA Annual*, 9–20.

Seely, M K (undated). "Dr Charles Koch Namib Woestyn Navorsingstigting". *Information leaflet* published by Namib Desert Research Unit.

Seely, M K, 1984. "Studying biology in the Namib". *SWA Annual*, 83–88.

*Seely, M K, 1987. *The Namib – Natural History of an Ancient Desert*. Windhoek: Shell Oil SWA Ltd.

*Smithers, R H N, 1986. *Land Mammals of Southern Africa*. Johannesburg: Macmillan.

Söhgne, G, 1976. "Tsumeb – a historical sketch". *Scientific Research in South West Africa* 5. Windhoek: SWA Scientific Society.

Stuart, C T, 1975. "Preliminary notes on the mammals of the Namib Desert Park". *Madoqua* 11 (4), 5–68.

Tarr, J, 1986. "Namibia's rare and endangered Damara tern". *Rössing* (May 1986), 2–5.

Terblanche, D J, 19. "The man-made island of Sandwich Harbour". *SWA Annual*, 89–113.

Tilson, R, Von Blottnitz, F and Henschel, J, 1980. "Prey selection by spotted hyaena (*Crocuta crocuta*) in the Namib Desert". *Madoqua* 12 (1), 41–49.

Van Doorn, T, 1987. *Windhoek on foot*. Windhoek: T. van Doorn.

Van Huyssteen, C N L, 1983. *The Lonely Grave in the Fish River*. Roodepoort: CUM Books.

Van Zijl, J J, 1986. "Inleiding tot die spoorwegverhaal van Suidwes-Afrika". *SWA Annual*, 117–121.

Viljoen, S, 1988. "The desert-dwelling elephant – hardy survivor". *African Wildlife* 42 (2), 111–115.

*Von Breitenbach, F, 1986. *National List of Indigenous Trees*. Pretoria: Dendrological Foundation.

Von Koenen, H and Von Koenen, E, 1963. "Namib Desert Life". *SWA Annual*, 106–109.

Von Koenen, E, 1964. "Golden Moles – Lost and found". *SWA Annual*, 110–111.

*Walkden-Davis, A, 1985. *Shell Tourist Guide – SWA/Namibia*. Windhoek: Shell Oil SWA Ltd.

Wendt, W E, 1972. "Preliminary report on an archaeological research programme in South West Africa". *Cimbebasia, Ser. B*, 2.

Willcox, A R, 1984. *The Rock Art of Africa*. Johannesburg: Macmillan.

Williams, A J, 1987. "Conservation management of the Walvis Bay Wetland with particular reference to the coastal bird numbers and their conservation significance". *Report commissioned by the Association of Round Tables in Southern Africa, South West Africa/Namibia Area, Walvis Bay Round Table 36.*

*Williams A J, 1987. *Popular Checklist of the Birds of South West Africa/Namibia*. Windhoek: Department of Agriculture and Nature Conservation.

INDEX

LEGEND

Maps

🏠	Rest Camp	◀	Border Post
▲	Campsite	✈	Airfield/Landing Strip
✳	Viewpoint	⊙	Waterhole
✚	Hospital	☗	Museum
ⅰ	Information Bureau	1	Hotel
✉	Post Office	▲^{2}	Places of Interest
Ⓟ	Police Station	🚌	Bus Terminus
♏	Hot Spring	⌂	Day Camping Facility
🏊	Swimming	▦	Sanddunes
♟18	Golf Course	⋯	Built-up Area

⌒	Perennial River	▬	Main Road
~--<,	Non-perennial River	—	Secondary Road
+++++	Railway Line	—	District/Farm Road
.—.	International Boundary	.....	Other Road
		▨▨▨	Park Boundary

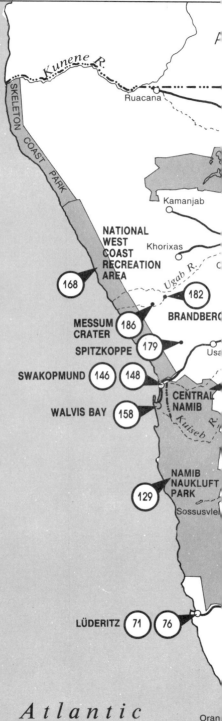

ORIENTATION MAP: NAMIBIA

Kunene R.

Ruacana

SKELETON COAST PARK

Kamanjab

NATIONAL
WEST
COAST
RECREATION
AREA

Khorixas

Ugab R.

(168)

(182)

BRANDBERG

MESSUM (186)
CRATER

SPITZKOPPE (179)

Usa

SWAKOPMUND (146) (148)

CENTRAL
NAMIB

WALVIS BAY (158)

Kuiseb R.

NAMIB
NAUKLUFT
PARK

(129)

Sossusvlei

LÜDERITZ (71) (76)

*Atlantic
Ocean*

Oran